THE MAN WHO STOLE PORTUGAL

Books by Murray Teigh Bloom

THE MAN WHO STOLE PORTUGAL

MONEY OF THEIR OWN

The Man Who Stole
PORTUGAL

Murray Teigh Bloom

CHARLES SCRIBNER'S SONS
New York

This book is for Amy and Ellen.

ACKNOWLEDGMENTS

MOST OF the research and interviews for this book were conducted during three trips to England and Europe between 1963 and 1965.

My London researches were aided immeasurably by Heather Chapman and those in Paris by Francis Schell. From Stuttgart, Arno Alexy very ably conducted several difficult searches and interviews in various parts of Germany. During my long stay in Portugal extensive sight translations of the lengthy trial records and contemporary newspapers were done for me fluently and efficiently by Peter B. Miranda. In Amsterdam, Aad van Leeuwen was helpful in opening certain sources.

For a full set of the transcripts of the three London trials, plus other important documents, I am deeply grateful to Sir James Waterlow, Bart.* Other useful assistance was provided by Helen Romer of Seaford, Sussex; Lynn Grossberg of Caracas, Venezuela, and Tomé Vieria of Lisbon.

Background information on the banknote business was provided by the late William F. Hunt, Chairman of the United States Bank Note Company and Frederic Colclough, Chairman of the American Bank Note Company, both of New York. In London several officials of Thomas De La Rue & Company Ltd. were equally helpful. W. van Andringa de Kempenaer, managing director of Johan Enschedé en Zonen of Haarlem, a gracious host, also provided particularly useful data.

Some sources in Lisbon and London have asked me not to mention their names so that I can only offer them a vague salute and my repeated thanks.

I am indebted to my old friend, Dr. Alfonso Quiroz Cuaron, Director of the Division of Special Investigations of the Bank of Mexico, who first interested me in the Portuguese banknote case several years ago.

Gratitude, too, to my tireless typist, Sherley A. Raices for decoding my manuscript against a deadline.

Finally, there is a continuing debt to the MacDowell Colony of Peterborough, New Hampshire—one of our great social inventions—for granting me the boon of a stay long enough to finish this book.

* The London trials required some 2100 pages of legal-size transcripts. The Portuguese trials covered 75 volumes, 32 annexes, for a total of 22,000 pages.

CONTENTS

PROLOGUE:
House of Lords, **April 28, 1932**

ix

Contents

EPILOGUE: 1932–1964

PROLOGUE

LONDON / April 28, 1932

NOT UNTIL the trial's last day in the House of Lords did one of the five Law Lords provide a capsule superlative.

On this day in the Chamber of the House of Lords, the supernally gothic meeting place of the British peers of the realm, Baron Macmillan of Aberfeldy corrected the oversight.

He said the highest court of appeal in the Empire had been considering "a crime for which in the ingenuity and audacity of its conception it would be difficult to find a parallel."

In the small press gallery at the northern end of the eighty foot chamber the reporters recorded the encomium with its awkward syntax. The only one who didn't was an unemployed London reporter who had been looking in on the long series of trials for Edgar Wallace, the awesomely prolific mystery writer of the Twenties.

When he was 14, Wallace worked for the crime's victim, Waterlow & Sons, as a proofreader's boy at 4/6 (about $1) a week. For years he had followed the case out of sentiment and professional interest. Several times he announced he would do a book about it. He died in Hollywood in February, 1932, the book unwritten.

After the Law Lords rendered their verdict on this morning Wallace's friend confided to another reporter:

"Ahh, Dickie would never have done the book, anyway."

"Why not? It's one of the great cases . . ."

"Too great . . . Take a London pavement artist who makes a living doing chalked sunsets. You pass by, take a look and put a few coppers in his hat because you like his simple, bright-colored pictures. Then late one summer afternoon there's a little shower. When the pavement dries he starts another sunset in colored chalk. Suddenly he knows no one is looking and he looks up. The sky has a magnificent double rainbow with gorgeous violets inside and reds outside. The sidewalk artist knows he can't compete with *that*. So he picks up his hat and chalks and leaves. Well, Dickie could never have done a book about this case because it would have made all his made-up stories look like he was short-weighing his readers. Like the pavement artist, Wallace knew when he was completely outclassed."

1924

LISBON / November 24, 1924

AT TEN P.M. a young, chain-smoking Portuguese businessman on the verge of bankruptcy and disgrace sat down at his office typewriter to compose an impossible crime.

He tapped away steadily at the 1918 Smith with its old-style six-row keyboard. His staff of five—an office manager, three clerks and a typist—had long ago left the second floor office in the deserted downtown commercial section of Lisbon, the Baixa. By 11:30 he finished the four-page document that would help make him the richest man in Portugal in a year, the richest *and* the most powerful in two. He was twenty-eight.

Most of the great modern white-collar criminals operate from the *inside*, utilizing a position of established trust to achieve their embezzlements and frauds.* The successful forgers and counterfeiters working from the *outside* must rely on polished skills, fierce attention to detail and well-trained associates to make an effective criminal combination.

Artur Virgilio Alves Reis, the amateur composer of crime, had none of these advantages. In terms of his targets—the Bank of Portugal and the world of banknotes—he was a complete outsider; and nearly a penniless one at this moment in 1924. Nor did he have any particular criminal skills. Worse, he was often careless with detail. And the three men he had chosen to help him could never be told the whole truth because anyone with a scrap of sense would know this insane scheme had no chance of success.

* For example, Ivar Kreuger, the match king; Philip Musica, the president of McKesson & Robbins, and Anthony DeAngelis, the great salad-oil entrepreneur who swindled New York and London financial firms out of $150,000,000. Why should anyone think the head of a large, reputable corporation is a crook? If strict controls were imposed on *all* trusted persons, comments Criminologist Donald R. Cressey, embezzlement could be prevented, but very little business could be conducted.

3

In spite of his staggering disqualifications, Alves Reis did succeed. He won because he had the splendid, vaulting imagination of the half-educated, the assurance of the ill-informed, the ridiculous luck of the beginner.

The profound impact of his success gave Portugal its worst shock since the great earthquake of 1755, brought on the most enduring dictatorship of our time, wracked the Lord Mayor of London, ruined one of the world's great printing firms, culminated in one of the longest and costliest cases in British legal history.

Today, the ripples set in motion by Alves Reis' dazzling scheme are still discernible—in the life of Holland's most honored actress; the prosperity of several Portuguese families; the affluence of a leading French electrical appliance maker; and even in the acerbic debates in the United Nations over Portuguese Angola.

Most criminals are unimaginative copycats. They do what other criminals have done before. The clever ones add technical refinements, plot more elaborately, time more carefully. Yet trains bearing valuables have been held up hundreds of times in the past century and seemingly impregnable bank vaults have been entered over the weekend almost routinely. Every banknote issued since the Chinese invented paper money has been counterfeited. And thousands of checks are forged routinely every week. Alves Reis' crime which had *never* been done before also had an in-built limitation: it could not be done again. It was—and is— *the* unique crime, the great once-in-a-civilization rarity. He had conceived and put into operation the foolproof counterfeiting scheme.

Any reasonably intelligent person can see there are three major obstacles in the path of the counterfeiter. To begin with, the plates he could make or get wouldn't be even remotely as good as the government's own plates. Don't the best engravers and printers prefer the security of a good government or bank job to the furtive, impoverished existence of a criminal freelance? Poor plates, in turn, make poor bills. Soon some bank teller or even a vigilant storekeeper detects the bogus bills. Before long the entire protective apparatus of the state is turned against the counterfeiter.

Consider the second big obstacle: who can you get to take the risk of passing the bills in small shops and restaurants? Only the marginal men of the underworld, the losers whose every appearance is enough to make even the most casual shopkeeper give the bill a second searching look. The criminal wholesalers who might buy your banknotes at a great discount? They endanger you just as much by their natural anxiety to get rid of the false notes as quickly as possible, thus alerting the banks and the government immediately.

And lastly, of course, is the inevitability of detection, arrest and conviction. Counterfeiting threatens the state as no crime except treason. The sentences have to be severe and swift with a counterfeiter. It is more than merely justice that has to be done; it is for the state much more than appearances: it is *self-defense*. A corrupt official, a man who killed his wife's lover, a company embezzler—all these could hope for, or even buy leniency. But no state can afford leniency either when only a handful of coins or one million banknotes is involved.

These three obstacles are fairly obvious and many an intelligent professional criminal has tried to cope with them in the past. But Artur Virgilio Alves Reis was the first to evolve effective solutions. He came up with the perfectly logical counterfeiting scheme. Even his enemies—and there were many, naturally—had to concede the plan's blinding brilliance, its lightning logic. As his main enemy, the State, was to say much later, through one of its most eloquent minions:

> There was no such thing as any logical difficulties for Alves Reis. In him conception immediately precedes execution. . . . Endowed with a highly fertile imagination and mental activity that's astounding and almost feverish . . . he never wondered if a notion that crossed his mind would be feasible or not. . . . Everything that he imagines appears possible and even easy for him. Like the heart diastole and systolic movements, his astounding activity and boundless daring are no more than two motor aspects of the dazzling vivacity of his mental images and deep darkness in which his residual inhibitions are sunk.

✿   ✿   ✿   ✿   ✿

He was born on September 8, 1896, into a middle-class family with remote claims to historic grandeur. Although his father, August Guilherme Alves Reis, was a self-taught bookkeeper who had worked his way up to a partnership in a funeral parlor in the São Tiago district of Lisbon, young Alves Reis was never allowed to forget that his father was a cousin of the great Admiral Reis for whom a leading street in Lisbon was named.

Besides the funeral parlor, the older Reis developed other business interests such as money lending. In 1914 when his son might have gone on to the university after completing training at a local lyceum—the family savings were lost in an investment in the Portuguese Petroleum Company which dug too many dry holes in its search for Angola oil.

For a year young Alves Reis took a course in practical engineering and then abandoned it to get married. He met Maria Luiza Jacobetti d'Azevedo at a picnic on a beach near Cascais. She was the daughter of the chief clerk of a British-owned firm of customs specialists in Lisbon. Like Alves Reis, she, too, had a famous relative: her great-grandfather had been a prominent and prolific Italian playwright named Jacobetti. She had been sent to a local private French finishing school for girls where she learned piano, French, reading and writing.

She was four months younger than her 20-year-old groom, reasonably attractive with high cheekbones, an almost prominent nose and a disappearing chin. Like most Portuguese women she was rather short and inclined to plumpness. She was very much in love with her deep-voiced, well-dressed fiance. He was about 5'6" but his very broad shoulders made him seem shorter. He started losing his hair even before he was 20 and to hide his increasing baldness started parting his hair in the middle.

After a year of courtship they were married in August, 1916. Since they weren't 21, Artur and Maria needed the written, notarized consent of their parents—called an "emancipation"—to get married.

In 1916 Portugal entered the First World War on the Allied side. Instead of going to the European front a married Alves Reis was easily able to wangle permission to go to Angola. Before leaving he prepared a document that would gain him great respect in the colony: a diploma—No. 2148—from the "Polytechnic School of Engineering" of Oxford University. The fact that no such school ever existed hardly mattered.

For the wording of the Diploma, which he dated March,

1916, he simply translated the University of Coimbra diploma of an acquaintance. The grade of Bachelor, the diploma read, was awarded to Alves Reis for his application in the disciplines of:

> Engineering Science, Geology, Geometry, Physics, Metallurgy, Pure Mathematics, Mathematics, Paleography, Electrical Engineering, Mechanical Engineering, Applied Mathematics, Chemistry, Experimental Physics, Applied Mechanics, Applied Physics, General Civil Engineering, Civil & Mechanical Engineering, General Engineering, Mechanical and Civil Design.

Further, he was able "to direct industries referent to the grade in which he was specialized." In short, he had studied everything and could do anything.

The diploma was signed by the "Director of the Polytechnic" Henry Spooner * and the "Chancellor of the University" John D. Peel. To it was appended a gloriously imaginative "Golden Seal of Oxford University" and a rubber-stamped "Polytechnic School of Engineering."

In July, 1916, Alves Reis had a copy of his diploma notarized by a dimwitted, accommodating notary in Sintra so that those who wouldn't fully trust a foreign diploma would know it was authentic because a Portuguese notary, in effect, said it was.

In November, 1916, Alves Reis took his bride to Angola on the west coast of Africa, south of the Belgian Congo. There, in Luanda, the capital city and chief port, he easily got a job in the Department of Public Works, approving building plans and sewerage layouts.

Angola forms a rough rectangle of nearly 500,000 square miles—about twice the size of Texas and 14 times larger than the mother country, Portugal. When Alves Reis arrived, there were some 20,000 whites in the country, some 10,000 mulattoes and about 3,000,000 Negro natives denigratedly called "Jagas." In 1916 Angola was primarily agricultural since it lacked its own coal and iron. Coffee, corn, cotton, sugar, tobacco and rice were exported.

---

* God knows how he happened on *this* name. The Rev. William Archibald Spooner, was the Warden of New College, Oxford, at the time. He didn't know bolts about engineering but he fathered "spoonerisms"—the unintentional interchange of sounds in two or more words. For example: It is kistumary to cuss the bride.

As the only man with an Oxford diploma in Angola, Alves Reis quickly felt the need of additional opportunity besides his dull Public Works job. He got another job in the local railroad repair shops as a supervising engineer. He worked there from 5 A.M. to 9 A.M. and then reported to his office in Public Works.

Angola then had few farm-to-market roads and most of the colonists depended on the railroad to get their produce to the port of Luanda. The trouble was there were few operating loco-motives. Most of them were idle because spare parts could not be obtained from war-ravaged Belgium where the machines had been made.

Reis quickly realized that paperwork in the office would never get the locomotives repaired. Boldly, he did something that any Portuguese white-collar worker would rather die than do: he put on overalls.

In Portuguese, overalls are known derisively as a *macoco*, or monkey suit, and in a few days Alves Reis was laughed at as the "monkey engineer." He used to climb into the locomotive boilers to find out what was wrong. He obviously had some engineering aptitudes and when he told the mechanics what was wrong and how to repair it, he turned out to be right surprisingly often. He was still called "our monkey engineer" but now it was said proudly. Inevitably he became known as the man who made the trains run. Not *on time*. Just *run*.

His suggestion that new locomotives be bought in the U.S. was quickly adopted. The idea was a good one but the American machines presented certain problems Reis had not anticipated. They were longer and heavier than the Belgian locomotives and when they arrived in Luanda some of Reis' jealous fellow engi-neers were certain the monkey engineer had made a terrible blunder. By employing certain standard stress-and-strain formu-las they proved conclusively to the railroad director that the new machines would be too heavy for their bridges.

Reis didn't know enough mathematics, let alone engineering, to dispute them on paper so he proposed a demonstration. He rode with one of the new American locomotives to the first bridge out of Luanda. The train stopped and he announced to the crew and passengers that if none of them trusted his conclusions he was ready to be a passenger—along with his wife and baby son,

Guilherme. The crew and passengers were shamed into going along. The train passed safely over the bridge—and all the other bridges, too. It was a great triumph.

As his reputation grew so did his rank. In March, 1918, he was made Inspector of Public Works and later that year became Acting Chief Engineer of the Angola Railways. Still, he sought new challenges.

A friend who had a tobacco farm was about to lose his crop through a lack of sufficient rain. Reis rounded up 50 natives and in a week built a rough irrigation canal through a hillside, using wooden conduits. The crop was saved with the diverted water of a nearby river. His grateful friend gave him half the proceeds of the crop.

Reis fell in love with Angola in spite of the many tropical diseases that were endemic there. Later he analyzed the nature of his overwhelming attraction to the country:

> I had sailed along Angola's extensive coast-line; I had under-taken many arduous journeys inland, studying carefully the re-sources of the country and I was now lost in wonder as I recalled the immensity of the riches of its soil and subsoil. Every kind of produce both of the temperate and torrid zones can be raised there, as though nature had wished to display to man her might and ca-price! In the subsoil, gold, silver, copper, tin, iron, and diamonds furnish the means required to make the Angola of tomorrow one of the most prosperous lands of the whole African continent, whilst, to enhance the tale of its natural riches, there are tablelands where white men find climatic conditions second to none in Europe. How the promises of Mother Earth stimulate and madden her children!

In May, 1919, when he was not yet 24, he decided it was time to make his fortune in Angola. When he resigned from the post of Acting Chief Engineer of Angola Railways the local Official Gazette made clear the governor of Angola was sorry to lose him. "Alves Reis had discharged his post with great zeal and com-petence thus serving the Colony and the Republic well."

He traveled throughout the colony buying up crops and sell-ing in Luanda. With his excellent railway connections his pur-chased crops always received priority—and timely transportation. He traveled with his wife—the two baby sons were left in their home in Luanda in the care of trusted native servants. In many

Angola villages Senhora Reis became the first white woman visitor. On their white horses and topees both were splendid relics of 19th century colonialism—and 20th century commerce.

He prospered and late in 1919 he went to Europe to pick up some war-surplus bargains. He acquired a trainload of French sandbags made of heavy paper which he sold to Angola as jute bags. He had deceived the purchasers but they didn't complain very loudly when they found the reinforced paper bags were as good as jute for their needs.

On the way back to Angola he found in Lisbon a warehouse filled with 20 unused but rusting German tractors. He was able to buy them for little because no one had been able to make them work. He hired two mechanics and with them worked a long week putting the machines in working order and painting them. He was able to sell them as new to an Angola importer.

In 1922 Reis decided it was time to return to Lisbon. He had accumulated profits of 600,000 escudos [then about $30,000] and felt he had completed his apprenticeship in the world of international business.

He returned to Lisbon in great style. With two partners who put in some capital he created A. V. Alves Reis Lda. [Limitado]. He rented a large 12-room apartment for 1,000 escudos a month, a high rental for Lisbon even though it was only $50 a month. He hired a cook, maid, seamstress and a chauffeur to drive his Nash sedan—his firm had acquired the Portuguese dealership for the American car—and furnished his home and office splendidly. He was the first businessman in Lisbon, he boasted, who had a private apartment adjoining his office so he could rest when he worked late.

The firm prospered moderately on its shipments to and from Angola but Reis was personally short of cash because he had overinvested in the South Angola Mining Corporation which had yet to produce a ton of iron ore. Worse followed: in September, 1923, Angola was in a great financial mess. The Angola escudo, inflated endlessly by the Ultramarino Bank of Portugal, had almost no buying power. Transfers of currency between Angola and Portugal were prohibited.

Reis looked around hastily for new capital. Some friends interested him in trying to clear up the tangled affairs of Ambaca, the Royal Trans-African Railway Company of Angola.* The company's shares had fallen to a few escudos each and foreign stock and bondholders were demanding action on unpaid dividends and interest.

Reis' interest in Ambaca heightened considerably as soon as he discovered there was $100,000 in the company treasury, lent by Portugal to pay off bond coupons. The temptation was too great. Later, he said, he just had to

> set in motion all that stagnant capital. To gain this end I had only to buy up a sufficient number of shares to enable me to have myself elected chairman of the company. There was no time to be lost. A bold stroke would settle everything, but were I to pay heed to my scruples I should inevitably fail. In the materialistic world to which I belong, there are neither honest men nor rogues—there are only victors and vanquished. So I had no hesitation in gaining control of the Company and making use of the shareholders' money.

But how could a nearly bankrupt businessman get capital to buy the shares of the Ambaca Company so that he could loot it? Alves Reis had discovered the secret of fast checks and slow boats. In connection with his Nash car distributorship he had opened a small checking account with the National City Bank of New York. He loved to issue checks on the New York bank because it took at least eight days for a check to reach it by sea. With eight days' free use of large sums a smart fellow could do much, particularly if he was careful to cable the money to the New York bank by the seventh day. And even if you forgot—or couldn't get the money in time—why it wasn't too difficult for you to persuade your creditor to try depositing the check once more. A stupid clerical error at the bank. So the check would make another sea voyage and, like certain wines, would travel well. With a little luck and some ordinary business lies a man could have free use of large sums for up to 24 days.

With some $40,000 worth of checks issued on National City Bank, Alves Reis bought control of Ambaca. When he controlled the railway company's reserves he was able to make good the checks.

Using the remaining $60,000 he bought control of the South

---

* Still Royal although the Portuguese monarchy was deposed in October, 1910, with a minimum of violence.

Angola Mining Company. He talked the company up with the zeal of a born tout and the shares rose even though its mining engineers had yet to turn up a worthwhile core of ore.

Early in 1924 he was introduced to José Bandeira who was supposed to represent an important Dutch financial group interested in the Angola oil fields. Since the South Angola Mining Company owned some oil claims as well, Alves Reis was eager to meet Bandeira. They hit it off well, Reis recalled, and

> Bandeira left me with the impression he had talked with a white chieftain of Angola. The next morning I ran into Bandeira waiting for a street car. I gave him a lift in my chauffeured car. At my office Bandeira was so impressed he asked me to give him option rights on the mining company stock and volunteered to introduce me to his friends if I ever went to Holland. As soon as I realized he had excellent connections in The Hague I decided to use him, just as we might use lemons: we squeeze them and discard them. Bandeira was for me an agent, a blind collaborator in my plan, a mere instrument for the attainment of my goal.

In May, 1924, Reis went to The Hague and Bandeira introduced him to his friends, Hennies and Marang.

> I was greatly charmed by Hennies. He knew about world finance with great precision. . . . He was more of a financier than a businessman, more practical than theoretical, clear in his logic, a sharp mind tested by failure and triumph. He was used to the whims of destiny.

Reis was somewhat less impressed by Karel Marang.

> A typical Dutch trader, smart rather than intelligent but deeply versed in trade deals.

They reached an informal agreement to make some trading deals in Angola, mainly involving shipments of German beer. The possibility of Hennies and Marang buying stock in the South Angola Mining Company seemed dim. Both men had the disconcerting habit of asking what the ore production of the firm was; *promises* they discounted at 100% immediately.

When Reis returned to Lisbon in June he found his firm faced by its worst crisis: his two partners wanted to get out. They had learned of the Ambaca reserve fund gambit and feared their partner was heading for jail.

On July 5th Reis was arrested and taken to Oporto that same evening. The charge, that he had embezzled $100,000 from the Ambaca company, had been made by three members of the Ambaca Board of Directors. Two of them were also directors of Oporto banks and they had used their influence to have him brought to Oporto for questioning. "A city where I knew nobody," Reis mourned.

Hennies and José Bandeira had arrived in Lisbon that very day. When they heard Alves Reis had been arrested they decided to return to The Hague. But Senhora Reis who knew how much her husband had counted on an association with the Dutch financiers, went to their hotel and pleaded tearfully for them to go to the Oporto jail to talk to her husband. He could explain everything.

In jail Reis was eloquent in his denunciation of the jealous political enemies who had conspired against him. Hennies asked Reis why he didn't solve his problems by selling the mining company stock and putting the money back in the Ambaca treasury. Reis went into a long involved explanation—how could he tell them the stock was almost worthless?—and the two visitors left him with much self-congratulation on their not getting involved. In Lisbon, Hennies wired his Angola agent to divert the shipment of beer he had consigned to the Alves Reis company. When they returned to The Hague they did not expect to hear from Reis again. And he had once seemed *so* promising.

In order to raise money for his defense and possible restitution to the swindled Ambaca stock and bondholders, Alves Reis had to liquidate all his assets. He wrote frantically, almost incoherently, to his wife from the Oporto jail:

> My Dear and Holy Wife,
> Ferreira [his trusted office manager] has just arrived and I know that until yesterday nothing had happened to the house. . . . Despite my 27 years, I have more experience than all the others . . . I have lost all hope of getting out of this prison before the trial. . . . Don't worry about the money, my love; do exactly as I tell you about the sale of the house and the payments to be made

from the sale of the jewels and the money will come as long as the auction will produce enough. Everything indicates that the whole thing must be done urgently. The jewels and silver you don't sell bring with you here and in the two hours that we can talk every day we can deal with everything.

Don't worry, love, life is like that and we must resign ourselves. . . . Your husband, dear wife, always helped everybody, now nobody helps him. What a great lesson! Kisses for the kiddies. And bring me some bedsheets.

> Millions of kisses from your
> loving husband

Alves Reis spent 54 days in the Oporto jail. When he stopped feeling sorry for himself and bitter at the ingratitude of those he had helped in the past, he started to do some thinking about the causes of his predicament. Clearly, the prime cause was a simple lack of money.

What was money, anyway? Mere paper! Portugal had long abandoned the gold standard. Look what Germany had been doing officially with its cascading inflation of banknotes. When the government needed money it simply kept the presses going. Look at Hungary . . . look at Italy . . . everywhere the money presses were running overtime.

And it wasn't even the state itself that kept this privilege in Portugal. Portugal had given this power of making a piece of paper have legal value to a semi-private institution: the Bank of Portugal. "Such an enormous privilege," Reis wrote, "can make the state into the slave of the holders of this great power."

He had Ferreira bring him everything he could find on the Bank of Portugal and its organization: by-laws, history, annual reports, clippings.

Under the law of 1887, he found, the Bank of Portugal had the exclusive license to issue banknotes in that country, to the amount of twice its paid-up capital. Most of the Bank's stock was held in private hands and the government itself controlled the rest. The Bank's considerable annual profits were proportionately divided between the private stockholders and the government.

Reis found clues suggesting that by 1924 the Bank, in order to accommodate a hard-pressed government, had issued notes to the extent of more than a hundred times the Bank's capital. Every

time the government was hard-up—all too often—it merely
turned to the Bank of Portugal and ordered it to issue more banknotes. Since the banknotes were not convertible to gold or silver
after 1891 the only expense involved was the cost of printing.
Fortunately, Portugal's inflation wasn't anywhere near the insane
level of Germany's in the early Twenties.

Between 1918 and 1923 there had been a six-fold increase in
the number of escudos issued by the Bank of Portugal. Naturally,
the more paper issued the greater the fall in value of the escudo
in terms of uninflated foreign currency. For example, in 1918 a
British pound was worth about eight escudos, or roughly about
60¢ per escudo. But by 1923 you could get 105 escudos to the
pound, or less than 5¢ per escudo.

As the pattern became clear, Reis was also encouraged by
another discovery. He had worked out a fairly complete chart of
the functions of the Bank's various departments. To his relief and
amused amazement he found there was no department specifically charged with seeing there were no duplicate numbers of the
banknotes or that the numbers coincided with the Bank's own
issue. The bank would get the dirty, old bills from its branches
and other private banks. These would be washed and pressed and
then sorted out by series and number for re-use.*

> I worked and reworked my estimates [he wrote later] to find
> out what was the most conservative figure for an issue of banknotes
> by me that would not throw out of gear the official bank machin-
> ery. The best figure was 300 million escudos or some £3,000,000
> [then about $15,000,000]. What great achievement, what splen-
> did undertakings I could initiate for Portugal and Angola with
> this money!

The courts of Portugal suspend all operations during the
summer months and Reis had all of July and August to work out
the rough steps of his plan. At his trial on August 27, 1924, the
judge acquitted him on the charge of embezzlement but did
order him held on a charge of fraud—issuing a $5,000 check on

---

* Although the Bank of Portugal had been patterned pretty much after
the grandmother of all central banks, the Bank of England, there were
key omissions. When a note, no matter how little worn, was returned to
the Bank of England the serial number was noted and the note retired
from further use. A new one would be issued in its place. A poor country
such as Portugal could not afford the luxury of eliminating filthy lucre.

the National City Bank of New York without adequate cover. On this charge Reis was released on $10,000 bail which he raised by the sale of jewelry, cars, and some loans from friends. In addition he raised another $5,000 to cover the rubber check and with consent of his placated creditors was able to get the case moved to a civil, rather than criminal court, where it was more likely he could win his case.

After 54 days in prison he emerged a secret but potential conqueror of the Bank of Portugal. He rushed to a beach resort near Oporto where his wife and three sons—the third had been born in May—greeted him with tears and kisses. Then that evening he found that his friends had not deserted him at all. In a leading Oporto restaurant he was given a *Banquete de Homenagem,* a Banquet of Homage, a fairly common social occasion in Portuguese commercial life. The banquets are used to celebrate a man's promotion in the firm or when his business has put over a big deal.

"My friends," said Reis between tears, "you have rehabilitated me in my own eyes with this great occasion."

Outside rehabilitation would also be useful.

> I skillfully utilized the press of Lisbon and Oporto by getting them to run accounts to reveal to the public the political and financial cabal that had sent me to prison unjustly.

It was not as difficult a public relations feat as it sounds. In Portugal there is no easy way of distinguishing between news and ads. Most columns are for sale and paid advertisements are used for far more purposes than in the U.S. press.*

Copies of these newspaper "vindications" were sent to Hennies and Marang. Reis knew he would need their help in getting out his private issue of banknotes.

> But I never dreamed of having Hennies or Bandeira or anyone else become my accomplice. A secret is only a secret only when it is one man's secret. Nor would I accept being a subordinate to Marang, Hennies or Bandeira. And I was sure they would not accept being subordinate to an Alves Reis. No, the only way to win

---

* Even grateful patients take ads saying that "only thanks to the brilliant work of Dr._____ was my life saved . . ." There is a suspicion that that most such ads are often sponsored jointly—by patient and doctor.

them over would be for me to pretend to be acting on higher orders
—those of the Bank of Portugal itself.

To reach Marang and Hennies, Reis had to go through his
first contact with them: José Bandeira. But his letters and wires
to José in The Hague were unanswered.* For one who had been
a prisoner, José bore an unreasonable superstition: he looked
upon all other ex-prisoners as bearers of bad luck.

In October, 1924, Reis' persistence had effect. José became
curious enough about a new proposition of making a $5,000,000
loan to Angola—with a 2% commission to those who could arrange it—to wire Reis that he would be glad to meet him in Paris.

From Paris, José took Reis to Hennies in Berlin where he
was staying at the Hotel Bristol.

> Hennies greeted me affably and showed great interest in my
> plans but I could see that he wasn't too keen on the idea of a mil-
> lion pound loan to what he considered a bankrupt colony. We had
> dinner alone and gradually I led the conversation around to the col-
> lected data I had on the secret issues of the Bank of Portugal. Later
> in my suite at the Bristol I showed him my file on the Bank. I con-
> vinced him that there had been such secret banknote issues to help
> the government and the Bank of Portugal. When I saw that Hen-
> nies had fallen for the bait I pretended to be doubtful as to the suc-
> cess of my contemplated financial operation as I knew nobody
> abroad to whom I could entrust a secret order for the manufacture
> of paper currency. Hennies thought there wouldn't be any diffi-
> culty in manufacturing Bank of Portugal notes once the contracts
> gave the necessary powers for any printing firm to do so. The next
> day he introduced me to his German lawyer who told me just what
> conditions would have to be specified in such a contract in order to
> get a German banknote firm to handle it.

When he returned to Lisbon in mid-November, 1924, Alves
Reis had a fairly clear idea of how the first fraudulent contract
was to be drawn. He didn't worry about the contract's *logic*.

The document that Alves Reis prepared in his office this
November evening was patently foolish—and considering his

---

* Long distance lines to and from Lisbon in those days were mainly
reserved for government use, Indeed, until 1952 long distance calls from
Lisbon were rare and very difficult to place.

long-term goal—totally inadequate. It was as if the builders of a moon-rocket were to depend mainly on a roll of scotch tape, two paper clips and three nails.

The contract he contrived postulated an international group of financiers who were going to lend the Portuguese African colony of Angola £1,000,000 (then about $5,000,000). In exchange they were to get the right to issue banknotes for the colony to the value of $5,000,000. There were other details but the whole undertaking had the pointlessness of an expensive counterfeiting of U.S Confederate States Money—in 1966.

In November, 1924, Angola's finances were at the worst in its 400-year history as a colony. Its currency was not convertible into any European currency, including the Portuguese. Trade was meager, bankruptcy common as malaria. Most of the Portuguese settlers would gladly have left if they could find someone to buy their businesses or farms. Angola didn't have any gold or other immediately valuable natural resources—oil was not to be discovered in any important quantities for another thirty years—and its exports were falling off.

Portugal, often called the Vatican's Quinta [farm] in turn, joked bitterly that Angola was its own poor farm. Clearly no banker who ever took a good look at the colony's balance sheet would *lend* it £1,000,000. For that kind of money it might be worth *buying*—after all, it was twice the size of Texas or nearly 500,000 square miles—but it was certainly not a good risk for a loan.

Not only was an Angola loan as risky as roulette but the whole idea that a sovereign government should permit an outside group to duplicate its currency for private use was unthinkable. The last time anyone mentioned it was 1914 when Alfred Loewenstein, a hard-nosed Belgian financier, offered his invaded and war-ravaged country a loan of $50,000,000 to insure stabilization of the Belgian franc. All he asked for was a low rate of interest—plus the right to print Belgian banknotes.* He was

---

* A somewhat different case in 1945 involved the U.S. Treasury turning over Occupation Currency plates to the Russians so they could print Allied military marks and pay their troops. Because U.S. military authorities permitted G.I.s to convert military marks into dollars—as a morale booster—the U.S. Treasury was out some $530,000,000. In July, 1945, alone, when American soldiers in the Berlin sector drew $1,000,000 in pay, they

turned down as fiercely as if he had proposed renting the royal family to stud.

The very wildness, the obvious hopelessness of the scheme made it impossible for Alves Reis to ask wiser men for their opinion. It was just as well.

"Gullibility is the key to all adventures," warned G. K. Chesterton, in what some might take as an encouragement of the amateur in crime. "The greenhorn is the ultimate victor in everything; it is he that gets the most out of life."

A beggar clothed in the vestments of a Prussian officer had acquired fantastic powers, Alves Reis remembered from the story of the Captain of Koepenick. Similarly, a ridiculous document clothed in the *papel selado,* the official seal paper of Portugal might acquire great dignity and importance.

Then, as now, *papel selado* was the universal solvent that converted all business contracts, all public contacts with government into the stuff of sanction.

The stamped paper can only be purchased in stationery shops which have a license to sell them. They are still needed for all official business whether you apply for a job, a transcript of a birth or death certificate, deeds of sale or an application for a passport. Today, tourists have to sign these stamped papers even for car rentals. The fold down the middle provides four lined sides. When preparing the document not a line must be skipped. If you misspell a word you simply repeat the word and add "digo" ("I say"), or correction. The only printing on the Official Seal paper which is issued by the government is a line at the top of the first and fourth pages which simply says *Imposto do Selo* (Stamp Tax) 1$50, the Portuguese way of writing 1-½ escudos. (About 8¢ in 1924.)

Ordinarily, business contracts typed on *papel selado* require revenue stamps corresponding to the value of the contract. But since "the government was involved" Alves Reis decided the stamps weren't required. But there was no getting around the need for the notarizations. Indeed, Reis welcomed this touch:

managed to send home to the U.S. some $3,000,000. The Russian troops, warned that their occupation marks would not be convertible into rubles, bought G.I. wristwatches and Parker pens for $1,000 each, cartons of cigarettes for $150 each.

they would enormously increase the look of authenticity the document needed.

Near midnight he closed the office, walked down the narrow street where he had parked his Nash sedan. An agency for the American car had been one of the unlucky ventures of A. V. Alves Reis Limitado and tomorrow he would have to sell the car in order to meet his office payroll. He drove past the nearby 110-year-old, five-story Bank of Portugal building. He threw it a kiss, a suitor certain of eventual conquest. He drove idly, savoring his last ride in the car. In the upper portion of the hilly city he passed the Army barracks near the old English Protestant Church and graveyard.

At midnight the Army sentry let out his traditional cry, "Twelve o'clock and all is well!" in a remotely recognizable English. This, like many of the orders in Portuguese cavalry regiments were still given in English, a relic of Wellington's presence. Alves Reis, who prided himself on his small knowledge of English, threw a vague salute at the sentry. All was not yet well but it would be before long.

He drove past the fine apartment building where he and his family had a grand 12-room apartment until a few months ago. With the downturn in his fortunes that, too, had to be sold, along with most of the furniture and his wife's jewels. Finally, he reached the second-rate Metropole Hotel where they had two rooms. The three boys were in one room and he tiptoed in to kiss the sleeping Guilherme Joaquim, six; Manuel Filipe, five, and the baby, José Luis, named after Alves Reis' new business associate, José Bandeira. In the bedroom Alves Reis took off his shoes with a sigh of relief,* undressed quickly and had the last of his daily quota of 100 cigarettes.

The next morning he took the contract he had drawn to the office of a friendly notary, Dr. Avelino de Faria. In Portugal every businessman must have a notary witness every contract, every business use of his signature. On starting a business every Portuguese "opens a signature" with a notary. Thereafter, the notary confirms his client's signature on every contract by comparing it to the signature he has in his files. The notary is one of

---

* Like most Portuguese men, he prided himself on his small feet. To make them seem even smaller, he wore shoes a size too short.

the great sinecures of Portugal: every time he confirms a client's signature he gets 75¢. Better still, he also gets 1% of the value of the contract so that a deal for, say, $100,000 would net the notary $1,000. Part of his fee the notary turns over to the state. In return the notary is supposed to read the contract carefully to make certain it does not contain any illicit or even criminal provisions. The notary is not allowed to assess a fee against contracts made with a government agency.

The notary wasn't in, but his assistant was. Without reading the contract—after all, everyone knew Alves Reis was a legitimate businessman of some standing—he added the notary's stamp and signature. After lunch Alves Reis took the contract with the notarial seal to the British consulate. Each foreign consulate, he knew, had a copy of the official signatures of the Portuguese notaries. In a few minutes the consular clerk, without reading the contract, verified the fact that it was indeed the signature of Notary Avelino de Faria on the contract. He placed the impressive British consular stamp on the document, collected his $2.50 fee and returned the contract to Alves Reis. Later that day Reis sent his confidential clerk, Ahrens Novaes, to the French and German consulates so that they, too, would authenticate the signature of Notary Avelino de Faria. By evening Reis had an impressive but still incomplete document.

Now he had his office manager, Francisco Ferreira, Jr., a former Army lieutenant, retype the contract on *papel selado* in both Portuguese and French in adjoining columns. Ferreira, enormously flattered that his employer had let him in on so secret a state document, did a much better typing job than his boss; and he also improved his employer's schoolboy French in the translation. When he finished typing Alves Reis told him he was going to get the necessary official signatures.

That night after his employes left Reis got the signatures —by tracing them. He appended the signatures of Francisco da Cunha Rego Chaves, the High Commissioner of Angola; Daniel Rodriguez the Minister of Finance and Delfim Costa, a technical representative of the Angola government. He didn't have to worry how accurate his forgeries were—after all, the consular stamps would vouch for their authenticity. He carefully cut off the two pages of notarizations from the original *papel selado* and bound it to the new one with tape and sealing wax. On the soft wax he carefully pressed a signet ring with the Portuguese coat of arms. Then as a final touch he appended two new Portuguese banknotes—one for 1000 escudos (then about $50) and another for 500 escudos. Presumably these were the banknotes that the agreement would permit the international financial group to have duplicated in return for its loan of $5,000,000 to poor Angola.

Now Alves Reis was ready to present the impressive contract to two of the three men he had selected to help him in his great scheme. Karel Marang and José Bandeira were staying at the Avenida Palace Hotel—then Lisbon's finest—and had been patiently awaiting a look at the magic contract Alves Reis had been talking about for several weeks.

As he drove to the Avenida Palace, Reis rehearsed his little talk about how difficult it had been to secure the contract from the government, how few were in on the secret, how confidential everything must be kept. A pity, he mused, he couldn't tell them how clever he had been in preparing the contract, for unless they believed the contract was genuine he would not be able to get their cooperation.

Karel Marang van Ysselveere * would have appreciated how clever he have been. But, of course, he could not be told. He was going to finance the operation.

PARIS / November 28, 1924

IT HAD BEEN a frustrating week for Karel Marang.

At his office in The Hague he got the telegram from Lisbon that the contract was about to be signed. Quickly he decided to

* Y appears only in Dutch words and names of foreign origin. In Holland Marang spelled the name IJsselveere and the IJ diphthong was pronounced as the *ai* in aisle. Abroad Marang would simply spell the last part of his name with a starting Y.

combine the trip south with a nettlesome piece of business in Paris. It was so delicate and personal he didn't mention it to his friend and colleague, José Bandeira, the younger brother of the Portuguese Minister to the Netherlands. Through José, Karel Marang had first met Alves Reis.

Since he couldn't discuss his Paris business with José, Marang arranged that they would leave The Hague separately on their way to Lisbon. José, who had an extraordinarily active sex life, would simply think Marang wanted to do some intensive visiting of the Paris *bagnios de luxe* such as the Sphinx. Marang didn't know him well enough—did he know *anyone* that well? —to admit that his overwhelming passion was not titillation but titles.

In Paris, Marang had a rendezvous with a baron.

Baron Rudolf August Louis Lehmann, Minister Plenipotentiary of the Republic of Liberia to the Third French Republic and the League of Nations, lived in a large ormolued apartment at 80 Avenue du Bois de Boulogne, just beyond the Porte de Neuilly. It has since become Avenue Foch, then as now *the* most fashionable street to live on in Paris. Two Rothschild mansions were on the same street.

While he waited for the Baron, Marang quickly took in, with firm approval, the lofty ceilinged room encrusted with marble, gilt and silk.

Before visiting the Baron, Marang had done some checking. The Baron was an *Officier de l'Inspection Publique* for "contributions made to French education"—a typical staging area for seekers of the Legion d'Honneur—and he belonged to three fashionable clubs. He had a chateau in the country and was married to an American lady, the former Charlotte Dell.

Marang's most important finding was that the Baron was *not* listed in any of the German, Austrian or Dutch nobility archives or even those of the Holy See for a possible Vatican title. The Baron, born in Amsterdam in 1870 of prosperous German parents, had a few tufts of hair on his almost bald head, a heavy fringe of iron-gray hair around the back of his head and a spiky moustache. His forehead sloped upward through a series of skin ridges and there were rolls of fat on his neck. He dressed with care.

The Dutch visitor was quickly dissected by the Baron. He saw a tall, moustached, handsome fellow of about 40 who spoke a careful but unidiomatic French. His hair and eyes were brown and there was a small port-wine birthmark on the left side of his neck.

Marang, the Baron deduced, had money at one time— probably a war profiteer—but now was probably undergoing some difficulties: the benchmade London shoes were beginning to show faint cracks due to lack of proper care and he had probably walked to the house from the nearest Metro stop. There was dust on his shoes and his face showed some perspiration. Now what did this fellow want?

Marang told him. To strengthen his request Marang had brought with him documents that attested to the fact that he was, indeed, the Consul General of the Central American republic of San Salvador and he was also Consul General of Persia to The Hague.

Marang wanted his Liberian diplomatic passport renewed. It was now, alas, ten years out of date. It had been issued in 1914 by Count Matzenauer de Matzenau, a Serbian who was then Liberian Minister to Imperial Russia. The passport declared that the bearer, Karel Marang, was the Secretary and Counselor of the Liberian Legation in Petrograd.

What was a Serbian doing as Liberian Minister to Russia? Baron Lehmann, a Netherlander who was now Liberian Minister to France, knew. The impoverished Liberian Republic which in 1923 had an annual budget of $380,000—nearly all derived from customs duties—clearly could not afford the expensive apparatus of paid representation abroad by its own nationals. In 1909 the government was officially declared bankrupt by a visiting American commission. A small international loan in 1912 enabled the government to continue on a modest level that certainly did not include representation abroad.

So long ago Liberia learned from even wealthier countries and farmed out its diplomatic posts to Europeans who, for the honor and diplomatic privileges, undertook to represent Liberia abroad.* The privileges were mainly social but potentially profit-

---

* Not until 1944 did Liberia begin paying its Ambassadors and Ministers abroad. Naturally they use Liberians for these paid posts. The current cost: about $1,000,000 a year.

able. A European acting as a Minister Plenipotentiary or consul general could use diplomatic immunity to smuggle much-wanted and highly taxed goods such as coffee and cigarettes and even autos.* He could sell various non-existent posts in his legation to other Europeans who wanted the honor and the diplomatic passport that went with it. If he was greedier—and more desperate—he could even use the post for a certain amount of discreet espionage for certain powers.

In October, 1914, Marang had purchased his Liberian diplomatic passport from Count Matzenauer for $1100. It had been worthless even then: Matzenauer had been dismissed from the Liberian diplomatic corps in 1913 for varied abuses of his post that even the easy-going Liberian government couldn't tolerate. Since Liberia had not recognized the Soviet Union the Marang passport was clearly invalid on at least two counts.

Marang took the news with a certain calm. He wasn't overly surprised although he hated to be shown up as a dupe who purchased a diplomatic document from a man who had no right to sell it. But in October, 1914, when he bought it from Count Matzenauer, then passing through neutral Holland, there was no easy way to check.

For the $1100 Matzenauer was also going to perform other duties: he would guarantee to get Marang into the *Almanach de Gotha*. Most people didn't know that the standard reference volume also published separate handbooks in German covering the lesser nobility. Listing in these handbooks came only after application to the *Almanach's* editor, Herr Hofrat Wendelmarth. The applicant had to include a historical account of his family enclosing letters patent, a description of the family's coat of arms, and a list of all surviving members.

Matzenauer made it clear that he would take care of these "annoying" details. He had done so many times before. At Matzenau Castle in Prosenyakovsei in Serbia (now part of Yugo-

---

* How little has changed is indicated in a *New York Times* item of March 22, 1965, from Buenos Aires. A Washington order forbidding U.S. diplomatic and government personnel from selling their cars and other personal belongings at a profit while serving abroad, aroused anger. "The transactions of Americans are undoubtedly slight compared with similar activities by some members of other diplomatic missions. These missions openly admit that part of their maintenance costs are covered by selling duty-free goods."

slavia) he had a splendid workshop for this kind of work. Was *he* - a real count? The Gotha handbook said he was.

In 1924 Italy's new dictator, Benito Mussolini, promulgated a curious law: everyone bearing a title not authenticated in the Italian Herald's office would be liable to a fine of 5,000 lire or $300. The Italian Herald office estimated only 10,000 of the 250,000 titles actually in use were genuine. The fines shot up with the title: the would-be duke must pay 70,000 lire, or $4200, the count $2400 and a baron or *one who wanted to be known as a baron,* only $1800.

In France the situation was no better, although the Chamber of Deputies didn't have the taxing genius of a Mussolini. There, one authority estimated, out of every 100 titles used only five were genuine—and those five, alas, existed in confusing duplication. There were eight Counts of Andigne, eight Counts of Bearn, ten Counts of Chabanne and nineteen Counts of Rochefoucauld; and fifty princes or princesses de Broglie.

Only in his own country, the Netherlands, Marang mused, was there a sober scarcity of titles, legitimate or not. In 1915 he had bought the title of the Manor of d'Ysselveere—les Krimpen, which enabled Marang to add van Ysselveere to his name.* The only difficulty was that the Dutch authorities would not accept the change; his own Dutch passport still bore the plebian Karel Marang. Ysselveere was a tiny village near the city of Dordrecht —about 15 miles southeast of Rotterdam—where he was born on July 13, 1884. Marang's father was a debt collector who used primitive strong-arm tactics.

An indifferent scholar for the most part, Marang became an apt student of different ways of making money with little capital. By 1914 he had accumulated a modest bankroll—just in time for his great opportunity.

He became one of many suppliers of wheat, ham, chocolate and oils to the Germans. He assumed the Germans would win.

---

* The general stereotype of the Dutch—the thrifty, solid, no-nonsense Dutch—makes Marang seem terribly atypical. Yet in some ways he resembled a far better-known seeker of Dutch honors: Martin Van Buren, the 8th President of the United States. Although he began life as the son of a poor farmer and tavernkeeper and rose to the highest honor his country could bestow, he felt something more was lacking. In his retirement he made many valiant efforts and finally corrected the deficiency. By methods not known he was able to obtain an ancestral coat of arms from Holland which he displayed prominently in his home.

Besides, it was easier to communicate with and get paid by the Germans. Trade with the U.S. and Britain was hampered severely by the German submarine warfare policy while trade with Germany was almost unfettered. Neutral Holland's only source of coal, iron and steel was now Germany.

True, the Dutch traders with Germany had to contend with the Netherlands Overseas Trust, a body of prominent merchants and bankers who saw to it that no goods were exported to Germany unless such exportation was permitted by the Allies. But there were ways to get around the restrictions and the border was remarkably elastic. A few hundred guilders was usually an effective and literal head-turner for many customs men.

Marang's main contact was a member of the German Purchasing Commission named Adolf Gustav Hennies, who had a Swiss passport. Hennies said his father was Swiss, his mother Brazilian. The arrangement was a sensible commercial one: Marang gave Hennies 10% of the gross value of his German shipments as a "commission."

It was profitable until early 1917 when the Dutch created their Netherlands Export Company with firm control over all exports and imports with a 5% limit on profits—compared to the 40–50% most exporters had been making. Until the U.S. entered the war Marang was able to bring coal over by the boatload and then transship it to Germany via Nord Deutscher Lloyd Line for which he acted as Dutch agent.

By the time the U.S. entered the war the export profits were down ruinously. There was little to export. Bread and coal were already severely rationed in Holland. Marang smuggled chocolate to Germany and kept on making good profits but by early 1918 even that was unobtainable and for the rest of the year he had a severe trading loss because he had to maintain a large staff.

From 1920 to 1923 his import-export firm, Marang & Collignon, prospered by shipping coffee to Persia and the Middle East and various African vegetable oils to Germany.

In 1922 Marang bought out his partner and ran the operation from his home in The Hague. There the first floor was given over to his offices and the upper three stories were living quarters for himself, his wife and two sons, and servants.

By early 1924 the firm was in trouble. Coffee prices had fallen and Marang was overextended. Before Marang's trip to

Paris in November, 1924, his bookkeeper showed him a sour statement: Marang & Collignon owed banks more than $100,000. By great effort Marang had been able to renew the several bank loans by agreeing to a higher interest rate.

Why should a businessman facing economic disaster be so interested in getting another diplomatic passport? To Marang who was meagerly educated and came from a lower-middle class family these foreign honors were the great equalizer. With them, he felt, would come more business opportunities.*

That night he took the Sud Express to Lisbon. Baron Lehmann had turned him down completely. And insolently.

LISBON / November 30, 1924

AT DINNER that night in a private room of Silva's restaurant in the Chiado—the expensive shopping district of Lisbon—Marang went over the contract for the fourth time. It was, he agreed with Reis, a *Negocio da China*, a Chinese deal, the Portuguese businessman's shorthand for a business transaction in which you stood to make a lot of money without much trouble, a relic of Portugal's older imperialism in the Far East.

Though he resisted Reis's engulfing enthusiasm, Marang could see no serious obstacles once they got a banknote printer to turn out the authorized notes. Everyone knew about Angola's floundering finances, knew Portuguese officials were underpaid and susceptible. Finally, all Europe knew that the trick of issuing more and more banknotes was the favorite device of desperately indebted governments after World War I.

---

* It helps credit ratings, too. Even today in France any step up in the Legion d'Honneur hierarchy of six classes increases the lucky man's credit by thousands of francs at his bank.

Still, Marang thought, he was the one the others were counting on to finance most of the operation. The business could cost him $10,000 or even $15,000 before it brought in a cent but the potential profits were of an order to make even the German contracts he had during the war seem niggard nonsense.

They talked long and late that night about who might print the banknotes. Their original idea was that Germany was the place—look at all the experience the Weimar Republic had with banknote printing.

Naturally this called for the advice of their expert on affairs German—Hennies. Marang assured Reis and José Bandeira that not only did Hennies know everyone who mattered in German financial circles, he also had certain arcane knowledge from the time he worked with the German Secret Service in the World War.

Reis nodded. This coincided with his own impressions of Hennies. Clearly the Swiss was *o altitudo*, a big shot—just as he, Reis, was about to become.

That night at the Avenida Palace Marang sent two telegrams. The first was to Marang's office in The Hague. He asked his office manager to wire £600 (about $3000) at once to Alves Reis in Lisbon. Reis had been quite insistent. He had incurred heavy obligations in order to get the magic contract signed. Naturally, he could not tell his new colleagues that the $3000 was needed desperately to help stave off his own imminent bankruptcy.

The second wire was to Hennies in Berlin:

CONTRACT SIGNED. NEED YOU IN HAGUE.

BERLIN / December 1, 1924

THE WAR OF 1914–18 which took ten million lives occasionally paid token interest on the great debt by giving some of the participants a second life. Adolf Gustav Hennies was one of the beneficiaries.

College students who first encounter Rimbaud's chilling line "I am another" get a philosophical analysis of just what the poet meant. For Hennies who had never heard of Rimbaud it simply meant that he had a new life, one almost immune to the powers of the police and the state.

The new life and identity commenced in October, 1914, in Brazil. It was, in fact, a third transformation. The second had started in New York in 1909 when he secured a small agency in Brazil from the Singer Sewing Machine Company. And the first? He preferred to forget that completely.

The second life in Manaos, Brazil—in the upper Amazon region—had been fairly prosperous but there had always been the sense of missed opportunity, of mistiming which he blamed on the inadequacies of his first life.

"To establish oneself in the world, one does all one can to seem established there already," wrote La Rochefoucauld for *arrivistes* of all centuries. Unfortunately, he never spelled out just how. Hennies was a good actor, a good talker, but his gestures and approaches were always slightly bigger or smaller than life—a contestant who held the rifle properly but who never, somehow, found the range.

The third transformation was thrust on him in November, 1914, when the Portuguese National Assembly voted to join Great Britain and France in the war against Germany. Hennies, who knew that his second identity was based on his first, which, in turn, was German, feared that Brazil would also join the war on the side of the Allies. In fact this didn't happen until 1917 but the German colony in Rio de Janeiro took fright and hundreds of German nationals in Brazil feared immediate internment as enemy aliens. Most of them frantically bought passage to Germany as quickly as possible. Hennies did some thinking first.

30

From certain sources he procured a false Swiss passport which gave him his new identity—Adolf Gustav Hennies, 33, the son of a Swiss father and a Brazilian mother. Occupation: international trader.

He left Rio in November on the old S.S. *Principessa Mafalda* for Genoa. At Gibraltar the ship was stopped by the British who interrogated each of the men aboard. The interrogation was routine. Each man was called into an office and interviewed in the language he claimed as his own—Portuguese for most of these returning Germans, of course—and then after a few routine questions the interviewer would excuse himself and leave the room. The German would congratulate himself on having fooled the British interviewer and relax. The worst was over. Ten minutes later the British interviewer would return, feign surprise at seeing the German still there and say in perfect German: *"Na, sind Sie denn noch da?"* (Are you still here?) The British caught five of the returning Germans when they blurted out replies in German.

Hennies who suspected a trick of this kind had steeled himself to avoid using German in any way. Ten days later he was in Berlin. A German friend in Rio had given him a letter of introduction to an official in Berlin and in January, 1915, Hennies was on his way to Amsterdam as a member of the large German Purchasing Commission there.

The material he purchased—much through Mijnheer Marang—was routed to Germany via Switzerland, particularly the items that were blacklisted for shipment by Holland and Denmark.

Hennies also did various little jobs for the German Secret Service forces operating out of neutral Holland. There was little danger. Espionage in Holland during the First World War was a polite task for gentlemen. Captain Henry Landau—a South African originally—was in charge of the Field Sections of the British Secret Service in Belgium and Holland. Later he described the idyllic conditions under which Allied and Central espionage sections functioned in Holland:

> The greatest tranquillity reigned. Our codes were left unguarded at night in an ordinary safe, an easy mark for any cracksman: our couriers came and went unprotected. Both sides had too many privileges at stake to run the risk of losing them. Their indi-

vidual officials, without the consent of the Dutch government, demanded favors, which both sides were only too glad to accord them; in return, we secured protection, and were given information about each other. Neither side was favored, and I think the Dutch, the Allies and the Germans were all delighted with the arrangement.

Hennies was 5'7" but carried himself so erectly that he seemed taller. His oval face had a non-Nordic olive-brown complexion so that he was seldom taken for a German. His black hair, combed straight back, was always carefully groomed. He dressed impeccably. From birth his right leg was shorter than the other and he wore a built-up shoe. The slight limp somehow added to his great dignity and self-assurance.

In 1916 when he was 35 he became the lover of Annaliese Angold, a 22-year-old German stenographer attached to the German Purchasing Commission office in Holland. At first as a joke, Hennies used to introduce her to Dutch friends as Fraulein Doktor Angold. The head of the German Secret Service in Belgium was known as Fraulein Doktor—"a good looking, buxom middle-aged woman with the disposition of a tiger," Captain Landau described her. *

Annaliese Angold was a mildly attractive blonde—a pawky pussycat rather than a tiger—who had fallen heavily for Hennies' man-of-the-world airs. She gradually began calling herself Fraulein Doktor, spoke vaguely of a Ph.D. in political economy and became an active aide to Hennies in many of his side-line deals.

By the end of 1917 Hennies was no longer certain that Germany was going to win. With Marang's help he quietly converted all his deutsche-mark holdings into gulden. Thereafter all his commissions were paid by Marang into Dutch bank accounts. By June, 1918, he had the equivalent of $90,000.

With the war's end came other opportunities for a man who had proved himself so deft a trade negotiator. Early in 1919 through his Berlin connections he was able to get himself appointed in East Prussia an "Abwicklungskommissar" or liqui-

---

* The original Fraulein Doktor was Elsbeth Schragmueller who obtained a Ph.D. in languages and economics from Freiburg University. As head of one of the German Secret Service sections in Belgium she became the only woman officer in the German army in World War I.

dator for reparations and arms deliveries to Poland. That country which had been ceded parts of Posen and West Prussia under the Treaty of Versailles was battling Lithuania over the city of Vilna; Czechoslovakia over Teschen; and the Soviet Bolsheviks over everything. Poland had become the great arms sink of Europe.

From his office in Insterburg in East Prussia, Hennies saw considerable opportunity. Every trainload of arms and reparations material went through his hands. The deduction of a small handling fee was to be expected. In addition he arranged some private deals with the Poles. For example, they were most anxious to get a large stock of hand grenades in East Prussia. The Poles were willing to bargain food for the grenades, even if they were short. They turned over American Quaker food shipments to Hennies for the grenades.

Hennies delayed shipment of the grenades until the Poles had shipped the food to Prussia. When the Poles opened the grenade boxes they found that they lacked the necessary fuses. The two Polish generals who had made the deal with Hennies were shot. Hennies sold the American food on the German black market for $50,000.

After leaving the liquidator job, Hennies went on to purely private speculations in Germany—still accompanied by Annaliese Angold. His greatest opportunity came at the end of the great mark inflation in November, 1923. The worthless paper currency was to be replaced by the gold mark, the Rentenmark, theoretically secured by a blanket mortgage on all German land and industry.

It took a barrel of the paper marks to get one gold Rentenmark but there were other banknotes that were as favored. For example, the German Railway's own gold mark banknotes in circulation were to be exchanged for the new mark on a one-to-one basis. From a friendly railway official Hennies learned that at the Deutsche Reichsbahn headquarters there were $750,000 worth of *uncirculated* goldmarks which would, in effect, become worthless after the Rentenmark exchange took place.

Hennies became part of a highly placed group of officials who saw a way to turn these goldmarks into a great private profit. With a special diplomatic passport obtained for him by the German Postmaster General, Dr. Anton Höfle, Hennies went to

London with the uncirculated goldmarks. There he was able to exchange them on the international currency market for pounds and Swiss francs. His share of the operation was worth $40,000. A few weeks after he returned to Berlin he was asked to take an even larger shipment of the railway goldmarks to London— $2,500,000 worth this time. He refused—on a hunch. A few weeks later the Postmaster and most of the others involved in this and several even worse scandals were caught up in Reichstag investigations. In 1925 Höfle killed himself in prison. Hennies had been questioned briefly but nothing more.

All through the postwar years he had kept in touch regularly with his old wartime colleague, Marang. They had profited on some joint export ventures to Africa and Persia—mostly coffee and beer shipments—but until Alves Reis had come along with his magic contract there had been nothing important.

When the wire came from Marang on December 1, 1924, Hennies called his mistress, Annaliese Angold, and told her they were going to The Hague. He also asked his attorney, Felix Lutz, to come along. The contract would bear a lot of looking into, Hennies knew. It sounded *too* good.

THE HAGUE / December 2, 1924

A RECENT PICTURE BOOK on The Hague has a lyrical comment on the city's unsuspected magical powers:

> The broad margin between imagination and reality which is the no-man's land where the Muses flourish, dreams blossom and adventures spring up out of the ground like mushrooms, is ever present in The Hague.

It was there in 1924, too. For José Bandeira the contract Alves Reis had secured represented great opportunity for a fortune at last. During the past three years while he was living with his older brother, Antonio, the Portuguese Minister to the Netherlands, in the narrow four-story building of the Ministry at 43 Bezuedanhout, José knew that his big chance was coming. Not only did he want it for himself and for Antonio but he *needed* it to show Fietje that she had given her love to a man among men, a doer.

Ordinarily, the meeting would have taken place at the suite in that splendid 19th century pile, the Hotel Des Indes, that Hennies usually reserved when he came to The Hague, or at Marang's offices, but Fate was stage-managing beautifully for Bandeira's plans. Hennies' usual suite was taken and they had been able to reserve only single rooms for him, his lawyer and his little friend, Annaliese. Marang's home, where he had his offices, was being painted. Everything considered, the best possible place would be the Portuguese Minister's home. Not only would this underline the official nature of the contract Alves Reis had secured but it would also emphasize the vital role José dos Santos Bandeira * had played in bringing together the key figures in this enormous undertaking. Now, at 43, José knew he was about to get the full radiance of Fortune's smile at last, after so many false dawns, so many shameful shadows.

The Bandeiras, a once-prosperous land-owning family from Chamusca, a small town south of Lisbon, had long ago left the land. Antonio, the oldest son, had entered the Portuguese Foreign Office after a spell of successful journalism. As a well-connected civil servant he had risen steadily to his present post in The Hague.

José, some seven years younger, had been less favored. He had, in fact, become the despair of his father.

In 1900, when he was 19, José left for South Africa to make his fortune. Within a year he had been nabbed for house burglary and given a three-year sentence by a Johannesburg court. He was released after two years and within a few months was sentenced

---

* About Portuguese names: José used to sign his name in full as José dos Santos Bandeira which meant that his father's name had been Bandeira, his mother's Santos. He was generally called Santos Bandeira to distinguish him from the other Bandeiras, rather like the English system of hyphenated names. Similarly, Artur Virgilio Alves Reis was generally called Alves Reis, rather than just Reis as we would do.

by the same court to four years for receiving stolen property. He came out in 1906 and two years later after trying various illegal enterprises without luck was finally reduced to supplying liquor to the natives. A court gave him one year. When he emerged he decided he had had enough of South African justice and returned to Portugal in 1912.

With his father's influence he got a job with Garland, Laidley & Company—they were shipping agents for Cunard and other lines—and for a time he seemed to do well. But in October, 1914, he took $1600 from the firm's safe and fled to Mozambique. (His father, already in a tight financial squeeze, solemnly undertook to reimburse Garland, Laidley for his son's theft. Paying off at the rate of $16 a month, the old man succeeded in repaying the firm by November, 1922.)

In Mozambique an old friend of his father's found José a job with the Mozambique Railway. Within a year José dipped into the firm's till and lit out for South Africa. His father's friend repaid the money and there was no prosecution.

José returned to Lisbon in 1921 and soon was invited to live with his bachelor brother, Antonio, the newly-appointed career Minister to the Netherlands. Perhaps, in a new land, with the steadying influence of his older brother, poor José would find himself.

Thanks to the knowledge of Dutch he had picked up in South Africa from his Boer friends, José had learned his way around The Hague quickly. He also learned that his older brother wasn't quite the steadying influence he had been depicted by their father.

Antonio was earning $200 a month from the Portuguese Foreign Office which paid its foreign representatives rather niggardly. Nearly all nations in the Twenties acted on the assumption that their Ambassadors and Ministers had private means. Several countries, particularly in Latin and South America paid their envoys nothing at all.

With the $200 a month, the house and three servants plus a small entertainment allowance, a prudent Antonio might have gotten by. But Antonio Bandeira was not prudent. He was a compulsive gambler, deeply in debt to several Dutch bankers.

Although Antonio was popular in The Hague's foreign set

there were some diplomats to whom Bandeira was anathema. He confined his affairs largely to wives of diplomats. An ambassador's wife was his current mistress. The affair was conducted with great discretion—only the diplomatic set knew.

His brother José was much less discreet. He wanted everyone to know that his mistress was and had been for some years the well-known Dutch actress, Fie Carelsen. He called her Fietje and was, in her words, "the perfect, attentive lover." They were inseparable at garden parties, concerts and legation affairs.

She was considerably taller than José who was 5'5" but the handsome actress didn't mind. José did. They seldom danced together.

"It isn't a *big* love," Fie Carelsen told friends, "but very warm, enduring and sweet. He is the most attentive man I've ever known."

For José the affair with Fie was not only a great upward step compared to the women he had known in the past but also brought a great change in his luck.

In 1923 he heard of bids being received in Macao, the Portuguese possession off the coast of China, for harbor works. He suggested that Marang and his group ought to submit a bid and then sell the contract to a Dutch construction firm. With his brother's influence, José pointed out, their bid would have a preferred consideration. Marang got a Dutch firm interested. They submitted a bid and got the contract. José got a 2% commission which netted him about $80,000, his first real money.

Now flush, he began looking around for other opportunities. He heard about the South Angola Mining Company, controlled by a Portuguese named Alves Reis, an expert on Angola. In the process he also became a fervent admirer of Alves Reis.

José was not forgetful of his obligations. He gave $10,000 to his brother Antonio, always pressed by respectful but firm creditors.

The black sheep, the family rascal was making good at last. José's father who had just finished paying off his younger son's 1914 theft from Garland, Laidley, wept with joy when he heard of his son's new prosperity. But José didn't send his father an escudo. It was best to forget the troubles of his "green years."

Late in November, 1924, José began dropping excited hints

about the big deal Alves Reis had cooked up for his group. "It's very big," he would say, "the biggest chance I've ever had."

In the morning of December 2, 1924, the Bandeira brothers played host to Marang, Hennies and the latter's Berlin lawyer.

José Bandeira, more ebullient and optimistic than ever, was all for Hennies immediately exploring the possibilities of a German banknote firm turning out the notes stipulated in the contract. But Hennies who had been reading the contract carefully and talking to his attorney, was a cautious skeptic.

"Before we go any further," he said, "I think we should have a better understanding of Alves Reis. Yes, I know you've met him and talked to him and been impressed but what do we *really* know about him? Is he the kind of man who *could* have gotten a contract like this? From what I've been able to find out he's still in trouble with some company manipulation and he's almost bankrupt. Why should the Portuguese government give a man like that an incredible contract like this?"

They turned to José Bandeira who had introduced them to Alves Reis. José was nettled.

"What do you take me for? Of course, I've checked on him."

In the first place Reis, he said, was a big engineer. José had once seen his engineering diploma—it was from Oxford University, no less. Reis had once been in charge of the state railways of Angola and then Inspector of Public Works in the colony, the highest technical post in the colony. He was very well connected with the Portuguese High Commissioner to Angola, Rego Chaves. An intimate, in fact. José had been present a few days ago in Lisbon during a talk between Alves Reis and Rego Chaves and the High Commissioner consistently used the "tu" form of address to Reis which is only used in Portuguese for friends or intimates.

(José's vanity wouldn't let him add that the High Commissioner had addressed *him* as "Meu amigo" which is never used to an equal. In his pique at being addressed as an inferior, José had missed a slurred by-play between Reis and Rego Chaves which made it quite clear that the High Commissioner had used the "tu" form to Alves Reis simply because Reis was a former student of his in the lyceum.)

José was about to go on to explain the circumstances of Reis' present involvement in a suspected embezzlement of stock from a company he headed, when Marang interrupted.

"Adolf, aren't we borrowing trouble? If the contract is genuine, as I think it is, they'll simply turn us down and then we'll know. In that case I'll be out the £600 I advanced Reis but that will be the end of it."

Hennies agreed Marang's approach was both generous and logical.

"All right, let us assume the contract *is* genuine," he said. "You want me to approach some German banknote firm to get the notes printed. Out of the question. In the first place my name was thrown around in the Reichsbahn goldmark affair and I might be suspect. Also, I don't think that a German firm would be right, psychologically. Germany has just been through the world's worst inflation of banknotes. Right now any German-made escudo notes would bear an unnecessary degree of suspicion. Why can't we go to the firm that made the 500 and 1000 escudo-notes for the Bank of Portugal?"

Marang had anticipated this. "I asked Reis this, too, and he said we shouldn't. His friends in the Bank of Portugal said we should get another firm to keep the affair as secret as possible. But there is another way. Coming up from Lisbon on the Sud Express I ran into a Dutch businessman I know. I talked to him about the problem of getting banknotes printed and he recommends a Dutch firm, Enschedé, in Haarlem. They print the Dutch banknotes and I think one or two other countries, too. Why don't I try them first?"

Everyone agreed it was a fine idea. Haarlem is only a 25-mile drive from The Hague.

HAARLEM / December 2, 1924

SINCE 1815 Joh. Enschedé en Zonen N.V.—John Enschedé & Sons, Inc., in American terms—has been the exclusive banknote printers for the Dutch government. In 1865 it began making Netherlands postage stamps as well. In addition, the firm, founded in 1703, had also become one of the world's giants in the field of fine printing. As an engaging promotion booklet put out by Enschedé warns gently:

> Reader, beware of asking an Enschedé man about his company! Ten to one that for the next half hour you will find yourself listening to a lecture on the history of the printing trade. . . .
>
> Rumors that promotion of staff members depends largely on being sufficiently familiar with the genealogical details of the House of Enschedé must be emphatically contradicted. Still no one will deny us the right to be proud of the tradition built up by seven generations over more than two and a half centuries of skillful and progressive management.
>
> A century and a half of banknote printing has trained us to shoulder heavy responsibilities, to identify ourselves with our clients, to partake in the development of their projects from the very beginning, to advise impartially, to share with our customers their joys and their sorrows!

One of the minor sorrows—not mentioned in the promotion booklet—was the impartial advice given on December 3, 1924, to a stranger named Karel Marang van Ysselveere.

Marang came in late in the afternoon of December 2nd.

Boudawijn Franciscus Enschedé, who had just been made a director of the firm at 30, talked to Marang.

Marang was excited but well-spoken, even cultivated, the director later recalled. "I suppose I should have been suspicious of the van Ysselveere part of his name—such an obviously false name—but business was business."

Young Enschedé turned Marang over to Albertus Dithmar Huijsman, the 36-year-old secretary of the firm. As was customary, he received Marang in the firm's museum. This large room off the main offices of the plant contains numerous samples of the

40

fine banknotes and stamps the firm has printed, plus stunning reproductions of great paintings.

"Marang was a tall, impressive gentleman, not without a certain pomposity," Huijsman noted. "He was obviously disappointed about the fact that he was not received by one of the
partners but I explained that he could see them only after the
purpose of his visit was made known."

Marang said his visit dealt with a highly important, even
secret, project; he could talk only to principals.

"If you only knew of my important diplomatic connections,"
Marang added, "you would know I cannot speak to a mere intermediary."

Finally, Marang grudgingly began to disclose some information. Mr. Huijsman took notes:

> He pretended to have in hand an important order for the man-
> ufacture of banknotes for a Western European nation, which coun-
> try normally used to spread the printing of same over various com-
> panies. The aim of his visit was to become acquainted with our
> working methods and which measures were practised against
> breach of trust.
>
> At a point when I had almost lost patience, he let me know
> that the country in question was Portugal. Not having the least sus-
> picion, I said I was very honored indeed with this inquiry. He then
> produced a Portuguese banknote and asked if we could print the
> same. My answer was yes, although I added it would have to be in
> a different style.

Marang reacted quickly. "It must be the same, the exact
same note."

"That's impossible," Huijsman replied. "But if that's what
you need why didn't you go to the firm that printed the original
notes. They have the original printing plates."

Marang was about to give up. The two Portuguese banknotes that Reis had appended to the contract—one for the 1000
escudos and the other for 500 —did not bear *any* maker's name.

Such a peculiarly embarrassing predicament! Here he was
the bearer of a top-level, secret contract signed by Portuguese
officials who had somehow neglected to give him some very basic
information: the name of the firm that printed the notes. Why
should they have kept such data from him?

At this moment Marang reached into his pocket and withdrew his wallet. From it he pulled out another 500-escudos note —bearing the picture of Vasco da Gama, the great explorer. At the bottom of the front of the note was the name of the banknote maker in thin, tiny capitals:

WATERLOW & SONS LIMITED, LONDRES

Huijsman told Marang that his firm would not like to imitate the work of Waterlow & Sons because (a) it wasn't ethical and (b) his firm wouldn't be able to imitate them exactly anyway.

Marang thought for a minute. "Would Enschedé agree to act as an intermediary in having the notes printed by Waterlow? Better still, could your firm order the notes from Waterlow and take care of the whole business?"

Huijsman asked: "Why don't you go to Waterlow's directly?"

Marang murmured vaguely about "the inherent difficulties of controlling the banknote issue" and how much more secure everything would be if it were one banknote firm dealing with another. Huijsman, although a nephew of Charles Enschedé, one of the partners, was a very junior member of the firm. He knew this called for approval on a higher level. He promised to let Marang know the following morning.

On December 3rd Marang appeared at the Enschedé offices again. Huijsman told him that his firm could not undertake to handle the whole deal but perhaps they *might* act as an intermediary. He gave Marang a letter of introduction to Sir William Waterlow of Waterlow & Sons Limited of London:

Haarlem,
3rd December 1924

Sir William Waterlow,
Waterlow and Sons, Ltd.

SIR—We have the honour to introduce to you the bearer of the present, Mr. K. Marang van Ysselveere, of The Hague. The said gentleman visited us in accordance with an order of Portuguese bank notes begging us to take the making of these notes upon us. Examining the specimen shown us we think the work is more in your line and so we advised Mr. Marang van Ysselveere to discuss the matter with you. We think it would be possible the order in question will be executed by your firm and the delivery of the notes is to take place by the intermedium of our firm. We should feel obliged by hearing your opinion about the above and remain, Sir, Yours respectfully

JOH. ENSCHEDÉ EN ZONEN

Marang was pleased. For a complete stranger to Enschedé it was an excellent letter of introduction. Even more to his liking was the somewhat cryptic but easily deciphered line—"and the delivery of the notes is to take place by the intermedium of our firm." This showed clearly that Enschedé thought the contract was valid. So much so that *if* Waterlow got the job Enschedé expected a commission.

With the letter Marang left in his chauffeur-driven Winton-Six for the drive back to The Hague. At his home he packed quickly and told his wife and private secretary, J. E. T. de Jong, that he would be going to London on important business. He phoned José at the Portuguese Legation to tell him of the letter of introduction and requested another letter. He needed a power of attorney to act for Alves Reis. After all the contract was made out to him, not to Karel Marang. They had discussed such a power of attorney in Lisbon and Reis had promised to mail it.

José was glum. "It hasn't come yet. What'll we do?"

Marang knew exactly.

After listening, José persuaded his brother, the Portuguese Minister, to give the Dutchman an impressive letter on the best, thick stationery. It was handwritten and bore the Legation's seal:

> I, the undersigned, the Portuguese Minister in The Hague, do hereby certify that the bearer of this letter, Karl Marang van Issel-veere, a Dutch citizen and businessman, bears a general power of attorney issued by Artur Virgilio Alves Reis, engineer, a Portuguese citizen residing in Lisbon.
>
> The Hague, Dec. 3, 1924
Santos Bandeira

After all, they knew the power of attorney was on its way.

Marang had his secretary, de Jong, wire for a reservation at the Great Eastern Hotel in the City of London. It was next to the Liverpool Street Railroad Station and convenient for continental businessmen visiting firms in the City. His chauffeur drove him the 12 miles south to the Hook of Holland where Marang caught the cross-channel boat to Harwich.

On the boat Marang remembered Alves Reis' strange insistence that under no circumstances must the original maker of the banknotes be approached. Marang troubled himself only for a moment: Waterlow had not made the two notes appended to the Reis contract. He did wonder, though, why Reis had been so insistent.

LONDON / December 4, 1924

WHYTE WAYS, the 18-room Waterlow home in the northwest London suburb of Harrow Weald, was done in the traditional cottage and farm manner rather than in any of the bastard stockbroker Tudor or Gothic revival architecture of the period. It was a good, solid house—a fine match for its owner.

At 53, Sir William Alfred Waterlow was an erect, solidly built 6'2" with a rather commanding presence, almost archetypically representative of the upper classes. He kept in trim with golf and tennis. His tennis style was essentially defensive. He used a tricky cut serve and was good at retrieving difficult backcourt shots but he avoided playing the net where the real tennis players are often separated from the would-be.

His impressive appearance plus a knack for remembering names and faces had helped him in his rise. Unfortunately the good first impressions were later eroded somewhat because of his monumental stubbornness and insistence on having his own way. Although he was a member of the Conservative Club in London and a consistent donor to party funds, he had been turned down the one time he applied for a chance to represent a Conservative constituency in Parliament. It was one of the few major disappointments in his life.

Before he left Whyte Ways this morning for the City, Sir William walked through the two acres of gardens and talked to his three gardeners about winter care. Now that Britain had had its first Labour government in history—it had lasted less than ten months—he, like many other Conservatives, felt it useful to know "what the workingman was thinking." The difficulty, Sir William found, was that the workingmen he was likely to be able to talk to—the eight servants at Whyte Ways or the 7,000 hands at the firm—somehow all sounded like Conservatives when he talked to them.

In the large company Daimler taking him to the City he read about the follow-up of the Zinoviev letter exposé which had broken late in October. In it the Third International, the foreign arm of Soviet Russia, had supposedly instructed British subjects to provoke revolution.

Sir William recalled with pleasure the firm way he had told off a company director who suggested Waterlow go after the Soviet banknote printing, when the Labour government had given the Reds recognition. The Conservatives had properly denounced the treaties with Russia, of course, and any Waterlow approaches would have been a waste of time. But Sir William had rejected the suggestion because he knew the suspicious Russians would no more entrust their banknote printing to capitalists than they would assign their widespread espionage to a foreign contractor. The relationship between a government and its banknote supplier was too intimate to endure the stresses of opposed ideologies. It was, he mused, as he thought of the great banknote inflation Europe was enduring then, rather like the relationship of sinner and confessor.

He read some of the manuscript of the company history to be published shortly. For the past few months he and other members of the family had been talking about the firm—and the family—with John Boon, an elderly ex-newspaper editor who was writing, "Under Six Reigns—the House of Waterlow" to celebrate 114 years of company existence. The only printing firm he could think of with a longer history was that Dutch firm, Enschedé.

Why celebrate 114 years? That wasn't special in itself but 1925, according to some genealogical studies, was the 300th anniversary of the arrival of the first Waterlow in England to escape

religious persecution on the Continent. In 1625 Walran Waterlo, a
native of Lille, came to Canterbury where he was a silk weaver.
Later the Canterbury settlers came to London to join relatives
and friends who had been driven out of France by the revocation
of the Edict of Nantes, which had given the Huguenots equal political rights with the Catholics.

The first Waterlow to enter the printing trade, James, did so
crabwise from the copying business. Early in the 19th century he
was a law writer: he copied legal documents for law firms.

The pay was low, the work arduous. Then in 1811, according
to the official Waterlow history:

> The turn in his fortunes came when he conceived the idea
> of employing lithography and printing as a substitute for copying
> where many copies of legal documents were required thus effect-
> ing a saving of both time and expense . . . notwithstanding the
> opposition of the law stationers, the Admiralty and the Judicature
> approved the innovations. Meanwhile he had taken his sons Alfred,
> Walter, Sydney and Albert into partnership. . . .

In 1844 when the development of the new railroad system
was at its height the Waterlow firm had twenty employes. Alfred
Waterlow saw a great opportunity and seized it. He and his
brothers developed new types of machinery and paper particularly suited to the printing of timetables and tickets. The innova-
tions were successful and the firm grew larger each decade. Stock
certificates for the railroads and other Limited corporations were
turned out by the thousands.

But in 1877, the year after the founder, James Waterlow
died, the firm encountered its first internal difficulty. The sons of
the founder separated. The eldest, Alfred, formed the firm of
Waterlow Brothers and Layton which retained most of the legal
and general printing business. (Layton had been associated with
the firm since 1839.) Alfred took his three sons, Alfred, Jr., Her-
bert and Walter into the firm.

The other firm, Waterlow & Sons Ltd., was formed by Sir
Sydney Waterlow and his sons, Philip, George and Charles. Sir
Sydney, very much the public figure was first Sheriff, then Alderman and finally Lord Mayor of the City of London, the crowded
square mile that makes up London's great financial district; he

also became a Member of Parliament. Sir Sydney was an innovator—he conceived and set up the first telegraphic communications system for the London police—and a philanthropist. He was the founder of the Industrial Dwellings Company which erected 6,000 low-rent tenement apartments in London. Sir Sydney's firm took over the original company's railway printing work plus the printing of foreign currency and postage stamps which the original firm had started doing in 1850.

Both offshoots thrived and got along with a minimum of friction by avoiding competitive spheres. They might have remained separate entities if Alfred's grandson, William Alfred Waterlow, hadn't decided in 1914 that the banknote printing business was a desirable one.

William was born April 23, 1871, to James Jameson Waterlow, one of the four sons of Alfred, the eldest son of the founder. William's father, James, was the only one of the sons who didn't take an active role in the firm.

James died a few months before this second son, William, was born and the lad was raised largely in the home of his grandfather, Alfred, now the head of Waterlow Brothers & Layton. Alfred sent his fatherless grandson to a good public school, Marlborough. After he was articled to a solicitor, Sir Thomas Paine, and in 1896 was admitted as a solicitor. In less than a year he joined his grandfather's firm, Waterlow Brothers & Layton, from a rather advanced apprentice perch as director.

In 1904 when he was 33, William Waterlow married an Edinburgh lady, Adelaide Hay, 32. They met during a golf game. The marriage was a good one and produced two sons. Waterlow did not make and keep friends easily and his wife became his confidante in business matters.

His reputation in the printing trade grew and in 1914 he became president of the Federation of Master Printers of Great Britain, after having served as Master of the Stationers Company, one of the 81 ancient guilds of the City of London.

As Managing Director of Waterlow Brothers & Layton he pushed the growing firm more into foreign banknote work, sometimes taking accounts away from the rival firm run by his cousins. But the snatched job that rankled them most was the local one for 100,000,000 British Treasury notes of £1 each. William got the order because he promised to deliver the first four million notes in five days. He got the order on August 2, 1914—the day Germany had declared war on Russia, when formal mobilization orders were issued in France and Germany.

On August 6th when the banks reopened—the August Bank Holiday had been extended three days by official proclamation —they had 2½ million of the new pound notes printed by Sir William's firm on postage-stamp paper rather than the fine linen-cotton paper which the Portal family had been supplying the Bank of England for its banknotes since 1724. The new notes were smaller than the traditional Bank of England currency and were signed by Sir John Bradbury, the Permanent Secretary to the Treasury. Inevitably, they were called Bradburys.

There was a certain amount of criticism from bankers who felt the Bradburys were not particularly good examples of banknote printing. In the great haste some banknote bundles were delivered wrapped in uncut sheets of the new banknote. But they were delivered on time to let the banks open. It was a great printing coup.

Later Waterlow & Layton also won the contract for printing several million ten-shilling notes but had to share the overall order with a competitor, Thomas de la Rue & Company.

As the demand grew for paper money Waterlow & Layton built a new banknote printing plant at Watford. In addition to the £1 and 10 shilling notes they also did the notes for the several Scottish banks which traditionally printed their own notes and certain English county banks which had permission to issue their own notes—a right that wasn't removed until 1921.

On January 7, 1919, William Waterlow was made a Knight Commander of the Civil Division of the Order of the British Empire, for the services he and his firm had rendered the Crown during the war. The honor was a comparatively low one—ranking below the Knights Grand Cross and the Companions of Honour but above the Knights Bachelor. In any case he was now Sir William Alfred Waterlow, K.B.E.

In some respects 1919 was a bad vintage year for honors. The postwar harvest had been too bountiful. Lloyd George who had been a leading member of the Asquith cabinet succeeded him in December, 1916. In getting rid of Asquith, Lloyd George caused a schism in the Liberal Party. The new Prime Minister boldly looked ahead to creating a new party of his own after the war. In Great Britain as in the U.S. political parties are built on only partly visible golden foundations. To get the money Lloyd George began selling honors—to almost anyone who could afford them. The going rates were £10–12,000 ($50–60,000) for a knighthood and £35–40,000 (or $175,000 to 200,000) for a barony.* Besides the flagrant commercialism which produced many sharp questions in Parliament and the House of Lords there was also widespread feeling that too many of the honors of the 1919 postwar list had gone to home-front warriors rather than those who had served on the fighting fields of France and the Near East. An anonymous and mordant bit of verse circulated widely in London in 1919, particularly in the City:

THE O.B.E.

> I knew a man of industry
> Who made big bombs for the R.F.C.
> And pocketed lots of L.S.D.
> And he (thank God) is an O.B.E.
>
> I knew a woman of pedigree,
> Who asked some soldiers out to tea,
> And said, "Dear me" and "Yes, I see,"
> And she (thank God) is an O.B.E.
>
> I knew a fellow of twenty-three
> Who got a job with a fat M.P.
> Not caring much for the Infantry
> And he (thank God) is an O.B.E.
>
> I had a friend, a friend and he
> Just held the line for you and me,
> And kept the Germans from the sea,
> And died—without the O.B.E.
>   Thank God,
> He died without the O.B.E.

---

* In the U.S. honors-hungry society the range for purchased honorary degrees today is also about $35,000 on up to $200,000, depending upon the prestige of the college, of course.

Sir William was understandably sensitive about the general criticism. At the outbreak of the war he was 43 but he remained an active member of the City of London National Guard in which he held a commission. In addition to the services he had rendered the Crown through the great mass printings of the much-needed banknotes he had performed certain printing services for the British Secret Service during the war which he never discussed publicly but alluded to mysteriously from time to time.

The service rendered was counterfeiting. In 1917 the British Secret Service asked the help of Waterlow and Thomas de la Rue in making imitations of German, Austrian and Bavarian stamps, to be affixed to envelopes in those countries bearing Allied propaganda messages. The letters were mailed in the appropriate country by neutrals and agents.

In an even more secret operation Waterlow was called upon by the Secret Service to counterfeit Imperial German banknotes. Waterlow engravers helped make the plates which were run off in a specially-guarded section of the Bank of England's printing works.

Because of his many overt and occult services to the Crown Sir William naturally felt his O.B.E. was a just one. It certainly wasn't purchased. But this didn't prevent his cousin, Edgar, who was a year older and openly envious, from sometimes saying how glad *he* was not to have any honors in the gamy year of 1919.*

Sir William's firm skimmed the cream of the wartime banknote business and had every intention of going after a great deal more of the overseas banknote printing now that several new countries had come into existence. This led to the opening of merger talks by Waterlow & Sons. There was no sense in the Waterlow cousins bleeding each other with price-cutting. Their non-Waterlow rivals, de la Rue and Bradbury, Wilkinson would be the only beneficiaries of such a consanguineous rivalry.

The secret merger talks began early in 1919 and were concluded with an announcement on January 21, 1920. The new head of the firm was Sir Philip Waterlow, chairman. His son Edgar and Sir William Waterlow became joint managing directors.

---

* "Knighthood is a cheap commodity," wrote Max Beerbohm, long before he became Sir Max. "It is modern Royalty's substitute for largesse and it is scattered broadcast. Though all sneer at it, there are few whose hands would not gladly grasp the dingy patent. After all a title is still a title."

In the interests of family harmony—and because he didn't control enough stock in Waterlow, Layton—Sir William took a secondary role. At the time he had little doubt that his second cousin, Edgar, would succeed Sir Philip, his father.

He didn't—because Thomas de la Rue filed suit against the newly reconstituted Waterlow firm. The complaint alleged that for some time—probably since 1913—de la Rue and Waterlow & Sons had a secret agreement not to bid too vigorously against each other in seeking security printing work from the British government. The successful bidder would give a percentage of its profits to the other firm. These payments had been made several times to each other but apparently in 1919 or 1920 Sir Philip Waterlow had welshed on a payment due to de la Rue. Hence the suit.

Sir William Waterlow was particularly outraged as, indeed, were many Waterlow directors who hadn't known of the secret agreement. But worse emerged. It became clear that Sir Philip Waterlow had been pocketing the secret rebates from de la Rue rather than putting the money in the Waterlow treasury. Sir William who had dug out this particularly heinous bit, brought it to the attention of the other Waterlow directors. As a result the de la Rue suit was settled out of court on April 10, 1923, for £30,000 (then about $150,000). Sir Philip was retired as chairman and replaced by Sir William. Why not Edgar Lutwyche Waterlow, the son of the outgoing chairman? Edgar, it appeared, had known of his father's pocketing of the de la Rue rebates. He had allowed filial silence to overcome his corporate obligations to his fellow Waterlow directors.

Thus on November 9, 1923, Sir William Waterlow had become chairman and joint managing director of the Waterlow firm at £10,000 a year, plus a car, chauffeur and expenses.* His second cousin, Edgar, was the other joint managing director but Sir William now felt he couldn't trust his cousin and some of his cousin's supporters among the directors. Henceforward the Waterlow firm would be a house divided in the upper reaches of management. Sir William expected Edgar to be seeking any wedge that would enable him to topple his cousin from the chair-

---

* With the income tax then only a 5/ on the pound or $1.20 for every $4.86 of income, Sir William's £10,000 salary would be equivalent today to at least a $150,000 salary and tax-free perquisites.

manship. In turn, Sir William knew there would be many company matters which he could not safely confide in his cousin. As long as he kept Waterlow & Sons profitable he would enjoy the support of the other nine Waterlow directors.

Sir William quickly got working. On January 1, 1924, the Crown announced that all British postage stamps would be printed by Waterlow. A few months later Sir William was also able to announce that the firm had secured the contract to print Latvia's banknotes. The firm's net profit of £114,910 for 1923 soared to £198,657 (nearly $1,000,000) for 1924. The stockholders and the directors knew that their new Chairman was firmly in command.

After getting his knighthood Sir William began thinking of his next goal: Lord Mayor of London. Dick Whittington could start his ascent with a clever cat but modern candidates rise through more mundane moves. In 1921 Sir William was elected chairman of the City of London School Committee. Then a year later, alderman for the Cornhill Ward of the London Corporation which meant that he had become one of the Magistrates of the City of London, a traditional steppingstone to the Lord Mayoralty.

His rise was noted jealously by his cousins. When Sir William became alderman in 1922 Sir Philip and Edgar Waterlow meanly proposed that part of Sir William's salary be deducted for the time he had given his aldermanic post.* The humiliating debate in the Board of Directors caused Sir William considerable shame but in the end the Board voted not to cut his salary. The issue was never raised again. Even if he wasn't giving the firm all his time Sir William was clearly making the firm far more profitable than Sir Philip had been able to do with his full-time efforts. Besides, one director pointed out, Sir William might be difficult and arbitrary but he wasn't the kind to pocket illegal rebates.

*   *   *   *   *

Since 1866 the head offices of the great Waterlow printing empire—including eight large factories—had been housed in a

---

* A friend of the Waterlows later described the relationship between the cousins in the words of Alain Lesage: "They made peace between us; we embraced, and we have been mortal enemies ever since."

rather modest four-story, yellow brick building in narrow Great Winchester Street in the City of London. Nearby are the Bank of England, the Stock Exchange and headquarters of the leading insurance companies.

On the morning of December 4th, Marang walked a bit out of his way to get to Waterlow's from the Great Eastern Hotel. It was a small tour of homage to the world's capital of business. In the narrow streets with the ancient names—Old Jewry, Cheapside, Poultry, Cornhill, Threadneedle—he looked admiringly at the morning rush hour crowds of black-suited, bowler-hatted men of the City—and the stockjobbers in their silk top hats. They seemed characters out of novels by the popular Galsworthy and many more seemed to belong in Dickens' pages.

As he entered the unimpressive street level door of Waterlow's, he glanced up and saw the coat of arms of a Royal Purveyor massed above the entrance. Inside he saw clerks and bookkeepers at work in the large groundfloor office. At a plain, wooden inquiry desk to the right as he came in, a uniformed commissionaire asked his business and Marang gave him the note of introduction from Enschedé to give to Sir William. Later Marang was escorted up a flight of wooden narrow stairs that creaked heavily as he mounted them. In a roomy, unostentatious first-floor office overlooking Great Winchester Street, Marang was introduced to Sir William.

He gave Sir William his visiting card which identified him as the Counsel General of Persia in The Hague, the letter from the Portuguese Minister to The Hague, and finally the contract between Alves Reis and the government of Angola.

Marang explained that he was a member of a Dutch syndicate coming to the assistance of the Province of Angola whose finances were in a bad way.

Sir William knew this. He had been following the misfortunes of Angola in the financial pages of the *Times*. In the past two years Waterlow had printed several low denomination notes for Angola. The orders had come directly from the Portuguese Embassy in London.

Sir William could not read Portuguese but he did have a working knowledge of French and was able to skim through the bilingual contract.

Marang explained that his syndicate was going to advance Angola $5,000,000 and in return the Bank of Portugal was going to permit the syndicate to issue the special printing of banknotes. These would be surcharged "ANGOLA" once they reached the colony.

The two notes Alves Reis had appended to the contract were of the so-called "poet" series; they bore the faces of Luis de Camões, Portugal's great epic poet of the 16th century; and João de Deus Ramos, a 19th century romantic poet.

When he saw the two banknotes Sir William knew they had been made for the Bank of Portugal by his great London rival, Bradbury, Wilkinson. Ordinarily he might have cut short the discussion with the foreigner by advising him to visit the nearby offices of the rival banknote printer. But why throw any more business their way? This might well be a way of getting Bradbury, Wilkinson out of the Portuguese picture altogether. So Sir William resorted to a polite evasion.

The two poet notes, he told Marang, had been done by "an American banknote firm." Technically, he was correct: Bradbury *was* a subsidiary of the American Bank Note Company but for Sir William not to have known that Bradbury was printing the Portuguese poet notes in London would have been the equivalent of General Motors not knowing that Ford was manufacturing its Mustang cars in the U.S.

Could Waterlow duplicate the two notes, Marang asked.

"We probably could," Waterlow said. "But we don't like to imitate another firm's products. In any case it would take several months of engraving work alone."

Marang had already made it clear the notes for Angola were to be taken to the colony by the new High Commissioner late in February, 1925.

"A pity," Sir William went on, "that you didn't bring us a note that we have made for the Bank of Portugal—the Vasco da Gama 500 escudos note." He had his secretary bring in a specimen book of banknotes which contained the 500 escudos note— and asked that Frederick W. Goodman, a Waterlow director who was in charge of the foreign banknote division, come in. Goodman had been with the company since 1881. His son, Vivian, had also entered the firm and had risen to a directorship, too. Waterlow had their support in his battle against his cousins.

Marang recognized the 500 escudos note immediately: it was another copy of the note he had shown the Enschedé people in Haarlem and had led to the note of introduction to Waterlow. Obviously, they would have to use this note instead of the higher denomination 1000 escudos note. No doubt Reis would have to get permission to do this from his corrupt friends at the Bank of Portugal—which inevitably meant another bribe to come out of the Marang pocket—but there was no other solution.

"Yes," he said firmly, "this note would do very well."

When Goodman, who looked rather like the late King Edward VII, came in, Sir William introduced him to Marang and provided a brief resumé of the discussion. Again, Marang stressed the importance of secrecy in the whole affair, particularly since the Banco Ultramarino normally was the only agency that could issue banknotes for the Portuguese colonies. Complicating matters, he went on, was the fact that two brothers, the Ulrichs, were serving as directors of the Bank of Portugal and the Ultramarino. For this reason very few of the Bank of Portugal directors were in on this very secret deal to find capital for Angola. In fact only the governor of the Bank and the deputy governor knew of it.

"In any case," Sir William said, "we would need the authorization of the Bank of Portugal to use their plates for this new issue of notes."

Easily arranged, Marang answered. As a matter of fact his personal secretary, José Bandeira, who was the brother of the Portuguese Minister to The Hague, was returning to Lisbon shortly and he would obtain the authorization.

"If any help is needed in Lisbon," Goodman volunteered, "perhaps our man there, Romer, might be able to help."

That was a good idea, Marang agreed. Perhaps their instructions to Romer could also be sent via his secretary, Bandeira. Mainly, though, he thought that Romer should be told how very confidential the matter was and that his intercession would not be necessary unless something unforeseen arose.

When Marang left that morning he knew how much 200,000

notes of the 500 escudos type would cost: £1500 (about $7500).*
He also had a letter of introduction for Bandeira to present to
Henry Gerard Wolfgang Romer, the Waterlow representative
in Lisbon. The letter Sir William dictated to Romer gave the details of the Angola contract and the fact that the authorization of
the Bank of Portugal was necessary. The letter concluded that his
intervention

> may not be necessary as of course we are in no way con-
> cerned in M. Marang van Ysselveere's business, but you will
> understand that we must have the Bank of Portugal's authority
> and they will furnish us also with the specific numbers that are
> to be used on these notes.

Goodman read the letter and decided that he ought to write
Lisbon, too, and delineate some subtleties for Romer. Sir William
could be airy-fairy about "we are in no way concerned in M.
Marang's business" but Frederick Goodman was very much concerned. It was vital not to let Bradbury, Wilkinson back into the
picture after all the work that Waterlow's had done towards oust-
ing them. Also it would be wise to alert Romer not to talk price.
So Goodman wrote:

> M. Enschedé had told M. Marang that the specimen notes
> annexed to his contract were probably produced by us, and, as of
> course you will understand, *we are not desirous to re-introduce our
> predecessor in any way to anything connected with the Bank of
> Portugal. We merely told M. Marang that from the appearance of
> the notes we thought they were American productions, as no im-
> print appears on them.* . . . We have arranged the matter of
> price with M. Marang.

To make doubly sure they sent a coded telegram to Romer
telling him an important letter was on its way and he was going
to have a visitor Monday morning. It was sent to Romer's cable
address: ENERGETIC LISBON.

---

* Or about 3.6¢ each. Rather on the high side. The U.S. Bureau of
Printing & Engraving turns out U.S. dollar bills at a cost of less than a
cent each. But the 500 escudos notes were more colorful.

LISBON / December 5, 1924

ENERGETIC LISBON as a cable address had been his own choice. It had a firm, no-nonsense ring; the *marque* of an alert, always-on-the-go special representative. As much as he enjoyed being Waterlow's own ENERGETIC he also relished coding and decoding his telegrams. Other salesmen might consider it a tedious bore but Romer never tired of reminding himself that it was as close to a military operation as one could get in business. A true Romer always liked to remember the great military past.

One of his famous ancestors, Wolfgang William Romer, had entered the service of the Prince of Orange as a military engineer when he was 18. As a colonel he accompanied Prince William of Orange to England in 1688 and the Romer family settled in Berwick-on-Tweed. Wolfgang William thus became the first of a long line of British military engineers named Romer. He designed defenses for the British in colonial Boston, New York, Barbados and in Portsmouth Harbor in England.

When he died in 1713 his son, John Lambertus Romer, was erecting military defenses along the Thames. One of John's many descendants who entered British military life was Major General Robert Romer. In 1869 our Henry Gerard Wolfgang Romer was born in Plymouth, England—one of 11 children born to the General and Mrs. Romer.

Unfortunately, when the General retired on half-pay three of his four sons decided not to continue the Army tradition. And Henry who would have liked to, was physically precluded: he lost the sight of his left eye in a childhood accident. After being educated at the Reading Grammar School—the equivalent of a U.S. high school and a bit more—the four Romer sons lit out for South America.

Henry had a good ear for language and in a few years acquired a considerable fluency in Spanish and Portuguese. He lived through a not-too-profitable variety of commercial ventures in the Argentine, Peru, British Guiana and Brazil. He traveled and sold: he settled and managed plantations; he golfed; he wrote travel and business articles for the English-language *Times* of Brazil. And then in 1913, when he was 44, he became a Special Foreign Representative of Waterlow Brothers & Layton of London.

Romer sold banknotes and was fairly good at it. He sold them to Bolivia and Costa Rica. The boom years most of South America enjoyed led to a considerable inflation which in turn called for more and more banknotes to be circulated by the central banks of those countries. He also secured orders for the printing of Costa Rican and Bolivian postage stamps.

South and Central America were particularly difficult markets. Ever since American Bank Note of New York began issuing notes for the northern states of Mexico in 1860 the American firm had sewn-up most of the continent by driving out other American competitors.

In 1922 Sir William Waterlow decided Romer had acquired enough seasoning in Latin America and was now ready to battle a competitor, Bradbury, Wilkinson. Although a London-based firm, Bradbury, Wilkinson had been owned, since 1903, by the American Bank Note Company, the very firm that had kept Romer from making more of a mark in his South American selling ventures. Waterlow planned to get even with American Bank Note by snagging an important Bradbury, Wilkinson customer— the republic of Portugal.

The business of selling banknotes to foreign governments has changed little in the past 50 years. Romer left no detailed accounts of his negotiations in Lisbon but recently in London another successful banknote salesman who knew Romer and had once worked for Waterlow, too, described just how banknotes are usually sold:

"Most Special Foreign Representatives are apt to be Scottish, Irish or American. English are too stuffy for the job. It calls for a lot of flexibility, an instinct for the jugular. Romer was British by nationality only. He certainly didn't look it. His skin was deeply tanned and his long residence in South America made him excitable and given to gesticulating with his hands when making a point. Bad for doing business in England but quite useful in the rest of the world. Not a bad chap. Even his mother would admit he wasn't particularly handsome: he had a squint in the bad eye and he tended to walk hunched over a bit—awfully unmilitary for that family. He was about 5'10". He had a fat toothbrush moustache and parted his brown hair in the middle. But he was good company at the bar and after a couple of drinks he'd pull out his wallet—just like the rest of us—and show you banknotes of the countries he had sold, like an Indian chief with his scalps.

"When Romer was sent to Lisbon his arrangement was pretty much what it had been in South America. First he got a special fee for the Lisbon negotiations, win, lose or draw. In addition his expenses while in Lisbon were covered totally. He had a small apartment in Monte Estoril. Oh, he was happily married: had a wife, two sons and a daughter living in Streatham, a London suburb. Being a Special is rough on family life but there's money in it: he got a 2½ % commission if he landed a deal and it could run up. A lot of these banknote contracts involve millions of dollars.

"As usual, Waterlow had a local bird dog on the scene long before Romer arrived. This was Robert Andrew Walker, a British national, but his father was Scottish and his mother Portuguese. Walker had a small ship supplies business in Lisbon that sold a lot of fishing nets during the First World War. He was about 35 then and when Romer arrived in Lisbon Walker was having a rough time. Like most banknote bird dogs he was on commission only and at this point he didn't have too much to show for the 16 years he had been representing Waterlow.

"The bird dog's job essentially is to find out who in government or the central bank to bribe or influence in other ways. Walker and Romer didn't get on too well. For one thing Walker felt that Romer lost them a sizeable contract on banknotes for the Ultramarino Bank, the only Portuguese bank allowed to issue notes for the Portuguese colonies. Apparently the deal had been set up and ready for signing when Romer talked about it prematurely. He must have been overheard by the local Bradbury, Wilkinson bird dog who passed the word on to the BW Special Foreign Representative, George T. Foxon, who got the business away from Waterlow. Actually, Ultramarino had been an old customer of Bradbury's so perhaps it wasn't too hard. Waterlow got a consolation prize—the printing of some small denomination notes for Angola.

"Naturally this soured Walker on Romer. Walker complained to Sir William Waterlow in London but they decided to leave Romer on the job, anyway. Don't forget, then as now, there were only a dozen or 15 qualified Special Foreign Representatives for banknote companies in the whole world. And there weren't many who could speak Portuguese fluently, as Romer could.

"Besides it wasn't the first time a big one got away from a Special Foreign Representative at the moment before signing. When a country is known to be in the market for banknotes the Specials who cover that part of the world for their companies descend on the capital city. Before they leave the home office they work out private codes. I'd have to have a list of the key people, perhaps four or five, plus code names for our competitors whom we knew would be on the scene. We needed the code names because we always assumed they'd try to buy copies of our wires from the cable clerk—just as we would. They'd spy on us; we on them. It wasn't too awkward usually because invariably all of us would be at the same hotel in the capital city. We'd be as nice as punch to each other and lie to one another over drinks or even dinner. Usually we'd keep our papers under lock and key, preferably in the hotel vault. When you'd want to look at your papers undisturbed you'd have your local bird dog call your stickiest competitor to the phone and hold them for twenty minutes pretending it was someone from the Central Bank who needed some vital information."

In October 1922 Romer got the contract for printing Portuguese notes away from Bradbury, Wilkinson which had printed a batch of ten million notes for the government under an October 1917 contract.

(Why didn't Portugal print its own banknotes? Before World War I the Bank of Portugal had done just that but during the war the serial numbering equipment on its note printing machinery fell into disrepair and replacement could not be obtained. One reason: the only source was the leading banknote printing concerns who made or controlled by patent most of the numbering equipment. Since no country would print banknotes without serial numbers Portugal had to turn to the private banknote printers. Just as they intended.)

"How did Romer get the 1922 contract? I don't know who was the key man here but it wasn't always simple bribery as it often is today in some of the new 'emerging countries.' For instance, there was a time when I landed a big contract in a Far Eastern country. First I ascertained that the key man was the governor of the country's Central Bank. I spent a month finding out everything I could about him. Well, I discovered his one great vanity: he prided himself as an expert on foreign affairs. When I found out he was going to visit England, I asked him if he would be interested in giving a special lecture in London before the Institute of Foreign Affairs of which I am an old member. I had no trouble setting that up and the governor was quite pleased. I went to London with him and made sure we had a fine dinner party before the talk and that there was good press coverage during it. I got him a temporary membership at my own club, several sets of free theater tickets and I made arrangements to have many items shipped back for him at no charge. I was a kind of public relations and personal service agency for two weeks and I got the contract,—£600,000, worth about $3,000,000 then. My end was $75,000 plus expenses.

"But until I had all the necessary signatures and I knew that half the contract fee had been paid in sterling in London I didn't relax for a minute. Too many contracts go sour after you've shaken hands.

"A London firm—not Waterlow—once tried to dislodge American Bank Note out of Canada. American had a seemingly invulnerable position in Ottawa but the firm felt *something* could be done. They hired a man out of one of the prominent merchant banking firms in the City, a firm with excellent Canadian connections. The chap had a good name and all that—right schools, regiment and everything. He could charm a fly off the butterdish. He came to Ottawa and did awfully well,—Empire preference and all that. Finally on a certain Friday he knew he had it sewn up; the contract was going to be signed on a Monday. Then on Saturday night he met the daughter of the key man at a party. He made a fast play for her and trotted her off to bed. It had been done before, I'm afraid. Somehow the gal's father learned of it and of course there was no signing on Monday. When the lad was sacked he asked to have a drink with me to cry on my shoulder. The bloody fool couldn't understand why the key man took things so hard: after all, the gal had been *willing*.

"Now an experienced man like Romer who didn't have the right school or regiment would never have gone offside when he had a contract nearly tucked away. Afterwards, possibly—but never *during*."

✻   ✻   ✻   ✻   ✻

The first order Romer had gotten from the Bank of Portugal was a small one, calling for the making of 600,000 notes of the 500 escudos variety bearing the likeness of Vasco da Gama the great 15th century navigator. (An escudo was then worth slightly less than 5¢ so that each note had a face value of about $25.) The total contract ran to some $23,000, including extra charges of $1,000 for the preparation of the watermark and some $2,500 for the making of the plates.

The contract also contemplated the printing of another 500,000 notes of the 1,000 escudos type but no definite order was given. In effect Romer had secured a wedge of the Portuguese banknote business with promises for more work. By February, 1924 Waterlow had delivered 400,000 notes to the Bank of Portugal, with the final 200,000 to be sent by ship by June.

After Romer's contract had been signed by all the parties in 1922, Frederick W. Goodman who had been a director of Waterlow's since 1906 and was in charge of the foreign banknote work, felt that a little mutual congratulation was in order. After all, Waterlow's had succeeded in breaking into the Bradbury, Wilkinson demesne. On October 27, 1922, Goodman wrote the directors of the Bank of Portugal to express

> . . . the extreme appreciation of our Board of Directors of the high honour conferred upon us by your Board in entrusting to us the manufacture of your Bank notes. As we have been contractors to the British Government for the manufacture of British Treasury Notes, ever since the inception of this form of currency, it would seem extremely apt, that we should act in a similar capacity to the Bank of our oldest ally, and we sincerely trust that the present in-

ception of this work may be the happy augury of a lasting and harmonious connection between us.

The style was the usual London-High Georgian of the period. And for the first two years of the contract, relations between Waterlow and the Bank of Portugal were smooth and amicable. On February 5, 1924, Romer got another order for another 200,000 notes of the Vasco da Gama 500 escudos type. The additional order amounted to only a $6400 printing job but it strengthened the Waterlow position. In order to get all of the Bank's note printing business, Waterlow suggested that Romer offer the Bank some special spring inducements and on May 1, 1924, Romer, in Lisbon, wrote the Bank a curiously prescient letter:

Dear Sirs:

I have the honour to confirm to Y. Ex. in writing what I have told on several occasions verbally to several high officials of your esteemed bank, which is as follows: In the event of the total order being granted to us, my firm proposed to supply free of charge the plates required for the stamping of these notes as well as those which may be necessary for the substitution of any of them *in the event, which it is hoped will never occur, that there should be any falsification of them.**

With the highest esteem and consideration,
I am,
for Waterlow & Sons Limited
HENRY G. W. ROMER

The Bank's director liked the special discount and on May 27, 1924, they wrote Waterlow they were giving them an order for 47–50 million banknotes, ranging from 500,000 notes of the 1,000 escudos type; a million notes of the 500 escudos, right down to 12,000,000 notes of the 5-escudos variety. The cost of each group of notes descended as the value of the note did. For example, the 1,000 escudos note (about $50)—cost nearly 3.3¢ to make, but the 5-escudos note (about 25¢) cost less than a penny each.

Through the magic of central banking, an abandoned gold

---

* Italics added.

standard and the necromancers of Waterlow & Sons Limited, the Bank of Portugal was going to convert 20 tons of steel, 60 tons of fine linen paper, and 80 tons of ink into nearly $125,000,000 of paper currency—at a total cost of $575,000. In all the world there was no greater bargain.

The contract had most of the standard banknote printing terms of the time.

Articles 10 and 11 provided the method of shipping the notes. They were to be sent

> . . . by the Company to the Bank, ready for use, in packets of 1000 good notes each, tied with ribbon and sealed, each packet comprising ten bundles of one hundred notes each, also tied with ribbon. These notes shall come grouped in alphabetical order of the Series and in each series in numerical order from 1 to 20,000.

The notes were to be sent every two weeks by English Royal Mail steamers because they have a special strongroom. The wooden boxes were to be lined with zinc and the outside hooped with wire and sealed at the joints. Twenty days after the steamer shipment arrived the payment for the shipment was to be made in sterling.

In all, a fine contract. Romer and Walker were congratulated by the London office and Sir William Waterlow was now convinced that his campaign to get more foreign banknote business was succeeding.

From Walker's grubby office in the downtown business district, Romer took a cab up to the Bairre Alto, the "high quarter" on a hill where a 200-year-old building housed the Royal British Club of Lisbon on Rua S. Pedro de Alcantara, smack in the middle of the city's biggest assembly of tolerated brothels. After doffing his bowler and dun-colored mackintosh, Romer stood drinks for several members who had been frank enough to admit they had a small bet going among themselves: most of them bet against Romer. They didn't think he could get the Portuguese business from Foxon of Bradbury, Wilkinson.

Then on the evening of December 4, 1924, Romer got a coded telegram from the home office. Decoded, it read:

IT IS VERY IMPORTANT TO AWAIT LETTER NOW IN THE POST INFORM YOU APPOINTMENT HAS BEEN

MADE HERE FOR A GENTLEMAN TO CALL AT WALKER'S OFFICE TO SEE YOU MONDAY MORNING PRIVATELY.

WATERLOW

He checked his code book and wired the home office:

UGORYATWAD AMEVG

Meaning:

REFERRING TO YOUR TELEGRAM 4TH AWAITING APPOINTMENT.

He went back to the British Club for a drink.

THE HAGUE / December 5, 1924

IN HIS OFFICE Marang was briskly optimistic. The London visit, he told José, had gone very well. The contract had impressed Waterlow—as had his diplomatic passport—and the only thing to be done now was for Reis to get specific permission from his Bank of Portugal cronies for the printing of the notes. A pity that they couldn't get Waterlow to do the 1,000 escudos notes. It was doubly profitable to get a piece of paper worth $50 for 3½¢ worth of printing than one worth only $25. Perhaps they would be able to work out something later on the 1,000 escudos note.

"Of course," Marang told José, "you won't go looking for this man Romer until you talk to Alves Reis. The fewer who know of this arrangement the better. Just give the Romer letter to Reis."

José was slightly nettled at the vaguely patronizing tone Marang often took with him. But he was more concerned with another problem.

"You know Reis won't like this. He said you mustn't go to the firm that produced the notes for the Bank of Portugal."

Marang shrugged: "I didn't. Waterlow didn't make the 'poet' notes appended to the contract. Another firm did them. An American one, Waterlow told me."

That evening José left for Paris on his way to Lisbon. In Paris he caught the Sud Express which made the run to Lisbon in 36 hours.

LISBON / December 7, 1924

JOSÉ CHECKED INTO the Avenida Palace Hotel and phoned Alves Reis to tell him he had great news. He had to see him right away.

When Reis got to the hotel, José proudly showed him the letter Sir William gave Marang to give Romer. Then he gave a detailed account of Marang's visit to Waterlow. He couldn't understand why Reis wasn't as overjoyed as he was at the way things were working out. All they needed was a letter of authorization from Reis' friends at the Bank of Portugal and the 200,000 banknotes—worth nearly $5,000,000—were as good as theirs.

"It was only my iron will that allowed me to keep my head," Alves Reis wrote later. He kept his head by bitterly criticizing Bandeira and Marang for not following the orders he had given them.

"If my friend, the High Commissioner of Angola, wanted me to contact Waterlow he would have told me to do so. The fact that my friends did not annex this 500 escudos note to the contract showed they weren't interested in this note—or in having Waterlow do it. Any fool could see that," he added scornfully.

When José suggested that they both see the Waterlow representative, Romer, Alves Reis told him it would be fatal to bring Romer into it. Too many people already knew of the contract. "No, the only hope now is for me to see my friends at the Bank and see what can be done to straighten out this mess."

On the morning of December 9th, Reis saw José again.

"I saw the High Commissioner and Governor Camacho of the Bank. Both are almost ready to call off the whole deal. Marang had exceeded the orders I gave him. They never wanted to bring Waterlow into the affair. But I finally was able to soothe Camacho. He agreed the authorization requested by Waterlow was natural and proper but he didn't want to exchange any correspondence with this British printer."

José was puzzled. "Why not?"

"Because there's nothing easier than for a letter to go astray; or to land in the hands of some bank employee so that the secret issue for Angola might become public knowledge at a time when it would be extremely unfavorable for monetary circulation to be increased."

Alves Reis couldn't tell José the real reason. Getting a letter of authorization from Camacho, the governor of the Bank of Portugal, to Waterlow, meant another elaborate forgery, one he wasn't prepared for. But perhaps he could rework the present contract so that, in effect, Waterlow would feel he had full permission. Maybe he could also squeeze more money out of Marang. Creditors were pressing Reis with biting vigor.

That afternoon José cabled Marang. To heighten secrecy he always cabled his brother, the Minister to The Hague, who would get the coded message to Marang:

DEAL CAN BE CONSIDERED CONCLUDED. WE CAN OBTAIN IN LIEU OF LETTER OF AUTHORIZATION DULY LEGALIZED CONTRACT IN NAME OF BANK SIGNED BY GOVERNOR AND ONE DIRECTOR, HIGH COMMISSIONER AND REIS. CONTRACT GIVES FULL PERMISSION HIGH COMMISSIONER FOR MANUFACTURE OF BANKNOTES. BANK GOVERNOR ALREADY IN DEAL BUT OTHER DIRECTOR'S SIGNATURE ESSENTIAL. WILL COST ONE MILLION ESCUDOS [$50,000] OF WHICH 100,000 MUST BE PAID WITHOUT FAIL ON DELIVERY OF CONTRACT WEDNESDAY [December 10th] AS DIRECTOR LEAVING FOR MADEIRA THURSDAY. IF MARANG AGREEABLE WIRE MONEY. BANK GOVERNOR CONSIDERS BUSINESS BADLY HANDLED LONDON. PROHIBITS DIVULGE CONTENTS OF THIS TELEGRAM TO LONDON FIRM BEFORE OUR ARRIVAL IN HAGUE.   JOSE.

In another part of Lisbon Romer was becoming worried. The caller he had expected three days earlier had yet to turn up. On the evening of December 8th he wired Waterlow (Cable Address: IMPRIMERIE, LONDON):

REFERRING TO YOUR LETTERS OF 3RD & 4TH INST. GENTLEMAN HAS NOT CALLED. BANK OF PORTUGAL HAS NOTHING TO DO WITH THE MATTER. BANK ULTRAMARINO IS THE BANK DEALING WITH PORTUGUESE COLONIES. TELEGRAPH WHAT I AM TO DO.

Earlier in the day he had sent a long letter to Sir William which expressed his impatience and great doubts with undiplomatic clarity:

. . . and it is now 10 minutes past 3 and I have been waiting the whole day for Mr. Bandeira who has not yet put in an appearance!!!

I cannot help thinking there must be some confusion in your mind with regard to the connection of the Bank of Portugal with Angola. The Bank of Portugal has never issued any Colonial notes to the best of my belief at any time!! So far as I know the Banco Ultramarino is the only Bank that has anything to do with Portuguese Colonial Notes . . . .

I cannot help feeling very nearly sure that these notes are not Bank of Portugal Notes at all but the Ultramarino. In any case, not having seen Mr. Bandeira I cannot say anything, but I think it well to let you know as soon as possible that to the best of my belief you are confusing these two Banks.

To some chairmen of banknote printing firms such a strong note might have been reason to start doubting, to start wondering about the unusual contract presented by a Dutch stranger. But Sir William was made of sterner stuff. Each of Romer's five exclamation marks only served to convince Sir William of his representative's lack of understanding. And the repeated emphasis on Sir William's "confusion" confirmed the Waterlow chairman's feeling that Romer was not only a boorish, conceited fool but also the one man who must be kept out of these delicate negotiations as much as possible. On the morning of December 9th he wired Romer:

YOUR TELEGRAM SHOWS YOU DO NOT APPRECIATE POSITION. DO NOTHING! SAY NOTHING! AWAIT CALL OF GENTLEMAN.

Not only did he return two of Romer's five gratuitous exclamation marks, but Waterlow also let him know bluntly just who was master.

When he received this wire Romer still wouldn't take the warning. He waited all day for the mysterious Bandeira to show up and when he did not, he wrote Sir William:

> I quite appreciate your cable and I certainly know nothing of the position but what I do know is that the issue of Portuguese Colonial Notes has always been in the hands of Banco Ultramarino and so far as my knowledge goes the Bank of Portugal have not only nothing to do with the finances of the Portuguese Colonies but it would be necessary to have a new arrangement with the Portuguese Government and a new Decree signed to enable the Bank of Portugal to issue notes for the financing of any scheme in connection with Angola. Not only that, but the papers at the present moment here in Lisbon being full of Angola finance, and the disastrous state of the Colony generally, I cannot help thinking that the Bank of Portugal would never consent to their plates being utilized for a Portuguese Colony whose finances apparently appear to be in a state of absolute chaos.
>
> Of course, up to now, not having seen Mr. Bandeira I am doing nothing and can do nothing, but I take the liberty of cautioning you in this proposed transaction, knowing many things that are going on at this present moment in Lisbon which I cannot refer to on paper, *I cannot but view the whole matter with very grave doubts as to how it will all come out.*

The prescient among us, especially those whose foresight has a logical basis, are clearly menaces to the rest and must be squelched properly. This, Sir William did in his letter:

> . . . and we must express our surprise that you do not give us credit for knowing that the Banco Nacional Ultramarino deals with the Portuguese colonies,* and our letters, if you had studied them, would have shown that special circumstances had arisen. Above all, not a whisper of this should reach the Banco Ultramarino.
>
> All we want you to do in this connection, after your interview with Mr. Bandeira and after he has fixed everything up with the Portuguese Minister of Finance and the Directors of the Bank of

* Romer wished he could answer *this* with an old Portuguese proverb: The man with a little knowledge soon displays it.

Portugal, is to safeguard our interests with the Bank by obtaining their full sanction for our using their plates and for producing these notes and to furnish us with the necessary numbers and schedules of signatures.

As Waterlow and Romer were exchanging their wires and letters, Alves Reis was busy manufacturing a new contract that he hoped would meet Sir William's demand for permission of the Bank of Portugal to use the 500 escudos plates.

It wasn't easy. First, he had to take the original contract that had been shown to Waterlow back to the British Consul in Lisbon for his notarization. Originally, Reis had not sought a British consular notarization because he never anticipated that a British firm might print the banknotes. This consular notarization, dated December 9th, now joined the earlier notarizations of the French and German consulates of November 25th. If Marang or Hennies noticed the discrepancy, Reis would be able to turn the weakness into a point of strength: his friends in high places were so influential that they were able to get the French and German legalizations on a prior date. Only the British wouldn't go along: they were too scrupulous.

The new contract was typed by Reis' trusted office manager, Francisco Ferreira, Jr., who had served in Africa. He had complete faith in his boss. But just to make sure, Reis explained that the signatures to the contract—those of Governor Camacho of the Bank of Portugal and Vice Governor Mota Gomes—would be added by them when he visited them at their homes.

In fact, Reis got their signatures by a somewhat more involved but far likelier way. He traced the bankers' signatures as they appeared on Portuguese banknotes. In order to get a larger version than the reduced one on the banknotes he employed a pantograph.

The new contract was shorter than the original.

CONFIDENTIAL CONTRACT

The undersigned,

Banco de Portugal, duly represented by its Governor Innocencio Camacho Rodrigues and its Director João da Mota Gomes Junior, as First Contracting Party, of the one part and the Government of Angola, duly represented by its High Commissioner Fran-

cisco da Cunha Rego Chaves, as Second Contracting Party, of the
other part, declare:

First: That the First Contracting Party authorizes the Second
Contracting Party to cause to be manufactured up to two hundred
thousand Bank Notes of five hundred Escudos and one hundred
thousand of one thousand Escudos of the issue of the First Contracting Party and of the types attached to this Contract.

Second: Each Bank Note will bear the special designations of
the Second Contracting Party, numbers series and signatures,
which shall be printed by the First Contracting Party.

Third: That the Second Contracting Party guarantees to the
First Contracting Party the privilege of the issue of Notes in Angola and that it will endorse to Artur Virgilio Alves Reis, Engineer,
a married man, all the powers granted by this Contract in the part
relating to the manufacture of Notes, which powers and conditions
are set forth in their entirety in the Contract to be drawn up on
this date between Second Contracting Party and the said Artur
Virgilio Alves Reis.

Done in Lisbon in the Agency General of the Colonies in the year
1924 on November 6 by me Delfim Costa as I certify. Done and
signed in duplicate there being no other copies.

With the new forgery made and the signatures copied, Reis
now sewed together the old and new contracts with a long shoe-
maker's needle and appended the page of notarial signatures separated from the original contract. He also attached a 500 escudos
banknote of the Vasco da Gama type on a separate sheet so that
if Waterlow refused to undertake the job he would be able to
take this banknote off before trying the contract on some other
banknote printers.

Sealed with wax and bearing the Portuguese coat of arms on
official seal paper, the new contract looked most impressive—to
José Bandeira. On December 11th, after reading through the
magic contract a third time—and each time characteristically
missing the point that Sir William had wanted a *letter* from the
governor of the Bank of Portugal—he jubilantly wired Marang in
The Hague:

WE HAVE IN HAND ENOUGH TO COMPLETE TRANSAC-
TION. LEAVING SATURDAY [December 13th]. DO NOTH-
ING BEFORE OUR ARRIVAL MONDAY. ASK ADOLF TO BE
IN THE HAGUE.

As José was sending the wire, a puzzled Romer was writing his stubborn employer again:

> . . . It is now Thursday midday and still there is no appearance of Mr. Bandeira and, according to the newspapers today, the unfortunate state of affairs in Angola have been very much talked about. . . . I am still of the same opinion and that is that nothing will be done in this connection . . . .

On Saturday, December 13, 1924, Alves Reis and José Bandeira left on the Sud Express for The Hague. The age of air travel was still a stuttering footnote. During the 36-hour trip to Paris, Reis rehearsed several scenes he might have to play in The Hague, mentally ticked off a number of questions he had to ask. José chattered with great animation about his favorite subject: women.

THE HAGUE / December 13, 1924

AT THE MEETING in Marang's office Reis deliberately did not show them the new contract right away. First he wanted a re-play of Marang's meeting with Sir William. Inwardly, he had the great respect of the Portuguese for the English businessman. He still didn't believe they would be able to fool a great British firm with this contract; would have much preferred that another banknote company, possibly German, should print these notes.

Again, Hennies patiently explained why he didn't think a German firm would be suitable and why he, least of all, should be the one to approach any banknote company in Germany. Finally Hennies and Marang convinced Reis that Waterlow was easily their best bet and the new contract was brought out.

Marang and Hennies read the contract carefully and both quickly saw what José Bandeira had missed: Sir William's specific request for a letter from the governor of the Bank of Portugal had not been met.

"But this contract is better than a mere letter," Reis argued. "Not only does it give Waterlow full permission but it even provides for another issue of notes in the future—the 1000 escudos notes—so that we won't need another contract when we are ready for that issue."

Somewhat reluctantly, Marang agreed. He would leave for London on the 16th and show the new contract—and the old, too—to Sir William.

Unquestionably Marang and Hennies noticed the minor discrepancies in the contracts: the fact that the second contract was undated, the curious gap in the dates of the notarizations. But it was rather like reading a good friend's letter and somehow overlooking a casual request for a loan. Or the lover who mistrusts but doesn't want his mistrust confirmed. More likely, they fully believed in the contracts and the scandalous corruption in Portugal that made them possible. The curious inconsistencies were mere details. Certainly Marang wouldn't have gone to London if he hadn't believed the contracts genuine.

Two days later—after wiring Sir William of his coming—Marang's chauffeur took him to the Hook again for the channel trip. Marang was pleased with the way he had finally persuaded Reis that Waterlow was really the *only* firm to do the notes.

In fact the only bad news to mar the day of his departure was a curt note from Baron Lehmann in Paris. The Liberian Ambassador to the Third Republic was still awaiting—with mounting impatience—the illegal Liberian diplomatic passport that Mijnheer Marang had obtained in 1913.

LONDON / December 17, 1924

WHEN HE ARRIVED in Sir William's office this morning Marang detected a greater cordiality than even on his first visit. When Sir William asked if he could have the contracts for his personal solicitor, Allen Ernest Messer, to go over, Marang said, of course. Sir William suggested he return about four that afternoon.

Since Messer couldn't come over until early afternoon Sir William asked Henry A. Woodbridge, a London notary, if he could (a) have his staff check the correctness of the French translation and (b) provide an English translation of the contracts. When this was done Woodbridge put his notarial seal and signature in attestation that the translations were "true and faithful" and that the contracts were properly legalized and notarized in Lisbon.

Solicitor Messer had a few caveats after going through the contracts twice. He noted:

1. The contracts are bound up in the wrong order. The contract between the Bank and the Angola government should have appeared before the one between the government and Reis.

2. The contract between the government and Reis is difficult to understand but this was not material.

In passing, he thought it a bit strange that the Dutch consortium that was going to lend £1,000,000 to poor Angola was going to get only £1,000,000 of Portuguese banknotes and no interest whatever but still that was really no concern of Waterlow.

He did think the contracts contained "sufficient authority for Reis to manufacture these notes and if they were manufactured by anyone authorized by Reis, the Bank could not possibly question their manufacture afterwards."

Still, to make sure he suggested that it would be "a good thing if Sir William wrote a private and confidential letter to the chairman of the Bank of Portugal" to get his specific authorization. On Sir William's request Solicitor Messer dictated just such a letter.

When Marang arrived later that afternoon, Sir William read him the letter he was going to send to I. Camacho Rodrigues, governor of the Bank of Portugal.

The letter told of the visit of Mr. Marang, of the two contracts, of the power of attorney that Mr. Reis of Lisbon had given Mr. Marang. Finally, it went on,

. . . You will realize it is impossible for a Bank Note manufacturer to print Bank Notes except with the direct authorization of the Bank, and I shall therefore be much obliged if you will kindly let me know that in accepting the order to print the Notes in question, and using the existing Plates for that purpose we shall be acting with your approval.

Marang approved completely.

"In order to insure secrecy, however," he added, "I would like to have my secretary, José Bandeira, the brother of the Portuguese Minister, deliver the letter in person to Senhor Camacho Rodrigues." Sir William thought that was a fine idea. To show his complete confidence in Marang and his secretary Sir William told his secretary, Alice Shaw, not to seal the envelope containing the letter.

He did more. He sent a wire to Romer:

WE CANNOT IMPRESS UPON YOU TOO STRONGLY BANDERIA BUSINESS MUST NOT BE MENTIONED TO ANYONE. STRICTLY CONFIDENTIAL.

That evening Marang returned to The Hague. He knew the banknotes were as good as theirs.

THE HAGUE / December 18, 1924

MARANG'S CONFIDENCE permeated the meeting in his office. Only Reis showed a niggling doubt: he would have to talk things over with Camacho Rodrigues on the tricky question of the letter of authorization. Actually, Reis was still trying to think of a way to avoid forging another document.

He covered his inner qualms by pretending to go over the contracts once again in Marang's office. As he told it later:

My eyes happened to fall on the notarial recognition and I quickly realized what a stupid error I had made in the forgery. The formula "I certify as authentic the above signature" should have been in the plural. Had anybody noticed this blunder? Could Waterlow's notary and translator have overlooked such a treacherous slip-up?

I asked Marang for the other Angola-Reis contract and once again the notarial recognition was in the singular. I was furious at myself. My mistake was so great nothing could excuse it. Meanwhile Marang had been called out of the office by one of his clerks and I rushed to his desk and with a fountain pen added an "s" to the words "assignatura" [signature] and "signatario" [signatory]. I heard Marang's steps outside and I hurriedly sat back on the easy chair I had been sitting in. My mood grew worse. I gave Marang the contracts and left to have lunch with Hennies at the Central Hotel where I was staying. My vanity was hurt. In order to forget the slip-up in the contracts I decided to forge a letter in the name of the Governor of the Bank, just to keep my brain busy.

My good star was still protecting me and a hidden hand was helping me . . . .

LISBON / December 22, 1924

ON THE SUD EXPRESS back Reis started to worry in earnest about the letter José was carrying from Sir William to Camacho Rodrigues. How could they be sure that with typical British efficiency Sir William had not *mailed* a copy of the letter to the Bank of Portugal?

In Lisbon he got another worry. The Portuguese Colonial Minister, without consulting the High Commissioner to Angola, had submitted to Parliament a bill authorizing loans of 200 million escudos (about $12,000,000) to impoverished Angola. The High Commissioner considered this a lack of confidence in himself and resigned. But as he thought it over Reis realized that news of the resignation in London would only confirm Sir William in his knowledge that the situation in Angola finance was desperate, that the Dutch "loan" was the only feasible solution.

"Fate," Reis said later, "was helping me by making everyone believe the High Commissioner didn't want any kind of financing other than that effected by constant and secret increases in monetary circulation—the kind I was ready to provide. If a political leader does that, it's perfectly legitimate; if I did it then it's a crime. What nonsense!"

Just to make sure Sir William heard the news and to quiet his own fears about a possible carbon of the letter being *mailed,* Reis wired Marang:

> HIGH COMMISSIONER HAS RESIGNED OWING TO COLONIAL MINISTER NOT BEING IN AGREEMENT WITH OUR TRANSACTION. CONSIDER SITUATION GRAVE. IF PRINTER HAS NOT MAILED COPY OF LETTER I CARRIED AND KEEPS SECRECY I'M CONVINCED SITUATION CAN BE NORMALIZED.

In addition to the fears which he couldn't share with any of his fellow plotters, he had an additional purely private one: his creditors were pressing him once more. It was time to hit Marang again. On the 24th Reis wired Marang directly:

> NO GOVERNOR SIGNATURE UNTIL £1000 RECEIVED. IF NOT FORTHCOMING QUICKLY I DECLINE ALL RESPONSIBILITY.

Marang knew Reis had him. Everything done so far would be useless without the letter from the governor of the Bank. The trips to London, the growing warmth of his relationship with Waterlow—all wasted unless he paid out this additional £1000 ($5,000). What shameless corruption must be taking place in Lisbon!

The following day Marang wired Reis that the money would be wired on Monday, the 28th, but that the governor's letter had to be ready before.

Reis had already gone to work on the much needed letter. How do you get the letterhead of the governor of the Bank of Portugal? You don't; you *make* one. Like this:

> A distant relative introduced me to the owner of a small printing plant. . . . In our talk I convinced the printer that I would

have a large order for him very soon. As I was about to leave I mentioned in passing that my friend, the Governor of the Bank of Portugal, had asked me to bring some engraved letterheads and envelopes from Paris. Alas, I had completely forgotten to place the order there. But I was patriotically certain that the work could be done as well—or even better—right here in Lisbon.

The stationery, designed by Reis, bore the words in the upper left hand corner:

BANCO DE PORTUGAL
Cabinete do Governador [Governor's Office]
Particular   [Private]

He also wrote the printer to take extra good care with the job and not leave any loose sheets of stationery lying around after printing because "someone might use them improperly." The job cost Reis 50 escudos or about $2.50. An escudo went a long way in Portugal then.

To heighten the illusion that the letter really was from the governor of the Bank, Reis decided to add the Portuguese crest. (Never having seen any Bank stationery he didn't know that its severe letterheads scorned such arriviste frippery.) The engraved crest was easy. He asked an engraver to prepare a seal for his club, the Portuguese Sport Club. In the center would be the Portuguese crest and on the periphery the name of the club. In a few days Reis told the engraver there had been a small change. He still wanted the crest but it had been decided that the name would be printed when the stationery itself was prepared. Reis took the engraved crest to his friendly printer.

When he had a hundred sheets and envelopes of the governor's stationery Reis composed his forgery. He wrote in Portuguese, since his English was poor.[*] At the same time he wrote another version of the letter by hand omitting addresses and leaving certain blanks for "Bank Notes" and other give-away words. He then asked a mining engineer who had often done translations for Reis to convert the letter into English. The translator had the impression he was dealing with stock certificates of some kind.

[*] Reis didn't know that the Bank of Portugal conducted its correspondence with Waterlow in Portuguese.

Reis went out of his way to congratulate Waterlow on its splendid caution:

> Although it is to be recognized that the Contracts held by Messrs. Marang & Collignon are documents sufficiently valid to free from all responsibility any printer, I cannot but thank your Firm for your attention and special care in consulting me before employing the Plates of the Bank which are in your hands and have great pleasure in informing you that you may accept the order from Marang & Collignon and use the Bank's plates.

Then, to make sure there wouldn't be any further slip-ups such as Waterlow's *mailing* a letter to the governor of the Bank, Reis included a prolix caution:

> You would highly oblige me by dealing directly with Marang & Collignon on all points connected with the printing of this Bank's Notes . . . and, should any further data be required from me, I should beg you to apply for it in a Confidential letter directed to Marang & Collignon or sent me, through their interposition, and in likewise Confidential form.

For the actual details of manufacture the letter was marvelously casual:

> The delivery of the Bank Notes may be made to Marang & Collignon, in London.
> As to the numerating, dating, signing, etc, of the Bank Notes, the same gentlemen are empowered to make the Bank Notes as they wish, that is, to have them numbered, signed etc, and printed by your Firm or any other, as they choose.

And, finally, if anyone at Waterlow's started wondering about two sets of similar banknotes afloat in Portugal itself there was a further reassurance that these notes would bear the overprint ANGOLA.

The signature of I. Camacho Rodrigues, chairman of the Bank of Portugal, gave Reis almost no trouble. He traced it from a 500 escudos banknote and enlarged it.

On another sheet of the Bank's stationery, Alves Reis performed one more forgery. This was a receipt for 100,000 escudos (about $5,000) "signed" by Mota Gomes, the Bank's vice governor, to acknowledge the bribe he had received. The receipt was sent by Reis to Marang to show him that the £1000 in additional bribe money Reis had insisted upon had been well spent.

José Bandeira arrived in Lisbon on December 27th with Marang's £1000 which he had been carefully cautioned not to turn over to Reis until he had the letter from the governor of the Bank in his hands.

In addition to acutely welcome money Reis also got a reassuring bonus: Marang had wired Waterlow and received confirmation from them that Sir William had not mailed a carbon of the letter given Marang for delivery to the governor of the Bank.

His confidence restored, Alves Reis decided it was time to carry the plot one step forward. José was the ideal tryout soul: if he saw flaws or objections in an hour of talks the matter was hopeless. The far sharper partners, Marang and Hennies, would spot the kinks in seconds.

"We will circulate the notes in Portugal and the Azores," he told José. "Camacho decided that this would be best because of the resignation of the High Commissioner of Angola. This means that we won't have to overprint the notes ANGOLA as we planned originally. In turn, however, we will have to use some of the notes to make investments in certain Angola enterprises."

One of the investments would naturally be the Angola Mining Company in which Reis was heavily involved. In effect, one of the conditions he imposed was that the new notes would be used to bail him out of a disastrous investment.

José thought it was a great idea. He wired his brother in The Hague that he had the governor's letter, that he had paid Reis the money.

And something else: Reis would need another £1050 within the next ten days because there was a promissory note of his due shortly. Again, Reis couldn't tell José or any of the group the real reason he needed this money. Without it he had no chance of finding out the exact combinations of Bank directors' signatures and numbering that were to be put on the new notes.

In The Hague, Marang wrote Waterlow that he expected the letter from the governor shortly and that he would be in London on January 6th and "trusting that you will have an opportunity to reserve a few hours for us, in order to be able to make a definite contract with you."

But Marang didn't send the £1050 to Reis. Surely there had to be an end to the insatiable demands of these corrupt Bank governors! No, he would not send any more money to Lisbon until he actually got a contract to print the notes from Waterlow.

The delay gave Reis his cruellest trial. For without the money he could not discover the secret of the exact combinations of Bank directors' signatures and serial numbers that were to be put on the new notes.

In principle the problem belongs to elementary cryptanalysis. The trouble is that you must first have a considerable number of coded messages—or banknotes in this case—to solve the mystery.

He was helped by a copy of the Bank of Portugal's regulations which he purchased at the Government Printing Office. In Article 223 of the regulations he found the requirement that the Bank's notes had to be signed by the governor or vice governor and one director. And the director's signature would alternate in each series according to the order of their seniority. Another publication, the report of the Bank's Administrative Council, gave him the seniority of each of the directors, alternated in each series of 20,000 notes. This he could learn only by studying several hundred 500-escudos notes. And to get those notes he needed the money which Marang was stubbornly refusing to send until he got the Waterlow contract in hand.

On January 5th he sent Marang a telegram of piteous desperation:

NON FULFILLMENT OF PROMISE TO SEND ME MONEY HAS PLACED ME IN TERRIBLE POSITION. MIGHT HAVE TO DECLARE BANKRUPTCY AT ANY MOMENT. YOUR PETTINESS IN THIS ENDANGERS ENTIRE OPERATION.

Marang was obdurate: no more money until he had the contract. It wasn't all pure obstinacy. He was within scowling distance of bankruptcy himself.

1. *Bank of Portugal Building in Lisbon, 1925.*

500 Escudos note of the 1922 series, with Vasco Da Gama portrait and sailing ships.
small detail beneath the central 500 figure at the bottom is the printer's little self-
ertisement: "Waterlow & Sons, Limited, Londres". This was one of the duplicated
es.

3. *Alves Reis on an expedition in Angola, 1920.*

4. *Alves Reis, Lisbon, 1925.*

6. *Alves Reis at his desk in Lisbon in 1953.*

5. *Alves Reis,*
in Lisbon in 1946.

7. *Alves Reis, Jr., Lisbon, 1964.*

8. Jose Bandeira, Arens Novaes, shortly after Reis' arrest in Dec. 1925.

10. Jose Bandeira, at The Hague, 1922, the time of the successful Macau port deal.

9. Jose Bandeira in the prison garden in 1926. He was allowed to wear his own suits while in "preventive detention".

11. *Jose Bandeira, in 1955, Lisbon.*

12. *Jose Bandeira in a Lisbon bar, 1960.*

13. *H.G.W. Romer,
photographed
about 1920.*

14. *Adolph Hennies, in 1924.*

15. *Fie Carelsen at the Longchamps Racetrack in Paris in 1925.*

16. *Karel Marang (left), the Dutch financier who operated from The Hague and later Paris, with his lawyer, Bemmel Suyk.*

17. Sir William Waterlow, in fu[ll]
regalia, at the Ascot Racetrack
in 1931, just before his death.

18. Antonio Bandeira, at right,
in full diplomatic uniform,
arriving for a formal reception a[t]
The Hague, September 1923.

1925

LONDON / January 6, 1925

MARANG ARRIVED the night before after a particularly rough crossing. Violent rainstorms and gales had been hitting the Channel and the British Isles. The Thames had flooded in many areas. The visitor's mood matched the weather. How had he ever allowed himself to get involved in a business venture where he put up most of the money and had little or no control over the operation? And to be dealing with an excitable Portuguese who was on the thin edge of bankruptcy!

He felt better in the cozy warmth of Sir William's office. Part of the warmth came from Sir William himself. He felt even more confident of his visitor than ever as a result of a credit report that had been put on his desk that morning. He had asked Stubbs, a leading British credit-reporting firm, if Marang was good for £5000 worth of credit.

The report read, in part:

> This gentleman is owner of export house of Marang & Collignon. He chiefly exports to Persia and the Levant and is reported to be very businesslike in his dealings. He is also Consul General for Persia at The Hague.

> Mr. Marang is further said to be possessed of means. . . . He always meets his obligations regularly so that business relations with him need not be objected to. Although he may be considered quite good for ample trade credit our informants are unable to decide whether a credit to the extent mentioned by you may be granted.

> He is also Consul of Legation for Liberia.

Clearly a man of substance and standing, Sir William concluded. And one in whom foreign governments reposed confidence and trust.

After Sir William had the Bank governor's letter translated

he decided that he had full authority to go ahead with the bank-note order and later that morning he drew up a Memorandum of Agreement. Waterlow & Sons Limited agreed

> to print and supply to Marang & Collignon 200,000 notes of 500 Escudos each as last supplied to the Banco de Portugal and exactly as one of the patterns attached to the Contract between the Banco de Portugal and the Government of Angola dated 6th November 1924, except that details of numeration, dating and signatures are to be supplied by the Banco de Portugal through Marang & Collignon, within ten days. . . .

> The price for the said Notes to be £1500, and the Notes to be delivered by the Company to Marang & Collignon in London on the dates following:

> 10,000 Notes by February 10th
> and
> 190,000 Notes by February 28th

The contract called for Marang to pay "all charges which may be incurred in respect of packing, freight, insurance, etc., for transmission to Lisbon or elsewhere."

Marang gave Waterlow his check for £1500. He remembered to send Reis a wire in English:

CONTRACT SIGNED. FIRST DELIVERY OF 10,000 PIECES ON FEB. TENTH AND REST BEFORE END OF MONTH PROVIDED I HAVE SERIAL NUMBERS IN A WEEK.

But he still didn't send the money Reis had asked for. The £1500 to Waterlow had put a severe dent in Marang's checking account. He would have to scrounge to pay this importunate fellow. Hennies who had been sharing expenses with Marang on the venture—so far they had invested nearly $40,000—would have to come up with more money quickly.

He wired Hennies in Berlin to send £400 immediately to Reis. That should keep him satisfied for a while.

       *   *   *   *   *

Late the next afternoon Sir William noticed the Marang file folder on his desk and remembered he had promised to write the Dutchman about some information he had requested.

In reply to your enquiry we beg to inform you that 1000 notes of 500 escudos measure 4¾″ × 7½ × 4¾″ and weigh about 5 lbs.*

In the file, too, was the most important letter from Camacho Rodrigues with its consent to the use of the escudos plates. Surely there should be some discreet acknowledgement that he had received this letter. In complete violation of the communication arrangements stressed by "Camacho" in the letter, Sir William decided to *mail* him the following:

I have the pleasure in acknowledging receipt of your confidential letter of 23rd December, the contents of which I have noted, and for which I am obliged.

Yours faithfully,
William A. Waterlow
Chairman of Waterlow & Sons Limited

He instructed Miss Shaw to send the letter in an unmarked envelope. She entered in her correspondence register the fact that Sir William had mailed a letter to the governor of the Bank of Portugal. She put the letter in her outgoing mailbox. Sometime late that afternoon it was picked up by Jim Nye, an office clerk, who copied the name and address on the envelope, noted that it would make the 6:30 P.M. pickup, and affixed a 2½ d postage stamp to it and then took it out to the GPO mailbox in the main hall of the Waterlow office building.

In well-ordered plots success or failure should never hinge on ridiculous details such as the non-delivery of a letter. But Sir William's discreet note of acknowledgement somehow never got to the Bank of Portugal so that Camacho Rodrigues didn't know he had sent a "confidential letter" to Sir William Waterlow. Alves Reis' extraordinary luck was still holding.

* Or worth nearly $300 an ounce. In 1925 gold was selling for only $20 an ounce.

LISBON / January 13, 1925

THE £1050 ARRIVED from Marang the day before—simultaneously with the £400 wired by Hennies which had somehow been delayed. Reis gave the extra £400 to José Bandeira who was returning to The Hague with the letter from Camacho containing the names of the Bank directors and the serial numbers that were to appear on the notes.

Working out the numbers and directors' names sequence had been done hurriedly by Reis. With 100 banknotes of the 500 escudos Vasco da Gama type obtained by him and his trusted assistant, Ferreira, in various banks, he was able to get a fair idea of how the Bank alternated directors' names and numbers. But in the great haste there were inevitable mistakes. For example he thought the Bank alternated directors' names with each 10,000 notes—actually it was 20,000—and he had not discovered that the Bank didn't number notes beyond the 1 AN series. Nor did he find out that the Bank never used two vowels together so that 1 AE and 1 AI were mistakenly ordered.* And there wouldn't be any W's or Y's. These letters don't appear in the Portuguese alphabet.

But Reis did get one important break. In the new forged letter by Camacho to Waterlow the banknote firm was asked which directors' names they already had on plates. Waterlow accommodatingly provided just such a list. It didn't strike Sir William how curious it was the Bank officers didn't know which name plates they had. For that matter it didn't seem to occur to Marang or Hennies how strange it was that the Bank governor didn't know which name plates were in the possession of the banknote firm which had been printing these very notes.

---

* In a similar situation another great banknote plotter, Friedrich Walter Bernhard Krüger received unexpected help from the enemy. Krüger, a Nazi SS major, was in charge of "Operation Bernhard" which manufactured $600,000,000 worth of British banknotes in World War II and had begun the manufacture of $100 bills. While trying to work out the U.S. Treasury's numbering code for the bills Krüger got a copy of *Life* magazine —from a Nazi agent in Sweden. An article on U.S. banknote making told just how the numbering system worked.

LONDON / February 10, 1925

AS A MEASURE of confidence in the venture, Marang spent the night at the Ritz Hotel instead of the more convenient and more modest Great Eastern where he stayed on his previous visits. The first batch of notes—some 20,000—were to be ready today. There were favorable auguries in the very air: London had just finished celebrating the 400th anniversary of the birth of that celebrated explorer Vasco da Gama.

At Waterlow's, Roland S. Springall, the assistant to Frederick W. Goodman, the Waterlow director who supervised all banknote production, took Marang to a nearby valise maker and helped him select a strong tan leather model to hold the first batch of notes.

At the Waterlow banknote factory in Scrutton Street after the 20,000 notes were packed—15,000 in the valise and 5,000 in a separate stout parcel tied with wire—Springall accompanied Marang in a cab back to the Ritz where a bellman took the 100 pounds of notes to Marang's room.

Marang thanked Springall profusely and said he looked forward to seeing him on February 25th when the next batch would be ready. Springall left and Marang stayed in his room—having lunch sent up—so that he could keep an eye on the valise and the package worth about $460,000.

Later in the afternoon he ordered a cab and went back to the Liverpool Street Station to catch the boat-train to the Hook of Holland.

THE HAGUE / February 11, 1925

THE MORNING WAS very cold. Marang's chauffeur had driven Reis and Hennies to the Hook to greet Marang and his valuable baggage. All of Marang's luggage bore orange diplomatic service labels. That and the fact that Marang had a *laisser-passer* signed by the Portuguese Minister to Holland got him through customs without the usual inspection. They drove quickly to Marang's house in The Hague.

The four mutually congratulated one another. Now that they actually had the first batch of banknotes it was time to come to a firmer understanding about just how the money was to be divided.

They sat around a mahogany table in the living room. The walls bore Raphael reproductions and Empire-style bronze ornaments nestled on every flat surface.

Reis suspected a rough bargaining session was to follow and had prepared for it. Originally, he wrote later,

> We had agreed to share the profits in *three* equal parts, one for Alves Reis, another for Marang and Hennies, and the third for José Bandeira. . . . Now Marang proposed that profits be shared in *four* equal parts, meaning that Bandeira and I should give up a sixth of our profits to Marang and Hennies. Marang argued heatedly that he and Hennies had put up the one million escudos ($50,000) to make the whole enterprise possible. Surely they were entitled to their expenses before there was a division of the profits. He didn't realize what a trap he had set for himself.
>
> I pretended to agree with Marang and would get Bandeira— who had stalked out of the room in indignation at Marang's demand—to agree. Yes, I said, Marang and Hennies were entitled to their expenses. But, then, surely, so were Alves Reis and José Bandeira. Now that the matter had been brought up they should know that "The Men" at the Bank of Portugal who had made the contracts possible would want 17 million escudos [about $850,000] for their "cooperation." Marang was trapped. He had to agree.

He had to agree because the alternative would be unthinkable. If Alves Reis had *not* promised such a generous bribe to the Bank officers it meant that they had *not* given him the contracts and splendid confirming letters. No, it would not bear thinking at all. The logical end-conclusion of such a wild thought was too frightening to contemplate for even a millisecond.

A chastened Marang drew up what he called their "Petite Contract" in French:

The undersigned Artur Alves Reis, José de Bandeira, Adolf Hennies and Karel Marang have agreed that the profits resulting from the loan made by them to the Government of Angola will be shared among them after deduction of expenses made by each so that each will receive 25% of the net profits. Of the next profits the first to be paid will be Marang: 1 million escudos [about $50,000] for the total expenses that he has put out so far. Next Alves Reis will receive 17 million escudos [about $850,000] for his expenses and charges that he has incurred. The remainder will be divided 25% to each of the subscribing parties.

Signed on February 11, 1925.

With the contract's signing certain old fictions were discarded. Obviously there would not be any loan of $5,000,000 to distressed Angola.

An expansive Reis reminded his partners that there were certain obligations that could not be forgotten: he had promised his Bank of Portugal friends a good part of the group's profits would be invested in certain Angolan ventures which he was certain would be vastly profitable. Angola needed help and Alves Reis for one, was patriotically determined to see that it got generous assistance.

As to the matter of distribution of the new notes. This would be under his supervision, as they had all agreed he was the best informed in this area. He and his staff of assistants would be able to do most of it by themselves but from time to time he would be calling on his partners for assistance.

That evening they worked out their short-term tactics. Reis and Hennies would go to Lisbon first without the notes to make sure that everything was working smoothly and that no hitches had arisen at the Bank of Portugal. If all was well, as they fully expected it to be, they would wire Marang and José Bandeira to come down with the notes. These two would wait in the Hotel Claridge in Paris—by now the hotel had become one of their many headquarters—for the go-ahead wire.

As Reis and Hennies boarded the train for Paris that evening, Hennies looked at his partner's matched and initialed valises and shook his head.

"Most unwise," he said. "The initials."

Reis was puzzled. "What's wrong with them?"

"My friend," said Hennies from the depth of his German

Secret Service experience, "there might come a time when you would not want to be readily identified by initials on your luggage. The wise man travels as anonymously as possible."

Reis smiled politely for the tip and said nothing. From here on in anonymity would be the very last quality Artur Alves Reis would ever display. Portugal was almost his.

LISBON / February 16, 1925

MARANG AND BANDEIRA arrived with the money the day before, a Sunday. There had been no difficulty at all at Vilar Fomoso, a lovely hamlet on the Spanish border where the Sud Express enters Portugal. With the orange diplomatic card carried by José and Marang's two diplomatic passports—Persia and Liberia—plus the fact that their luggage now bore the newly-created stickers for diplomatic luggage, the way had been smooth. Marang didn't even have to show the *laisser-passer* signed by Antonio Bandeira, Portuguese Minister to The Hague and dated February 12, 1925:

> The undersigned, Minister of Portugal in Holland, recommends to the Portuguese authorities the bearer of this document, Mr. K. Marang van Isselveere, who is going to Portugal on an official mission and requests that he be granted the usual facilities compatible with the Law.

Reis had given a lot of thought to the best way of getting rid of the 500-escudos notes quickly, safely and with a maximum profit. The *only* way, he concluded, was to get into the illegal foreign exchange business.

Like some other countries in Europe whose currencies were no longer convertible into gold, Portugal had an extensive illegal market in foreign currencies which were bought and sold at higher than official exchange rates. Businessmen, particularly the Port wine shippers, much preferred to have hard dollars or pounds in their foreign bank accounts than soft escudos at home.

The center of these black-market currency deals was Oporto, the dark-gray-stoned city of the north. Oporto was always much more sombre than Lisbon, infinitely more businesslike. On a gray rainy day—and there are many such in Oporto—it feels like Birmingham, England. Perhaps the weather and the grayness drove a disproportionate number of Portuguese of the north to migrate to America and Brazil and even Great Britain.

In the village cemetery of Moura in northern Portugal is the tombstone of a resident who "died of laughing." Hundreds of thousands of other Portuguese did their laughing only after they left Portugal for opportunity elsewhere.* As they prospered in the U.S. and Brazil they sent money to their families and close relatives in Portugal. When the dollars and milreis and pounds arrived in northern Portugal the recipients often went to certain brokers in Oporto to get an even better rate of exchange. The differential on the black market could be as much as 20% but most of the time it averaged between 8–10%. In addition to the foreign currency itself or certified checks on foreign banks there were also foreign currency permits—*permis*—which could be bought and sold at a premium.

Reis and his trusted office manager, Ferreira, quickly recruited a crew of free-lance black-market currency men known as *zangão* or drones. They were promised a 2% commission on all their transactions and given 500,000 escudos each in the new crisp 500 escudos notes. Reis took them to the Lisbon station to catch the 8 P.M. overnight train to Oporto. He trusted each of the free lancers but to make sure he had Ferreira accompany them.

In the first two days in Oporto the crew bought—by paying slight premiums above the current black-market prices—some £23,000 ($115,000) in exchange for their escudos notes. After paying them their commissions daily, Ferreira promptly transferred the hard currency to special accounts Reis opened.

* Portugal's emigration laws have been tightened greatly. But in recent years some 150,000 Portugese men have skipped over the border to get work in France, which has more jobs than workers. And like the earlier emigrants who went even further these men send home a good part of their earnings. In 1964 Portugal obtained $100,000,000 in foreign currency this way.

Another method of getting rid of the new 500-escudos notes was even simpler: Reis and his aides opened about a dozen new bank accounts in Oporto and Lisbon. They would deposit the new notes and several days later start making withdrawals. Most of the time they got back notes they had not deposited. Often they made deposits in the small town branch offices of the large Lisbon and Oporto banks. A few days later they would withdraw banknotes from the main branches in the two big cities.*

One of the free-lances played it cautiously the first day he got to Oporto. He went to the nearest bank to change one of his 500-escudos notes for smaller bills. If he were handling counterfeits he wanted to know about it right away. The teller examined the new bill minutely—and exchanged it for smaller bills with a nod. Portuguese bank tellers never smile.

Another of Reis' agents had a little more trouble. Adriano Silva who operated out of Braga, another important source of emigrants, was a little careless. He simply deposited the money in one bank in Braga, the Bank of Minho, instead of spreading it around in different accounts. The bank manager who vaguely recalled Silva had once been arrested for embezzlement, became curious enough to send two of Silva's new 500-escudos notes to the Bank of Portugal in Lisbon with a run-down on Silva's past. The Bank returned the notes with a brief comment: the notes were excellent and could be handled without fear.

One of the bank's employees told Silva. He rushed to Lisbon to tell his boss, Alves Reis. Reis was naturally pleased with the Bank of Portugal's comments on the new notes but perhaps it was also time to assert himself and defend the *honra e dignidade* of his agent, Silva. (Honor and dignity are always coupled in Portuguese so that it emerges as one amalgamated word, rather like lovingkindness in the Old Testament.)

As Reis told it later:

> The case was of much more concern to me than Silva ever imagined. I was starting to be "somebody" and I was quickly becoming one of the largest depositors the Bank of Minho had. [Alves Reis Ltd. had about $125,000 deposited in various

* Checking accounts were then quite rare in Portugal. Most businessmen completed their transactions with payments in large denomination banknotes.

branches of the bank by the end of February.] At the bank's main office in Oporto I was greeted with a great show of honor. I coldly set forth the situation and deplored it as having hurt the honor and dignity of my own trusted agent, Silva. They apologized profusely and Silva who was present earned the moral reparation he deserved. Naturally, Silva told the other men who were exchanging currency for me. If they had any doubts about the whole operation once, they no longer did. They now knew they were working for a man with important connections.

LISBON / March 1, 1925

MARANG AND José Bandeira brought the second batch of notes without incident. This time they had 30,000 notes worth nearly $700,000. Springall took Marang around to the same luggage maker and ordered two tan leather bags to hold the 150 pounds the notes weighed.

Marang's expenses in the venture were paid out by Reis and the money transferred to the Dutchman's account in The Hague. But Marang was even more pleased by the knowledge that his own honor and dignity was about to be upheld gloriously. Besides the money, he brought with him the authorization of the Holland Red Cross to represent it at the celebration of the 60th Anniversary of the Portuguese Red Cross. He also bore various gifts from the Dutch Red Cross which he was going to present on Sunday, March 1st, to the President of the Portuguese Republic, Texeira de Gomes.

After settling the money matters with Reis, Marang went to his room at the Avenida Palace Hotel to rehearse the speech he was going to give on Sunday—and to relish his forthcoming vindication.

In 1922 at the time of the celebration of the 400th anniversary of Magellan's circumnavigation of the globe Marang had ma-

neuvered mightily in The Hague to get himself appointed with
another honors seeker named Piet Wattel to represent the Dutch
Geographic Society at the anniversary dinners in Madrid and
Lisbon. But the affair had been marred for Marang by the bitter
attack launched against him by the Portuguese Minister to
Holland—Antonio dos Santos Bandeira—who had warned the
foreign office in Lisbon that

> Messrs. Marang and Wattel, two Dutch businessmen on their
> way to Lisbon, are going to express the Dutch Government's de-
> sire to have various personalities invested with Portuguese Grand
> Crosses and other honors, in exchange for Dutch honors. All this
> is mere maneuvering on the part of the two businessmen who do
> not enjoy the least category or situation here. They have not been
> directly or indirectly authorized to speak on behalf of anyone in
> this country and are only trying to exploit in their own interest
> the representation of the Magellan Committee, of which they are
> the mere couriers at their own request. Both of them belong to
> the class of small traders. Marang made a small fortune during the
> war and since then titles himself Marang de Ysselveere. Wattel
> enjoys the perhaps unfounded reputation of devoting the greater
> part of his activity in the acquisition of titles and honors for the
> use of moneyed parvenus.

Since diplomacy is the ultimate exercise of flexibility, Antonio Bandeira had now become a collaborator and even a friend of
Marang as a result of the banknote operation. Naturally when
Marang went to Lisbon this time he was a fully accredited and
honored representative of the Dutch Red Cross, thanks to Bandeira's intervention.

On Sunday the ceremony went off well and Marang's speech
—in French—was well received. He presented the Portuguese
Red Cross with a silver plaque from Prince Henry of Holland,
Queen Wilhelmina's Consort. In the shadowy world in which
honors are generated and granted, mutuality is the operative
word. So Karel Marang received the Plaque of Honor, the Portuguese Red Cross' highest award, and from the government itself
the Order of Christ for which he had been proposed by a local
politician named Barbosa de Magalhães. The latter award
pleased Marang greatly: with it went the right to wear a sliver of
red and white ribbon in the jacket buttonhole. The white in the
ribbon was so thin that if properly inserted the ribbon looked

very much like that worn by the French Legion d'Honneur, a distinction for which Marang had long yearned.

To cap the great pleasures of this splendid day a local paper ran a picture of Marang getting the Order of Christ—and mistakenly identified him as Prince Henry of Holland. Naturally Marang sent several clippings of the story of his awards to that skeptic in Paris—Baron Lehmann, the Liberian Ambassador to France. But Marang still didn't return the Liberian diplomatic passport that had been demanded several times by mail.

One of the features of the Portuguese Red Cross celebration had been the presentation by the Minister of Posts & Telegraph of a fine series of postage stamps commemorating the anniversary. The stamps had been printed by Waterlow & Sons. When photos of the presentation appeared in the Lisbon papers, Robert Walker, the local Waterlow representative, sent clippings to Sir William Waterlow. In London Sir William studied the photos carefully and was pleased to discern the face of his current customer, Karel Marang, near the President of Portugal. Marang seemed to be holding an award of some kind.

In all, March, 1925 was a great month for the renewal of honor and dignity of the members of the gang. And now it was the turn of Alves Reis, himself. He was sorely in need of moral vindication now that the money was rolling in. The stink of prison, the stain of failure had to be wiped out forever. "No man is rich enough to buy back his past," Oscar Wilde once mourned. But then he wasn't as rich or as powerful as Alves Reis was about to become. With the proper weapons a determined man could *reconstruct* his past.

Now Alves Reis contemplated exultantly the vindication that would soon be his. He had to wipe out the stain put on his name by those treacherous Ambaca Company directors who had caused his imprisonment. To do so Reis had to buy back his controlling interest. He spent 2,000,000 escudos (about $92,000)—which had cost him only $144 in printing costs—to get the shares. He knew they weren't worth much but he wanted desperately the pleasure of being restored to the position of majority shareholder and to throw out his former colleagues on the board. But he wasn't quite ready for the showdown. That would come in May when the directors of Ambaca were to meet.

LISBON / April 15, 1925

THE MONEY rolled in. Reis now had to show Lisbon what a big man he had become. He bought a fine four-story mansion, well-known locally as the Menino d'Ouro, the Golden Boy Palace. It was paneled with rare Brazilian woods and more importantly, for Reis, it had a cleverly concealed safe under the library floor. The odd name came from a Portuguese couple who struck it rich in Brazil. They were childless and endlessly prayed to the Virgin: they would give her as much gold as a son would weigh on his first birthday if they could have a child. In her 41st year the wife did become pregnant and in time delivered a healthy boy. The gold—some 22 pounds—was donated to the church on his first birthday.

The house also had a certain curse on it, the superstitious said. The Inquisition was supposed to have used its grounds as a burial ground for its victims. In fact when Reis added a two-car garage on to the structure to house his new Hispano-Suiza, the workmen did unearth many old bones.

He bought the mansion for a million escudos ($50,000) and spent another $25,000 furnishing it.* From Lisbon and Oporto jewelers he bought for his wife $50,000 worth of jewelry, including a pearl collar with 399 pearls; diamond earrings, broaches, bracelets, eight diamond rings; a platinum framed lorgnette—*and* a diamond encrusted platinum framed lorgnette for the evening.

In this month of burgeoning wealth there had been only one moment of danger. Hennies volunteered to bring one of the banknote shipments to Lisbon. He had a diplomatic passport as Commercial Attaché of the Liberian Legation, much more recently granted than the one Marang still held onto.

As Reis later recalled the incident, Hennies had with him some 40,000 notes worth 20,000,000 escudos ($1,000,000).

* To get modern equivalent of these and subsequent expenditures multiply the dollar equivalent by seven. A good white-collar job in Lisbon in 1925 paid $40 a month.

I saw him go to the customs counter but the Chief of Customs decided not to respect the diplomatic immunity conferred on Hennies by the Liberian passport. The situation was serious and I could see Hennies was worried. If the Customs Chief insisted on opening the trunk we were *all* in great trouble. I intervened and told the customs man the trunk was in transit and would go tomorrow to the Santos customs post, the embarkation pier in Lisbon.

We left the unopened trunk there and I took Hennies for a welcoming dinner at the Avenida Palace. I was careful not to show any concern. I said my friend Camacho Rodrigues of the Bank of Portugal would take the necessary steps. The next day I went back to the customs post at the Rossio Station and happily found another Customs Chief. I greeted him affably and described the difficulties his colleague had raised for diplomat Hennies the day before.

"It's not important, you understand," I said "but you know how zealous diplomats are of their privileges. Hennies plans to protest to the Foreign Office today and of course he needs a morning coat and striped trousers which happen to be in the trunk." I pulled out an elegant crocodile and gold key case as if I was ready then and there to extricate the needed suit from the trunk. The new customs man was as pleasant as his previous colleague had been dour. He deplored what certainly must have been an error on the part of the other customs man. He would certainly have no objection to releasing the trunk on presentation of a diplomatic passport. I rushed back to the Avenida Palace and told Hennies my friend Camacho had succeeded in getting the trunk released. All that was needed was Hennies' diplomatic passport. I sent my aide, Ferreira, to the customs post with Hennies' passport and the trunk was now released. Hennies now had further confirmation of how well I stood with the powers of Portugal.

The gang now had 70,000 notes in circulation worth some $1,750,000. As quickly as possible the notes had been exchanged for pounds, dollars and francs.

With so great an infusion of currency into the moribund Portuguese economy it was inevitable that a clamor should arise: Beware! Counterfeit 500 escudos notes were circulating everywhere.

Whenever a package of 500 escudos notes came through, the

Lisbon and Oporto banks sent them on quickly to the Bank of Portugal to be posted to their credit. Ordinary merchants accepted the 500 escudos notes with great reluctance. In some areas business came to a standstill because the sellers wouldn't accept the notes.

The Bank of Portugal naturally examined the notes as they came in for exchange. Its renowned expert on counterfeit notes, Senhor José Armando Pedroso, checked and rechecked the suspect notes. He measured them, magnified them for better examination, took samples of the ink off them, *smelled* them. His judgment was firm and unqualified: these were perfectly good notes.

The Bank sent discreet letters to its correspondents in all parts of the country: the rumors about counterfeit 500 escudos notes were totally unfounded. No such false notes had been uncovered by the Bank.

Still the rumors grew. In Lisbon, some of the wags were suggesting that new 500 escudos notes be tried on the elephant: *he* would know. The Lisbon Zoo had an elephant which could distinguish between silver and copper coins. The copper ones offered him would be taken by his trunk and thrown into the deep ditch that kept him within his island. A silver one he'd take to a box on the far side of his domain, deposit it and ring a bell-rope to get the keeper who would bring a bundle of grass—in exchange for the coin.

When people started snickering about money, Alves Reis knew, it was time for studied idleness.

> I ordered suspension of transactions with my notes. I told my trusted employees that the popular fear of the notes had reached the Bank of Portugal and my friends Camacho and Gomes [the governor and vice governor] had recommended caution and discretion.

Late in the afternoon of April 15th Reis had a visit from several business friends who warned him there were many false 500-escudos notes in circulation. Reis thanked them for the warning and added warmly: Yes, how true was that wise old Portuguese maxim: "Friends in the market are worth more than money in the chest."

Perhaps it would be wise to heed the warning. Besides he

was ready for the next stage of his plot. Now it was time to gather his associates in Paris to let them know what was going to happen next. He had his staff send wires to Hennies in Berlin and Bandeira and Marang in The Hague. All read:

MOST IMPORTANT MEET CLARIDGE PARIS APRIL 29.

To his staff he announced some important wheat and match deals that were on tap in Paris. Senhora Reis was told that it was time she acquired some fine Paris gowns to go with her impressive array of jewelry. Their three sons, supervised by a governess, and Mrs. Reis' personal maid, accompanied the family to Paris by Sud Express.

PARIS / April 29, 1925

THE CLARIDGE WAS then one of Paris' best hotels: right on the Champs Élysées and the first Paris hotel with an indoor swimming pool and Turkish baths. It advertised itself as "The only palace on the Champs Élysées." With its 300 rooms—each with private bath and telephone, a not-too-common combination in Paris in 1925—and its long colonnaded shopping gallery, it was the delight of the wealthy visitor. The elegant dining room was ruled forcefully by a very young captain of waiters named Henri Soulé. He was then only 23 and decades away from his autocracy of Le Pavillon restaurant in New York.

For this important meeting José brought his mistress, Fie Carelsen. Hennies came alone: his affair with his wartime friend Annaliese Angold, had recently lost its flavor. In Berlin she found another and more generous protector.

Fie Carelsen was then 35. She was tall, bony, with a wide mouth, enormous black eyes which lit up her thin, pale face. The fashion of the Twenties with its compression and concealment of the breasts fitted her well. It was the age of beige but she was bold enough to add warm colors. As one of Holland's leading actresses she could defy the conventions of dress as easily as those of sex.

She first met José Bandeira in The Hague in 1921, soon after her divorce. Her husband had been Jean-Louis Pisuisse, a leading Dutch actor. "A wonderful artist and a rotten husband," she said.

> My heart was bleeding when I met José—he was poor, very poor. Everybody criticized me for joining up with a poor devil. I didn't care. I loved him. I earned enough to live well. José would tell me: "When I am rich I'll buy you a sapphire ring." And when he had his first success with the harbor deal in Macao he did buy me the sapphire ring. I was so glad for him. I knew his pride had undergone difficult trials before that.

In The Hague, José was often at her handsome brick and marble house. It was furnished attractively in the vogue of the period: oriental bric-a-brac; cushions everywhere; maroon lampshades and many souvenirs of her travels in Europe and South America. And a Javanese maid.

In some ways her affair with the Portuguese adventurer was a European re-play of the memorable American encounter in the Twenties of the actress and the notorious gambler: Fanny Brice and Nicky Arnstein.* The two tall women had some surface resemblance but Fie, unlike Fanny, had no middle-class illusions about the joys of marriage. Never during her five-year affair with José did she hint at marriage or desire it.

"He often said: you would be less as my wife; more as my mistress. It was not a *big* love with José. But it was warm, enduring and very sweet. He was gentle, charming and allowed almost nothing to distract him from the one pursuit he was expert in: making love. I wasn't his mistress. We were lovers. He never supported me. I always paid my own way."

She knew she wasn't the only woman in José's life during this period. "But I suspect our affair was the first time he was proud of his friend. Of course, everyone in The Hague knew I was his friend. We made no secret of it."

She first met Alves Reis on one of his trips to The Hague late in 1924:

"I didn't like him. He didn't look you in the eyes. And he al-

* Retold recently in the Broadway musical, "Funny Girl."

ways talked of women, how he needed women, one every night. He made himself sound like a big Don Juan. I *think* he was trying to impress me but he never made any overtures.

"He was only interested in money and women. I'm sure he was unfaithful to his wife from the start. He didn't have the least sense of humor.

"The next time I met him was early in April, 1925, when he came up to meet José on some business. José brought me along because we were going to celebrate my birthday on April 5th. But soon after Reis arrived he took to his bed in his suite with a case of mild influenza. He was all alone in the city and a friend of my friend. I treated him with consideration, brought him his medicines, read to him and nursed him. When he recovered he was very grateful.

"What happened was that he heard José and me talking about a new Renault. José had half-promised me one but was afraid to buy it for me because I might have an accident. It wasn't a pose: when he had money José was most generous. So Reis broke in our conversation and said: 'Let *me* buy you a Renault. It's the least I can do for your kindness in nursing me while I was sick.' So I got the Renault from Alves Reis."

José didn't forget her birthday. She got a 3½ carat diamond ring.

Her doubts about Reis remained.

"José kept telling me what a big man Alves Reis was, how important he was in Portugal, what great plans he was setting in motion. And all I could say to José was: If he is so important why can't he speak French well?"

Hennies worried her.

"He had cold eyes and was a little bent over. He never looked like he had money. Sad-looking but very clever. In fact, he *looked* like a swindler. He always made me feel poor little José had fallen into bad company. José told me Hennies had a little friend, a German girl, but that was over. Hennies and I were very formal to one another: I always addressed him as Herr Hennies and he called me Madame Carelsen."

Because the men of the group were together so much on business, Fie naturally spent a lot of time with Senhora Alves Reis. It was not an association of Fie's choosing:

"She spoke very little French and was altogether too bour-

geois for me. She'd talk about food and dresses and the children.
She was short and dumpy and *that* didn't help. She wore very expensive dresses that didn't suit her and the many new pieces of
jewelry made her look like she was married to M. Rhinestone.
And they were genuine, of course. I think my affair with José embarrassed her. She once asked me why we didn't marry. I told her
I wasn't in love with José and after that we kept our talk strictly
to food and dresses."

Marang did not bring his wife to the Paris meeting.

"He always kept her in the background. I met her a few
times in The Hague but we were never friendly. Marang was
handsome, good-looking, and the tallest of them although inclined a little to pudginess. He was tight with a guilder but
dressed himself well. I think secretly he looked down on me for
associating with a Portuguese, a short one at that. With him, of
course, it was business."

Although Antonio Bandeira, the Portuguese Minister to Holland did not come to the meeting because he was well-represent-
ed by his brother, José, it would have been impossible for him to
do so, anyway. He was busy introducing his new wife to his family in Portugal.

"It was quite incredible," Fie recalls. "He was good-looking,
popular in the foreign set—particularly among the women—and
had had any number of affairs with very attractive friends.
Whom does he marry? A short, dumpy woman. Not charming. Or
rich. And he wasn't even in love with her! Why does a man do
such a thing?"

Antonio who was friendly to Fie partly because of her great
steadying influence on his younger brother and because he was
fond of her, told her the strange story. As Fie recalled it:

"The first hint I got that he was going to get married came
when he announced in March, 1925, that he was going to repair a
great wrong he had committed in his youth. March was also the
time José had paid off all of Antonio's many gambling debts and
gave him $10,000 for his help in the banknote affair. So for the
first time in his adult life Antonio was out of debt and had money
in the bank. It must have unbalanced him a little.

"I assumed that in his youth he had seduced this Portuguese
woman and that was the 'great wrong' that preyed on him. She

was always in love with him and wrote him often. I'm sure he never encouraged her. But then she decided to get outside help in her life-long efforts to become the wife of diplomat Antonio Bandeira. Once a year she would go to Lourdes to pray to Bernadette for the miracle of marriage to Antonio. Among all those diseased and crippled pilgrims she used to justify her visit by telling herself she was sick with her unrequited love for Antonio.

"When the miracle finally did take place she naturally went back to Lourdes to thank Bernadette for her miraculous intercession."

✳   ✳   ✳   ✳   ✳

The quarters they had at the Claridge represented clearly the difference in rank of importance.

"Alves Reis was the unquestioned leader." Fie recalls, "He had the largest suite. Marang had a smaller suite. José and I shared a large room and Hennies had a smaller room."

On the afternoon of April 29th, Alves Reis called the band together in his suite. He had sent his wife off shopping with Fie Carelsen and the governess had taken the children to the park.

As the informal chairman of the board it was necessary to inform his associates of certain developments—good and bad—that had taken place recently in Lisbon. They already knew that he had ordered a temporary cessation in the distribution of the remaining banknotes because of the flurry of warnings sent to the Bank of Portugal.

They were less clear about the second and more important development: the creation by them of the Bank of Angola & Metropole.

José voiced his fear first:

"Why do we need it? Just to pay salaries and rent?"

Reis was serenely superior.

"The opening of the Bank by us was strongly suggested to me by my friends at the Bank of Portugal. But an even better reason is that we *need* a bank. We've reached the limit of how far we can go just by using free-lance foreign exchange dealers to buy our pounds and dollars for us. Inevitably their turning up with only 500-escudos notes will direct certain unwelcome attention to them—and us. A bank can do these things simpler, through more hidden means—and we can also save the 2% commission we've been paying these drones."

It would not be an easy task to get the permission necessary from the Banking Council or the Inspectorate of the Banking Trade, Reis made clear. He had already made some preliminary inquiries and was told that things would go easier with the application if he dropped certain of his proposed directors such as José Bandeira—"a long jail record, you know" and Adriano Silva—"once arrested for embezzlement. Acquitted, but still, do you really need a director like that?"

Reis said he was sure José would understand why he would have to drop him as a possible director of the Bank. José nodded glumly: the mistakes of his "green years" would never stop running alongside.

The Bank's directors would include Hennies and Marang, men of substance—and no arrest record—who would both pledge substantial capital, as would Alves Reis, of course.

Another task was set for José, Reis went on. A terribly important one.

"Our Bank of Angola & Metropole will have certain goals. Through it, of course, we will be able to dispose of the rest of the banknotes we have from the first printing—and the subsequent ones. The Bank, too, will be our instrument for investing in real estate in Portugal and for acquiring control of certain Angola corporations. The profits should be considerable and much of that will be set aside for our ultimate goal."

Reis, an instinctive ham, paused for a minute.

"That goal, my friends, is mastery of Portugal itself. And the way we will achieve that without revolution or coup d'etat is by buying control of the Bank of Portugal."

Their startled reactions—the half-open mouths, the wide-open eyes—provided a warming sight for Alves Reis.

"Yes, the time has come for us to show our appreciation for our friends and colleagues at the Bank—Governor Camacho and Vice Governor Gomes—by giving substantial assistance in their secret battle against the backward directors of the Bank. When we have a majority of the Bank's stock we will be able to override the captious critics, the reactionary dead hands of the past. The quiet purchasing of available Bank of Portugal stock will be the task of our good José."

They congratulated Reis on his audacious planning, his splendid vision. Even Hennies volunteered a little speech in which he called Artur Alves Reis "one of the great financial geniuses of the age."

Reis was inordinately pleased with the unanimity of his group to his scheme. He had conceived this bold stroke while in prison in Oporto. This was the solution to that old roadblock that had ignominiously halted all counterfeiters: the inevitability of detection and vigorous prosecution by the state. But once he and his associates were in control of the Bank of Portugal the danger of prosecution would be over.

In his diligent study of the Bank's by-laws Reis discovered that *only the Bank of Portugal could initiate action against counterfeiters of its banknotes.* But if he and his friends were in control of a working majority of the Bank's shares why should they tolerate the presence of any Bank official who would want to initiate such misguided action?

Once they were in control the unauthorized issues of banknotes would be regularized secretly and evidence of the illicit acts removed. * The new administration of the Bank of Portugal would sweep very clean, indeed.

Before he left Lisbon for Paris, Reis had arranged for his trusted office manager, Ferreira, to keep him informed of any new developments in the matter of the public mutterings about the new 500-escudos notes.

On May 7th Reis got a telegram from his aide:

TWO BANK DIRECTORS GOMES AND [Ramiro] LEAO LEFT FOR PARIS BY SUD EXPRESS.

Were they on their way to London and Waterlow's? It would be a good idea to "receive" them when they arrived at the Gare d'Orsay at ten that evening. He suggested to José that they go to the station and Reis would talk to the Bank directors to find out what, if anything, the Bank was going to do about the rumors of counterfeit 500-escudos notes in circulation.

They went to the Gare d'Orsay that evening. Reis suggested

* A sensible arrangement even when criminal acts aren't involved. In Great Britain when one party's ministers replace those of the defeated political group, the permanent civil servants wisely remove everything from the files that might embarrass the past government. The process is sometimes called "The Battle of the Filing Cabinets."

that José should stay discreetly in the background as an observer.

The difficulty of finding Mota Gomes and the other director was one that Reis didn't dare tell José about: he didn't know what Mota Gomes—his supposed close collaborator—looked like. But he spotted two men he took to be the Bank directors and followed them closely out to the taxi rank. A third man, whom he took to be a director, too, came to meet them. This was Emidio da Silva, a well known professor of economics who was later to become an economic elder statesman à la Bernard Baruch. He was a Bank director, too.

Reis followed them more closely as soon as he heard them speaking Portuguese. He overheard da Silva ask Mota Gomes if there was any truth to the rumors of a large number of false 500-escudos notes in circulation. Gomes answered quickly:

"Rumors, just rumors. There are no false 500-escudos notes. Just before we left Lisbon we agreed to publish in yesterday's papers an official statement denying in a positive and clear manner such a harmful rumor."

The three got into a cab and Reis overheard them saying, "Grand Hotel." Crazy with joy, he ran back where José was waiting—and watching.

> "Mota Gomes could only speak to me briefly.[*] He told me that we can soon put the remaining notes in circulation because yesterday's papers carried a statement categorically denying the circulation of false notes. I have an appointment with him tomorrow at the Grand Hotel. He's going to call me at the Claridge to set the time for our meeting."
>
> The next morning I left the hotel for a little walk. At another hotel I put in a call for Alves Reis at the Claridge. My family was out and the operator asked for a message. I said that Mota Gomes would see Alves Reis at 4 P.M. After lunch with Bandeira during which I showed him the message slip I took him to the Portuguese Travel Office on the Champs Élysées and there I bought two Lisbon newspapers of yesterday.

[*] A universal ploy, discovered independently by finaglers all over. In New York City at this time, for example, it worked this way, according to *The New York Times:* A lawyer would lie in wait for some official on the way into City Hall. He would dart over on the steps with hand outstretched. He would say something like this: "That was some ballgame yesterday, wasn't it?" The official would smile and nod, and go in. And the lawyer could go back to a client observing from the plaza to say: "I told him about that proposition and he said yes—you saw it."

The papers had the Bank's announcement as he knew they would. It ran:

NOTES OF 500 ESCUDOS

The Administration of the Banco de Portugal inform us that there is no foundation for the rumor current in some localities of the country that there are in circulation false 500 Escudos Notes.

José was again impressed, naturally, at how privy his friend and partner, Alves Reis, was to all the Bank's plans.

At 3:45 Reis left the Claridge for his "interview" with Mota Gomes. While in the lobby of the Grand Hotel he had another of his incredible strokes of luck. He spotted Mota Gomes at the concierge's desk and approached close enough to overhear the vice governor of the Bank of Portugal inquire about a seat on the boat train for London.

In a whirl of fears Reis walked back to the Claridge. Surely the banker was going to London to see Waterlow & Sons. Even if that wasn't his *main* purpose he would unquestionably drop in while there to pay a courtesy call on the Bank's chief supplier of banknotes. And then, in all innocence, wouldn't Sir William say something to the effect that he hoped Senhor Mota Gomes was pleased with the new issue of 500-escudos notes they had printed for use in Angola?

The terrible possibility required some kind of early warning system. Marang.

At the Claridge, Reis found another reason why he had to get in touch with Marang without delay. Awaiting him was one of his trusted aides—Ahrens Novaes. He had been sent by an increasingly nervous Ferreira, Reis' office manager, to tell the boss another Bank of Portugal director, Caeiro da Mata, was on his way to Paris. Four directors floating around northern Europe! Wouldn't *one* of them drop in on Waterlow's in London?

Yes, Marang would have to do some quick scouting in London. He phoned Marang in The Hague.

He had just received word from Lisbon, he said. Some of the "opposition" directors of the Bank of Portugal were going to London. It would be a wise precaution if Marang went to London to renew his acquaintanceship with Sir William and warn him and his key aides that some of the directors of the Bank of Portugal were opposing the regime of the governor and the vice governor with the aim of deposing them. (Sir William, Reis knew, would immediately sense the possibility that a new regime at the Bank might want a new supplier of banknotes.) And finally, Reis suggested to Marang he should ask them to let him know if and when Waterlow's had been visited by *any* of the Bank's directors.

Marang quickly agreed a trip to London was called for. He would have visited Siberia if Reis asked him. His share of the banknote operation profits had made him wealthier than he had ever been before. In the previous month he purchased *two* new American automobiles, a Lincoln and a Kissel. Last week he paid all his debts to the Rotterdamsche Bank, some $40,000. And just this week he and Hennies formalized their business relationship when the German became Marang's full partner in the trading firm of Marang & Collignon. All over Europe splendid new opportunities were opening up now that he had an abundance of capital and didn't have to pay ruinous interest charges to banks. In fact, things were proceeding so splendidly that soon he would be able to borrow all the money he wanted or needed—without interest. From the Bank of Portugal.

LONDON / May 9, 1925

SIR WILLIAM DID not see Marang on this visit. He was at the Second British Empire Exhibition at Wembley. On this great day when the Exhibition had been opened by King George V and Queen Mary more than 100,000 visited the exhibits. The Waterlow's Pavilion in the southwest corner of the Palace of Industry was a popular feature. It was in the charge of Sir William's older brother, Colonel James F. Waterlow, but Sir William was, of course, on hand when the King and Queen visited the Waterlow Pavilion.

In the Pavilion, according to the book, "Under Six Reigns" ("Being some account of 114 years of progress and development of the House of Waterlow under continuous family management") the

> finished product of printing in all its forms is here displayed to the visitor. South American, Portuguese, Swiss, at least half the nationalities of the world, can here see specimens of their currency.

The King, a noted philatelist, particularly admired some of the postage stamps Waterlow's had printed and

> the King paid a compliment to the firm and to Colonel Waterlow, on the admirable character and scope of the exhibit. Among other visitors to the Pavilion has been a long succession of Foreign Ministers . . . and many other foreigners of great distinction.

There weren't too many Portuguese visitors but those who came noted with pride that their own land's 500 escudos note bearing the face of the great Vasco da Gama, looked particularly handsome among the assorted banknotes.

John Boon, the author of the handsomely bound souvenir book concluded:

> There has been no attempt on his part to exalt the House of Waterlow at the expense of other businesses: the statements made are statements of fact. Nothing has been exaggerated . . . Waterlow's was founded more than a century ago—it has gone from strength to strength, under Waterlow guidance. There is no certainty in earthly affairs, but it is not too much to hope that in A.D. 2025 there will be occasion to chronicle another century of uninterrupted success on the part of Waterlow & Sons Limited.

Now that the Waterlow family was seemingly united once again all things were possible. On the book's cover was embossed the Waterlow coat of arms: a great snake swallowing its own tail. Inside the circle was a sheaf of wheat and the slogan: *Vis unita fortior.* (Union is strength.)

Marang stayed at the Carlton Hotel this time. It had seemed to him that the Ritz was getting rather too many *arrivistes* during his last visit.

When he dropped in at Frederick Goodman's office at Waterlow he was greeted cordially. The director called in his aide,

Roland Springall, in charge of the manufacture of the Bank of Portugal issues.

The relationship with Springall was carefully nurtured by Marang. When he had taken delivery of the last batch of notes— on March 3rd, there were 150,000 and it required some special handling. Marang thought they should try to get even stronger cases than on the previous two trips and Springall took him to another luggage maker. This time he ordered three trunks, each to bear 250 pounds of notes. After the Waterlow porters loaded the heavy trunks into two cabs Springall and Marang drove the short distance to the Liverpool Street Station Main Line Departure Cloakroom where the cases were unloaded and Marang received the 2d. (4¢) cloakroom tickets for each of the three heavy trunks with $3,600,000 worth of Portuguese banknotes in them.

Then Marang begged Springall to join him for lunch at Pimm's in Cheapside. Over coffee, Marang said he fully appreciated Springall's special attention and wanted to make him a little present. As Springall recalled later:

> He wished to make me a present of cigars. I said that it was very kind of him but I did not wish for any present. . . . I was quite pleased to do what I could in my capacity to help him in buying the cases and so forth, and that it was more or less a sideline to the contract. I told him I did not smoke and tried to turn him off . . . I have never smoked in my life. I saw my brothers start. But he insisted and not wishing to offend him I thanked him. Since he wished to mail the cigars to me at home I gave him my private card.

Marang suspected that it might be useful to be able to get in touch with Springall away from the office or even over weekends. The cigar ploy was simple but effective.

Now on this vibrant May day in Goodman's office Marang chatted with connoisseur enthusiasm about the running qualities of his two new cars, the Lincoln and the Kissel. They were well-equipped but they lacked one adornment he would love to have: the enameled plaque of a member of the Royal Automobile Club. Goodman a member of the club—as Marang had already ascertained—picked up the cue quickly and graciously. He would be pleased to second Mr. Marang for membership.

With personal matters out of the way, Marang went on to cover some business. As Springall recalled,

> The syndicate that he had formed was also with the Governor and Vice-Governor of the Bank of Portugal . . . and some of the other directors . . . it was an organization closely linked with the Bank of Portugal and the Government to help Angola . . . But there was an opposition side to the Board and that his side had been purchasing shares with a view to getting control of the Bank . . . In the opposition were the other members of the Bank of Portugal who were not in the know on this secret issuing of notes and the arrangements that had been entered into for the secret help of Angola. He seemed rather concerned at the time about the arrival in London of Directors. He had some information that some of the Directors were expected in London and asked if we had seen any, or if we had any visit. We had not had a visit.

As a personal favor, Marang asked Springall to let him know by telegraph when any directors did show up at Waterlow's. Springall promised.

Marang returned to The Hague that evening secure in the knowledge that he had set up an effective warning system for Alves Reis—and himself.

He left Waterlow's before the last afternoon mail came in *
—with a letter from Robert Walker, the Waterlow "bird dog" in Lisbon. In it he discussed the possibility of orders from the Bank of Portugal for a 1,000-escudos note and some of the lesser denominations.

As for the 500-escudos note:

> we shall in all probability receive repeat orders against our note at present in circulation which is very much liked, in spite of the fact that someone (presumably our competitors) have circulated a report that same has been falsified, this for reasons which you will understand.

Walker, like Romer, did not know that their 500-escudos note had been repeated 200,000 times without the knowledge of the Bank of Portugal. But as an old banknote hand he did understand the old trade trick of starting rumors of "counterfeit" against your

* In those happy days London enjoyed *four* daily mail deliveries.

competitor's products. Since counterfeits of *some* kind were almost always floating around you were bound to be right often.

And sometimes you might just be right enough to get the business away from the previous supplier. The banknote printing business could get rough. Accordingly, Walker followed the Portuguese maxim: he who has to live with bad neighbors must sleep with one eye shut and the other open.

THE HAGUE / May 21, 1925

"A LOAD OF CARES lies like a weight of guilt upon the mind: so that a man of business often has all the air, the distraction and restlessness and hurry of feeling of a criminal," noted William Hazlitt in one of his perceptive essays. But then how weigh the load that lies on the head of a businessman who *is* a criminal?

It was too heavy for Reis to bear alone in Paris. He left his family to continue sightseeing, shopping and absorption of culture while he went to The Hague to be comforted by the unperturbed Marang who would tell him of his smooth visit to London.

But the fearful wraiths travel faster than trains and they lay in wait when he arrived in The Hague. Now Reis was gripped with another consuming chimera: perhaps the Bank of Portugal would solve the problem of public grumbling about so many new 500-escudos notes in another way. Wouldn't it occur to them that it might be wise to withdraw the entire 500 escudos note issue and replace the notes with others? * In which case the duplica-

* Such a drastic measure had been considered briefly by the Bank—and discarded as impractical. A government spokesman explained later: "To withdraw the notes would mean throwing out the window the cost of the notes in circulation—about two million escudos. [About $100,000.] The bank of a poor country spending as it does every year millions of escudos to replace deteriorating notes cannot raise this expenditure to unbearable levels by withdrawing any type of note just because some country bumpkin refused to receive one such note in a cattle market."

tion of serial numbers would be detected quickly and the great plan would end ignominiously. Was he to be finished by another of history's mocking trifles? The English king and the ridiculous horseshoe nail; the marsh fever that afflicted Cesare Borgia while he was waiting with an army above Rome to take over when his father, Pope Alexander VI, would die.

Reis wired José who had returned to Lisbon to keep an eye on things:

PLEASE CHECK CAREFULLY IF SHARES ARE STILL IN CIRCULATION.

Like criminals and spies everywhere the band had adopted its own Aesopian euphemisms. "Shares" had a far more innocent sound than "banknotes."

José checked. The Bank of Portugal's official notice that there were no false 500-escudos notes in circulation had a reasonably calming effect. Businessmen accepted the notes with a tolerant shrug: *They* said the paper was good which meant it was as good as any other paper They issued. It wasn't much reassurance in an inconvertible world but enough.

José wired Reis in The Hague:

TWO TRANSACTIONS EFFECTED WITH BANK. NO SHARES FOUND OUT. ALL OTHER BANKS CONTINUE USING SHARES FREELY.

Much relieved, Reis returned to Paris. There he remained oblivious to the joys of a Paris spring because of his fears of the Gomes visit to London and possibly Waterlow's.

Every few days he would telephone Marang in The Hague: was there any word from Springall? Reis was fearfully certain the Bank directors had already been there.

On May 15th Marang wired Springall at his home in the London suburb of Chingford:

PLEASE WIRE IF YOU HAD ALREADY VISIT OF LISBON PEOPLE AND HOW ARRANGED. MANY THANKS.

Springall wired that there had been no visitors from Lisbon.

The visitors never came to Waterlow's and by May 26th Reis decided that if any Bank directors did visit London it had nothing to do with banknote printing. It was perfectly safe to return to Lisbon.

There still might be danger in Lisbon and a good family man would prefer to have his family away from the arena of battle. If she didn't know it before, Mrs. Alves Reis now got the first hints that the family wealth may have had its origins in a scheme that was *not* aided secretly by some officials of the Bank of Portugal.

When he left for Lisbon Reis told his wife to wait for his all clear telegram. There was still much danger ahead. If the worst came she had with her more than $150,000 worth of jewelry and large sums on deposit in various French, British and Swiss banks.

He boarded the Sud Express to meet triumph and vindication—or stupid defeat through mischance. If *They* beat him it would not be through superior intelligence; only bad luck—stupid, unreasoning chance—the wild element that keeps crime, like politics, from becoming a true science.

LISBON / May 28, 1925

A MILE-LONG TUNNEL leads into the Rossio Station in Lisbon. Now it is used only for local traffic but in 1928 the international steam trains would end the journey from Paris at the end of the dark tunnel. Although every train window would be closed the soot would cover even the first class Wagons-lit passengers.

This didn't matter for Alves Reis. Today he was armored with gold:

> Once again, calm and fortified in spirit I entered triumphantly in Lisbon. Friends gave me a royal reception at the Rossio Station. I was ready for the serious battles that lay ahead.

This afternoon in Lisbon he took care of the Ambaca matters at a stockholders meeting. Now that he was the majority stock-

holder things went more favorably. A resolution commending
Alves Reis for his fine administration of Ambaca was voted
unanimously. After the meeting more joy came his way.

A friend in the Public Prosecutor's office told Reis about
some highly irregular activities by the Oporto Commercial Bank.
It had been two directors of this bank who had taken the action
that led to Reis' imprisonment the previous year.

At a stockholders meeting of the Oporto Commercial Bank
Reis attacked the offending directors and gave copies of his evidence of their irregularities with Bank funds. Later that evening
some other Bank directors asked Reis for peace and harmony now
that Reis was also a Bank director. (Ambaca owned some of the
Bank's stock.) Reis said they could have peace only if the two directors were dropped. The proposal was not accepted. Reis
turned his evidence over to the Inspector of the Banking Trade
and the Oporto Commercial Bank was forced to close. The directors were later tried and found guilty of banking irregularities.

The affairs of the proposed new Bank of Angola & Metropole *
could not be resolved as easily. The Bank's facade was impressive.
Reis had persuaded a prominent retired Navy Commander, João
Manuel de Carvalho to accept the post of President of the Fiscal
Council of the new bank. Carvalho was personable and particu-
larly well-connected: his daughter was married to the son of Luis
Viegas, the Inspector of the Banking Council and a member of
the nation's Banking Council.

The new bank's application for permission to open its doors
included many commendable objectives:

—to finance development projects in Portugal and overseas.
—to enter into contracts with the state or bodies representing it
with a view to raising the value of Portuguese currency.
—to promote aid or participate in the creation and operation of
enterprises for commercial, industrial, agricultural and mining
operations.

Still, Dr. Mota Gomes, the vice governor of the Bank of
Portugal, whose consent was needed, was unhappy about the application and the "moral standing" of some of the signers of the
new bank's application. (Only Reis knew that his main opponent

* Meaning metropolitan Portugal, as distinguished from its colonies.

was the man who was supposedly his great friend at the Bank of Portugal.)

Reis brought other pressures to bear. He had Marang come to Lisbon to intercede with the President of the Republic. After all Marang was a valued foreigner the Republic had decorated twice for his endeavors in its behalf.

Unable to withstand the persistence of the President of the country *and* its Inspector of Banking Trade, Dr. Mota Gomes reluctantly withdrew his opposition—provided the new bank began with an initial capital of at least 20,000,000 escudos (about $1,000,000). This would put it on a par with leading Lisbon banks.

Reis hadn't forgotten his wife and children in Paris. On June 5th he wired her she could return when she wanted to. But now that her anxiety was relieved she wasn't particularly anxious to return to Lisbon. There were so many fittings for the 19 dresses and a coat she had ordered from Jenny de Paris for some $5,000. There were various pieces of jewelry she wanted at Cartier's. When he sent the wire Reis also wrote her a letter in which he urged her to transfer the safe deposit box they had in the Claridge safe to José, leaving everything in it, including the group's code book. He also included a cautionary note. The Spanish and Portuguese customs officers were sometimes difficult: he urged his wife to hide her jewels in her *peito* (bosom) at the French border and to leave them there until they passed the Portuguese border. The safe deposit box which Mrs. Reis looked through carefully also contained 22 sheets and 18 envelopes of the personal stationery of Camacho Rodrigues, governor of the Bank of Portugal.

If she hadn't known before that her husband had become the most daring crook in Europe she surely knew it now. The knowledge spurred her to new purchases. She wired her husband for more money. Fie Carelsen was also buying some clothing and needed money.

Alves Reis, the indulgent husband, wired Marang to give Mrs. Reis money when he arrived in Paris. So Reis wired his wife

MARANG ARRIVING JUNE 6 AND WILL GIVE YOU THE MONEY YOU NEED. WILL ALSO GIVE FIETJE 5000 FRANCS [$250] ON JOSÉ'S ACCOUNT.

But José who was ordinarily quite openhanded to his mistress had become alarmed at the way Fie was spending. He thought that Mrs. Alves Reis, usually the prudent one, was giving his mistress some wild ideas. He wired Fie:

IF YOU TWO PERSIST IN FOOLISHNESS WE SHALL NOT SEND YOU ANOTHER SOU.

On June 27, 1925, a decree was issued by the Banking Council authorizing the creation of the Bank of Angola & Metropole. Always ready to help old and trusted friends, Alves Reis had the original bank charter drawn up at the notarial office of Avelina Faria, who had notarized the original forged contracts that had, in time, made the new bank possible.

The new bank had 23 initial shareholders: friends, relatives and influential parties such as a deputy, a former Minister of Agriculture and a prominent professor of economics. Alves Reis, of course, was the controlling stockholder.

The shareholders were all Portuguese. Originally Alves Reis had intended to list his friend and colleague, Adolf Hennies, as a major shareholder but there was considerable uneasiness in official circles about listing a German. Everyone knew that Germany, deprived of its colonies by the victorious Allies, was eyeing the Portuguese colonies of Angola and Mozambique and was trying to make a deal with the British on them. Part of the suspicion stemmed from the outdated Anglo-German Treaty of 1898 which *did* provide for the partition of Portugal's colonies between the two powers in the event they came into the market. At least once a year the British Foreign Office had to reassure the Portuguese Minister for Foreign Affairs that there was no truth in current allegations that Great Britain had designs on or encouraged the designs of others against the Portuguese colonies. But several books by German colonialists such as Dr. Heinrich Schnee kept the suspicion alive. In one book Dr. Schnee quoted with obvious approval an English Germanophile, William Harbutt Dawson:

> "It is inconceivable that a decadent country like Portugal with a population of six million should have an empire of one million square miles."

Ten days before the Bank's charter was granted officially a confident Reis had spent $125,000 getting a building for the new bank on the Rua do Crucifixo in the downtown business district of Lisbon. He took an option on a building in Oporto to house a main branch and spent $50,000 for it when he exercised the option soon after. He also bought, for $88,000, the building which housed the offices of Alves Reis Limitado.

The new bank made large investments quickly in certain Angolan and Portuguese enterprises. With these expenditures the Bank of Angola soon felt the need for another issue of banknotes. What hastened the need considerably was the fact that Reis had 90,000 banknotes from the first order he couldn't use.

Reis hated to tell his partners he had made such a great blunder. It wasn't all his fault. Marang and his escudo-pinching in the early days of their association had limited the number of Bank of Portugal 500-escudos notes Reis could analyze for the secret of the directors' names and numbering sequences the Bank used. The solution he arrived at hastily had been imperfect. He hadn't realized the Bank did not use double vowels in front of serial numbers; that the Bank's own series did not extend beyond AN. So in all, he had in the hidden safe in his Golden Boy Palace some 90,000 notes that might be spotted if they were put into circulation. Since the Bank of Portugal didn't bother checking the serial numbers of banknotes that were returned to the Bank in the normal course of business, the duplicated bills would pass easily. But a bill with prefixed letters that were never used by the Bank might be spotted accidentally by a teller who knew the Bank didn't use double vowels or letters beyond AN preceding the serial numbers. The risk was too great.

One night he opened the great safe under the floor in the library of the Golden Boy Palace where he and his family now lived with six servants. The idle 90,000 notes, worth some $2,250,-000, tore at his heart. The great things he could do with the money—if only somehow it was *safely* useable.

He held up a package of 1,000 notes and detected a vague odor of camphor. He had added several pounds of camphor to the safe in the hope this would absorb the smell of too-fresh ink on the banknotes. The notes now smelled of fresh ink *and* camphor.

The next day he had his aide, Ferreira, try an experiment with a few packages of notes. These were immersed in a bathtub filled with water and the juice of several dozen lemons. After several hours of soaking the camphor smell was gone but so had the notes' original color: they now had a reddish tinge.

Reis showed the great measure of trust he had in Ferreira by making fun of himself: "You see, Francisco, what a great magician I am? I turn big money into small shrimps."

Later Ferreira tried to dry the notes—some 2,000—with blotters. That was hopeless so he tried ironing them. He finally got them dry but the reddish tinge made them doubly impossible to use.

A week later Ferreira came to Reis with good news. He had heard of a new way to remove the fresh ink smell from banknotes: a strong solution of water and glycerine would do it. Reis gave him 500 banknotes to experiment with. These were soaked in the bathtub of the sumptuous living quarters attached to the Alves Reis private office. Six hours later Ferreira joyously found that the notes had, indeed, lost their fresh ink smell. After he dried them he found that they had also lost some of their size. They had shrunken a full quarter of an inch in length. Ferreira was disconsolate but his boss reassured him: "Don't worry. My friend, Camacho Rodrigues, will laugh with us when I tell him of our experiments. We could not use these notes in any case."

His partners, unfortunately, did not have as good a sense of humor. Ashamed to admit he had blundered, Reis gave them some long, convoluted explanations of why 90,000 notes could not be used. There were, he said later,

> three possibilities dictated by intelligence, prudence and ambition. Prudence told me to give up the idea of circulating the unused notes. Or I could pretend the Bank of Portugal had ordered the suspension of further circulation of our 500-escudos note issue. That is, that this was the end of the line and we should use our profits quickly to buy Bank of Portugal stock until we had enough seats on the Board of Directors to gain control. And the third possibility was simply to order another issue from Waterlow's.

His colleagues bought his lame explanations rather readily. Marang had been looking forward to a holiday trip to Norway with his wife. Hennies was off to Albania where he was exploring, for the group, the possibility of their getting in on the creation of a central bank for this troubled land, and acquiring various trade monopolies. And José Bandeira who trusted Alves Reis completely really couldn't care less. Now that he had lots of money he was living as he always dreamed he would live.

One day in late June in Lisbon José suddenly got a rich man's whim for another new car to add to the three he had recently purchased. He sent off a long telegram to Letourneur & Marchand on the Champs Élysées in Paris for a "Claridge" cabriolet on a Hispano-Suiza Boulogne-type chassis. He specified:

> All wood and steel trim, carefully finished wood interior, slanted windscreen (3 glass); handle-operated separation screen between front and back [this was to be chauffeur-driven, of course]. Small wooden cabinet in rear. Upholstery in black Morocco leather of first grade; hood in black cowhide. Floor to be covered with carpeting. Cushions to be filled with horsehair. Telephone between rear and front. Car red with silver trim and fenders black. Extra accessories: 3 Vuitton valises, one large, two small. And don't forget the Barker headlight dippers.

For a few months Reis had hoped that the Bank of Portugal would authorize Waterlow to print an issue of 1,000-escudos notes. Then Reis would have the Bank governor secretly "authorize" Waterlow to turn out a companion issue for Reis and his group. Obviously it would be preferable to have an issue other than the slightly suspect 500-escudos banknotes. But the Bank still did not give Waterlow's the order on the 1,000 escudos notes.

Now, Reis knew, they would have to get a re-order of the 500-escudos Vasco da Gama notes. There were still many Bank of Portugal shares to be purchased, many more investments to make in Angola. The Bank of Angola & Metropole needed more banknotes soon. It was time to return to the old typewriter and forger's equipment.

THE HAGUE / July 26, 1925

ALVES REIS ARRIVED on Sunday, July 26th, with the two necessary forgeries. The first had been a confidential letter to Waterlow & Sons Ltd., from I. Camacho Rodrigues, governor of the Bank of Portugal:

> Dear Sirs:
> In accordance with the instructions given to Mr. Marang van Isselveere and for its complete execution you are hereby authorized to print 380,000 banknotes of 500 escudos, type Vasco da Gama for the printing of which you can use the plates at present in your possession.
> As this order is the remainder of the first order placed with you, through Mr. Marang van Isselveere, the same conditions of payment, delivery, etc. will have to be maintained, viz:
> (a) payment of printing for the account of Mr. Marang
> (b) delivery of the total of the order, in London, to the same gentlemen.
> As this affair is strictly confidential we would request you to maintain the confidence observed on the first occasion and would esteem it a favor if you would kindly treat everything in connection with same, direct with Mr. Marang, who has the necessary powers to bring it to an end.
> Kindly note that by the 31st inst., and through Mr. Marang, we will send you the numbers and signatures that will have to be inserted.

The second letter listing the serial numbers and directors' signatures that alternated with each group of 5,000 notes were provided with almost perfect accuracy this time. Reis had had time—and a sufficient number of banknotes, of course—to work out the series relationships properly. This time he utilized every single letter, except vowels. And he allotted, properly, 20,000 notes for each letter series such as 1B, 1C, 1D, 1F and so on. He made only one mistake. He listed one of the Bank's directors as "A. Pereira Lima" when it should have been "A. Pereira Junior."

Reis had taken his wife and three boys to Paris where they were awaiting his return. After finishing his business in The

Hague he would return to Paris and then go on with them to
Carlsbad for the baths.

Like all Portuguese men, Alves Reis had a carefully cultivated concern for his liver. It wasn't just an aping of the Frenchman's inordinate liver-pampering. Because the Portuguese are
such enthusiastic eaters—and passionate devourers of sweets *—
every Portuguese male who had a lively concern for his health
knew that the liver had to be scoured and scrubbed at least once
a year so as to be ready for another year of hard eating. Middle-
class Portuguese men went to local spas such as Pedras Salgadas,
and Vidago but the rich preferred to go abroad. Carlsbad was
particularly favored in the Twenties.

There was more to talk about with Marang than just the
banknotes even though that was by far the most important item
on the agenda. Marang was vexed that they weren't going to be
getting 1000-escudos notes this time instead of the old 500
escudos. To him it was an obvious piece of business logic: if the
cost was the same it was always better to buy a product that you
could sell for $50 rather than one that would fetch only $25.

Hadn't Reis' friends at the Bank of Portugal been promising
him that he would be able to use the 1000-escudos plates next
time? Reis agreed that such promises had been made but a majority of the Bank's directors were against ordering the 1000-escudos
note as yet. So that would have to wait until they and their allies
at the Bank were in control. José had already purchased, through
intermediaries, some 4600 shares in the Bank of Portugal. They
still had a considerable distance to go towards control but that
would come in good time.

Since there was no alternative, Marang consented somewhat
gracelessly to the re-order on the 500-escudos note but he became
querulous again about the large investment he and Hennies had
made on Alves Reis' recommendation, in the South Angola Min-

* Portugese monasteries don't ape the French. Instead of making expensive liqueurs the Portuguese monks make certain kinds of pastries and
candies. Because of their shapes and colors these are popularly named, with
mildly mocking appropriateness, "Nun's Breasts" and "Bacon from Heaven."
But the pastry monks refuse to make cakes for the festival of São Gonçalo
in Amarante. Gonçalo is the patron saint of marriage and on Romario—the
first weekend in June—the Amarante confectioners make special cakes
which young men and women give each other as presents. The cakes are
shaped like penises.

ing Company which the Reis group now controlled. Marang
said he had heard reports from Angola that the company's mining
claims were worthless . . .

They were, indeed, but how could Alves Reis admit *that*.
How could he admit that he and his associates had poured nearly
$250,000 into a worthless set of mining claims. The classic re-
sponse of course, is to admit nothing—and attack. What about
the Albania business which he and José had been against from
the start? They had already put $50,000 into tumultuous little
Albania and now it looked as if the government of Italy would be
getting permission to institute a central bank for Albania, not the
Reis group. Besides, Reis pointed out, even if the iron ore claims
of the South Angola Mining Company hadn't proved themselves
yet the company still controlled hundreds of square miles on
which prospectors were also busily at work. If not iron it would,
eventually, be the more valuable oil that would turn up on the
land.

Still, Marang had to admit that Reis had managed affairs
very well so far. They were millionaires now and soon with the
new issue would be multi-millionaires—and the controllers of the
Bank of Portugal.

That evening Marang was host at dinner for Reis, Antonio
Bandeira and Count Simon Planas-Suarez, the Venezuelan Minister to Portugal. They dined at a hotel in Scheveningen, the popular seaside resort adjoining The Hague.

The inclusion of the Venezuelan was the result of a subtle
campaign Reis began after the Hennies incident with the Lisbon
customs official. In conversations with Marang since then, Reis
often suggested that perhaps the group ought to employ another
kind of diplomatic courier—one whose credentials were *completely* unquestionable. The second batch of notes from Waterlow would be nearly double the first order and as Marang knew,
they wanted to get the new notes into Portugal as quickly as possible. Piecemeal transportation of the past was no longer suitable.
Reis was sensitive to Marang's pride in his various diplomatic
passports and he managed to get the point across delicately.

Antonio Bandeira had suggested the Count as a likely
courier. He had known Planas-Suarez slightly in Lisbon and then
renewed the acquaintanceship when the Venezuelan gave a series

of lectures at the Academy of International Law in The Hague in 1924.

Marang suggested that he be rewarded for the considerable favor with a new Ford coupe but Antonio who had an empathetic knowledge of the Venezuelan diplomat's means, thought such a gift was "not in keeping with his high diplomatic status." Much more suitable—and far more welcome—would be cash. Say, 200,000 escudos (about $9,000). In their own 500-escudos notes, of course.

Since 1904 Don Simon had served Venezuela as unsalaried Minister Plenipotentiary in Austria, Italy, Greece, Holland, Hungary, Rumania and Yugoslavia and now in Portugal. He was born into a prosperous middle-class family in Caracas in 1879. His father, Ricardo Planas Torres, conducted a thriving import-export business with Europe and in 1882 he took his family to Paris for an extended stay. Young Simon returned to Caracas to attend Central University of Venezuela where he obtained a doctorate in political science and a law degree. Then he began writing the first of some 20 books: on international arbitration; extradition in Latin America; a history of diplomacy; the Central American Court of Justice, and one on Relations of Portugal and Latin America. And this year, when he was 46, a handsome, rather hard-faced diplomat, he had completed another volume: *The Monroe and Bolivar Doctrine in the International Relations of Latin America.*

He had considerable time for his books because the work as Venezuelan Minister was hardly arduous. He was polished, witty —so different from his dull books—and a welcome guest at diplomatic soirées. He and his wife were a popular couple in all of their posts and inevitably he picked up a number of foreign awards and honors, including the Order of Christ of Portugal and Commander of the French Legion of Honor. He was also a Count of The Holy See. Although in his university days he was pleased to be known as a free-thinker he now relished being a Papal Count. Indeed he *insisted* on being known as Count Planas-Suarez, even if his native land was ostensibly a republic. After all, its president, Juan Vicente Gómez was an absolute dictator; almost like a monarch. He was also a good friend.

Nor was Don Simon one of the many impoverished Papal

Counts to be found all over Europe after World War I. His wife, the former Angelina Yudice Rossi who came from a prominent family in San Salvador, had a moderate private income.

At this convivial dinner in Scheveningen, Don Simon was told Marang and Reis had a great number of "confidential documents" they wanted brought to Lisbon from The Hague as diplomatic baggage. Of course, they would be happy to cover Don Simon's expenses which would be fairly heavy since several trunks were involved.

Planas casually waved aside all idea of recompense for a favor. Good friends always wanted to help one another. But Antonio Bandeira insisted that his friends, Karel and Artur, would consider it even more of a favor if they were *allowed* to pay all the considerable expenses. Don Simon reconsidered. In that case, of course, he would be happy to accept recompense.

Imbued with the two useful "D's" of diplomacy—discretion and delicacy—he never once asked for any more information about the kind of "confidential documents" that filled several trunks.

Later that evening in The Hague, Reis congratulated Marang on the astute way he had handled the Venezuelan: "The diplomatic world lost a great talent when you turned to business." Marang was naturally pleased to hear confirmation of a self-evaluation he had long had.

He and Reis agreed that Marang would go to London on Tuesday evening, July 28th to visit Waterlow's on the morning of the 29th.

Marang looked forward to the visit. It would be good to see his friends, Sir William and Frederick Goodman. Only last week he had his chauffeur put the enameled plaques of the Royal Automobile Club on the three Marang automobiles. He would have to thank Goodman in person for his club membership.

LONDON / July 29, 1925

MARANG TOOK the night boat from the Hook of Holland to Harwich and he was grateful that it had been a remarkably calm 120-mile Channel crossing. Several of his winter passages had been acutely miserable.

In Sir William's office he was greeted warmly. He gave Sir William the confidential letter from the governor of the Bank of Portugal and Sir William called in Frederick Goodman to get the work started since Marang stressed the speed with which the huge new order was needed—in Angola, of course.

Although Marang already had with him another letter from the governor listing the directors' names and serial numbers that were to go on the plates, he decided it would be wiser to hold *that* off for a few days as he had in the past. He promised Sir William he would have the needed letter within ten days.

When he was closeted with Frederick Goodman, Marang thanked him for his sponsorship in the Royal Automobile Club. To show his gratitude he wanted Waterlow's to run off 11,500 stock certificates for the new Bank of Angola & Metropole.*

Goodman was pleased with the additional business, at how steady a customer Mr. Marang was becoming.

"There is one minor condition," Marang said smiling lightly. "We must ask that the usual Waterlow & Sons imprint at the bottom of the stock certificate be eliminated—as well as your usual watermark in the paper itself. Two large printing firms in Lisbon are active depositors in our bank and we don't want to ruffle them by going out of the country for our security printing requirements."

It was the best excuse Alves Reis could think of. When he first fell in with Marang's idea of letting Waterlow do the bank share certificates he hadn't thought out the implications.

After he reflected more fully, Reis realized some of his enemies might think it a too-curious coincidence that the bustling

---

* Mack the Knife's mordant questions in *The Threepenny Opera* were to the point: "What is a passkey, compared to corporation stock? What is robbing a bank, compared to founding a bank?"

new bank also had its stock certificates printed by the very firm supplying banknotes to the Bank of Portugal. Why take a chance? Let Waterlow's print the certificates—without any printer's identification.

Frederick Goodman promised to have the Waterlow engraving department come up with some suitable designs for the new shares in a few days. Later that day Sir William had the new contract for the 380,000 banknotes ready for signing. It was almost identical to the one that had been signed at the time of the first order. Of course, the total price was higher now: £2,850 (approximately $14,000). The first batch of 50,000 notes would be ready by August 28th with the remaining 230,000 a month later.

Marang signed with a flourish and wrote a check for the £2,850. He returned to The Hague that evening.

LISBON / August 1, 1925

JOSÉ HAD BEEN in Lisbon for the past two weeks. He brought Fie Carelsen to Portugal and was proudly introducing her to his family and friends. He was no longer little José, the ne'er-do-well with the prison record. He was now a *morgado*, a landed proprietor, the proud equivalent of an English squire.

He had spent $150,000 in buying three large estates: one from the Count of Guarda—the Quinta da Musgueria just outside Lisbon; another from the Marquis de Sagres and the third from the Marquis de Funchal. The country gentleman also had to balance his holdings with sound city investments. In Lisbon he bought a fleet of taxicabs, and a majority interest in a leading shirtmaker which had long supplied him with his own choice linen; and a popular barbershop in the business district.

Fie Carelsen recalls the visit to Portugal:

"We drove in his new chauffeured Hispano-Suiza to each of his new Quintas where he had installed various members of his family to see that things went well. I met an older sister and an ailing younger brother. You could see that they were still puzzled at the enormous change in José's fortunes in the past few years. They remembered vividly the scandals of his youthful crime and imprisonment and now he was buying Quintas from counts and marquis as if they were grapes.

"We went to all the sights of Portugal such as Sintra and Estoril. It was a splendid vacation. I was so glad for José. Everything was working out for him: rainbows every day.

"There were often gifts. José was very generous but the thoughtfulness that went into each was more important than their value. I remember in Lisbon when I was having some particularly bad migraine headaches he gave me a beautiful little gold pillbox with a note: 'If my great love can't cure your *mal de tête,* I hope this little box will succeed.'"

Since his mistress was one of Holland's great actresses it was only fitting that José should help the struggling theater of Lisbon. He lent the Ginasio Theater 640,000 escudos (about $30,000) to modernize and refurbish. He sent out feelers to see if he could purchase Lisbon's largest newspaper, *Diario de Noticias.* He was ready to offer 9,000,000 escudos (about $45,000).

During this giddy, soaring period he didn't forget the many other women in his life, the discards. To each of five former mistresses he gave handsome souvenirs ranging from $1,000 to $5,000. A prince would do no more.

When he lost $7,000 in gambling one night at the exclusive Club dos Patos (the Duck Club), his old buddy, Oscar Zenha, who had been promoted to José's private secretary, accompanied him. When Zenha's face grew long as José's losses mounted, Bandeira slapped him on the back and laughed merrily. "Oscar, if I lost only 350 escudos (about $10) would you make such a long face?" Zenha said even *he* could afford to lose 250 escudos. "Well, Oscar, believe me, I only lost 250 escudos tonight."

He couldn't explain to Zenha that the cost of printing 300 of the 500-escudos notes which he lost had cost only 250 escudos.

LONDON / August 6, 1925

SIR WILLIAM WENT over the new order handed him by Marang ten days ago and now noticed a discrepancy which he wrote about to Camacho. He also volunteered some information which the Bank governor surely should have known. But business details in Portugal were not always as orderly as in London.

> I have pleasure in acknowledging receipt of your letter of 20th July, which was handed to me by Mr. Marang van Ysselveere containing your instructions for us to print and deliver to Mr. Marang 380,000 (three hundred and eighty thousand) Banco de Portugal bank Notes of 500 escudos, type Vasco da Gama to be printed from the plates in our possession which we are proceeding with.
>
> In referring to this order as the "remainder" of the first order, I have assumed that it is a continuation of it, as the total number originally mentioned by Mr. Marang will be exceeded.
>
> When sending us the numbers and signatures to be printed on these notes, I shall be obliged if you will let us know if the numbers are to be printed in red as on the first part of the order, or in black as recently instructed by the Bank for future orders.
>
> Assuring you of my highest esteem,
>
> I am, Sir,
> Your obedient Servant

The letter was mailed to Marang in The Hague along with a letter for him about the share certificates for the new Bank of Angola & Metropole. Enclosed, too, were some sketches for the share. The letter to Marang concluded:

> We herewith enclose confidential letter to Senor I. Camacho Rodrigues which we shall be glad if you will have forwarded through the usual channels, and we shall be pleased in this connection to receive as soon as possible the Schedule of numbers and signatures required.

Marang promptly mailed the schedule of serial numbers and directors' names which he had received from Reis more than two weeks ago. To Reis, who was now in the spa at Carlsbad, he sent the letter from Waterlow to Camacho. Marang, of course, read the letter first and realized that Reis whose English wasn't too good would need assistance in framing the reply supposedly coming from Camacho. He had his secretary type a letter in English for Reis to use as a model in replying to Waterlow.

How did Marang think Reis in Carlsbad would be able to get the signature of Camacho, now in Lisbon, for the reply to Sir William? A good question.

THE HAGUE / August 8, 1925

"We have most of us contemplated committing a crime—and wished that particular crime could be committed quietly, impersonally, and without involving any danger of detection. But the darkest intentions are not bad enough, for to commit a crime, one must traverse, or allow oneself very gradually to drift across a borderline that separates wishful thinking from desperate acting . . . Is there any point in his progress at which the criminal recognizes that he has crossed the border, and that wild imaginings have assumed an uncomfortably concrete shape?"

—PETER QUENNEL.

DID KAREL MARANG know that he was deeply involved in a purely criminal enterprise instead of a desperately corrupt financial undertaking?

In his long search for honors, wealth and upper-class status Marang had, as most searchers do, cut corners, cheated on taxes, lied and finagled when necessary. But as far as anyone knew he had not engaged in any major, overt criminal act.

On this August day in his office when he celebrated his recent prosperity by acquiring still another American car, a heavy

Lincoln, is it possible he did *not* know he was a central figure in a criminal drama?

There is a notion held by some psychiatrists interested in psychic phenomena that the true function of the mind is to preserve sanity by filtering out most of the millions of random messages coming to us every second from other minds. When the filters fail or work imperfectly we become schizophrenic. "Voices" and "radio messages" bombard us from all over and we can no longer function through the maddening buzz of over-communication.

The sane not only can filter out the "messages" that do not concern them but they have an added safeguard: they need not "see" what they don't want to.

How much a sane Marang saw, heard or guessed remains problematical. Indeed, a fair case can be made that he never knew he was in a criminal enterprise—as Alves Reis intended that he shouldn't. Reis knew instinctively it would be wiser to have associates who *were* the roles, instead of merely acting them.

If Marang had doubts there were many solid reassurances available:

—After all, the Portuguese Minister to Holland *was* deeply involved. True, he had his weaknesses but still he was an honorable man, trusted implicitly by his government. And hadn't Waterlow & Sons, that paragon of the security printing world, carefully checked and *accepted* the contracts to produce the banknotes?

—It was true that his partner, Alves Reis, was going to be writing letters to be signed by the governor of the Bank of Portugal although the banker was in Lisbon and Reis in Carlsbad. But Reis had carefully explained to José Bandeira and Marang that "the Men" in Lisbon trusted him so fully that they let him have signed, blank letterheads for him to use when necessary.

—And, finally: their notes had been circulating now for more than six months in Portugal and not a susurrus of suspicion from the Bank of Portugal. Indeed, when there had been uneasy comments about the new 500-escudos notes in circulation the Bank promptly and officially set the minds of the rural merchants and bankers at rest.

CARLSBAD, CZECHOSLOVAKIA /
August 12, 1925

TODAY ALVES REIS had taken his wife and three sons to the photographer for a family picture. The pose he liked best showed him with a gray homburg, a malacca cane, banker's double-breasted gray suit, with a three pointed white handkerchief in his breast pocket. The somewhat fleshy, broad face was that of a man of achievement, a man who knew what he was doing. Although it was a warm day he insisted that his wife wear her new Russian mink coat. She hardly protested.

His three sons, carefully dressed for the occasion, were arrayed alongside Reis and his wife, in order of age. Alves, Jr., now seven, wore a popular Jackie Cooper cap and an open shirt collar. There was a small blue flower in his lapel which his father had put there. The two younger boys wore short pants.

Reis ordered two dozen copies of the photo to be made for mounting in the new stand-up, cut-out fashion, instead of with the conventional matted frame. He would send copies to his associates and to various members of his and his wife's family.

He had already shown great generosity to members of both families. For his wife's father he had purchased two income-producing apartment houses in Lisbon. For his own younger brother, Alvara Alves Reis, 17, he was financing business and language courses in Amsterdam and had promised him a good post in the Bank of Angola & Metropole when he finished.

For the correspondence he would have to handle while in Carlsbad Reis had taken a portable Corona typewriter. The frequent telegrams from his associates in Lisbon and The Hague had to be deciphered and then new answers enciphered. A nuisance. More than once he wished he'd thought of bringing one of his trusted office staff to Carlsbad to do the decoding and typing of the considerable correspondence. His wife had taken the boys' governess and her personal maid so that she could spend much of her time, when not taking the mineral baths, in shopping for Czechoslovakian glassware.

There were almost daily letters and telegrams to José in Lisbon who, when he wasn't introducing his mistress to friends and family, was keeping an eye on the group's affairs. But it never hurt to jog him occasionally, to remind him certain timetables were inexorable. Reis wrote:

> We have to have everything operating by Sept. 30th. The building on Rua Comercio is taking too long and though it seemed big enough originally you may be sure it won't be. Everything indicates that by March of 1926 the issue [controlling stock of the Bank of Portugal] will be ours but even without the issue the house is too small for what we have to do.

By now he could forge the Bank governor's signature free-hand and didn't have to resort to the laborious business of copying it from a banknote and then enlarging the signature. On one of his own Bank of Portugal letterheads he typed:

Dear Sirs,
    In reply to your favour of the 6th inst. I beg to inform you that I fully agree with its contents. With regard to the numbers I kindly request you to print same in red colour.
    Hoping the execution of this order will have your undivided attention, I remain, dear Sirs,

Yours faithfully,

I. Camacho Rodrigues

The small portable was slightly out of alignment but the letterhead was now familiar to Sir William and it didn't strike him as odd that the Bank of Portugal couldn't afford better typewriters.

Sir William was more concerned by a discovery made by Roland Springall. The latest order from Comacho through Mr. Marang was for notes to bear exactly the same serial numbers already born by 500-escudos notes printed the year before for the Bank of Portugal—in the Romer order. Of course, they had been told that the Marang notes would be overprinted "ANGOLA" once they reached the colony but, still . . .

Frederick Goodman in checking the directors' signatures ordered for the new batch, noticed that one of the names listed seemed to be in error.

Sir William was slightly perturbed. How should this be handled? He called in his personal solicitor, Messer, who had been so helpful in the past, clarifying certain points in the Reis-Angola contracts. Messer told Sir William that the errors should be pointed out to Marang and suggested a letter which Sir William sent out that day. The key parts read:

> There is, what we presume to be, a typist's error (which we mention below), but subject to this, these Notes are, until the overprinting has been done in Angola, identically the same including the series numbering as those ordered by the Bank in 1922. We presume the Governor has not overlooked this.
>
> With regard to the error mentioned above, one of the signatures appears as A. Pereira Lima, and occurs in eight places. We have no Director's signature agreeing with this—should it be A. Pereira Junior, as we have a signature block for this? If not, will you please send us the facsimile signature of A. Pereira Lima.
>
> Replying to your enquiry, 50,000 notes will be ready for you by the 28th August, as arranged.

At the same time Sir William enclosed a letter to be sent by Marang to Camacho.

Marang promptly wired Reis in Carlsbad in code about the Pereira mistake.

Reis was annoyed with himself for the stupid error. It was the third serious error he had made since he had begun this enormous criminal undertaking.* Somehow each time a solicitous providence also provided him with a means of correcting his mistake without too much trouble. Clearly, he was intended to succeed in his great plans. Of course, it would have been much more difficult if Marang had not won Sir William's confidence so that what might have been a dangerous seed of suspicion became only a grain of typing error.

He wired Marang:

PEREIRA JUNIOR IS SIGNATURE PRINTER MUST USE. NEVER PEREIRA LIMA. IF LETTER SAYS SO IT WAS A TYPING ERROR.

Then he went to the mineral baths for the last time. Thank God, the Carlsbad "vacation" was almost over. The prescribed mineral drinks made him nauseous.

---

* The first had been to use the singular "signature" on the contract. Then he failed to uncover the complete pattern of serial numbers for the first banknote order.

In The Hague, Marang wrote in his odd English to Waterlow that his

> . . . remark was exactly correct. So please use the signature
> block of Mr. A. Pereira Junior.
>   Regarding to the numbers, I thank you very much for your
> information and for your comfort I communicate to you, that
> especially, whereas the shares are destined for Angola, the
> governor has taken the same numbers.

For the first time, he felt sure enough that a specific message
from the governor was not required for the duplicated numbers.

PARIS / August 27, 1925

ALVES REIS HAD called the group together this Thursday morning
for an important meeting on the eve of their picking up the first
batch of notes of the second order from Waterlow.

This time he and his wife were alone in Paris. The children
had been taken by their governess for a visit to her sister in Stras-
bourg.

There were several key items on the agenda and the chairman called the informal meeting together at 11:00 A.M. in his
Claridge suite; an early hour for a Portuguese businessman.

First, the pickup of the initial batch of the new notes. José
would accompany Marang to London this time. He would meet
some of the Waterlow people so that he could make the pickups
himself in the future, if necessary.

Second, the matter of the banknotes. This time, Alves Reis
explained, there would be a somewhat different routine—
suggested, of course, by "the Men" of the Bank of Portugal. The
notes would be counted at Marang's offices in The Hague and
carefully taken *out of sequence*. A small security measure but an
important one. New bills in numerical sequence might arouse un-

wonted curiosity in some rural bankers and the result might be another May scare. For this work, Reis volunteered one of his office aides, Justine de Moura Coutinho. Reis trusted him completely. He couldn't talk any language except Portuguese so that there would be no opportunity for him to gossip with any of Marang's staff who might be curious about the stranger's presence in the office for several weeks.

Now as to the arrangement with Don Simon, the Venezuelan Minister to Portugal. He had agreed to facilitate the entrance of several trunks of "confidential documents" from The Hague to Lisbon for the group. In addition he would be glad to store the trunks in his apartment in Lisbon which also doubled as the Venezuelan Ministry. Unfortunately, the original fee discussed with him back in The Hague in July seemed to be subject to some misunderstanding—by Planas-Suarez. He wanted more. It would be up to José who had suggested him as a privileged courier to handle the bargaining for the group. Admittedly, he was going to be paid in their 500-escudos notes but still there was no reason to be profligate with the money: there were many more important expenditures ahead for the group.

José nodded confidently: "I will handle him." Now that he was managing director of the important new Bank of Angola & Metropole he was ready and even anxious to prove his worth as a financier and negotiator.

And the Albanian affair, continued Reis. While he had not been enthusiastic about the investment in that country he and José had been willing to go along with Marang and Hennies as co-investors. Now surely, it was time to cut their losses and clear out. The new Italian dictator, Benito Mussolini, was establishing a firmer hegemony in Albania and other foreign capital didn't seem welcome.

Marang wanted to defend the Albanian venture but his heart wasn't in it anymore. Reis was right. The $65,000 they had put into several ventures there—plus bribes—was not going to be productive. And their hope of getting the right to issue banknotes for the new bank in exchange for gold was no longer remotely possible.* He was tempted to comment sarcastically about the

---

* A week later, on September 2, 1925, the new National Bank of Albania was organized under Italian auspices and supported by an Italian loan.

larger losses they were likely to sustain in Reis' South Angola
Mining Company but why introduce a note of discord into a
meeting devoted to a furtherance of their mounting wealth.

There were minor items about the Bank of Angola & Metropole. Reis wanted to nominate his aide, Ferreira, as a director. He
knew how much Ferreira longed for the honor. He had long been
a faithful assitant who put in long hours at the office and had
never betrayed a confidence.

The nomination was seconded and passed unanimously.

Some discussion followed on the further real estate purchases
the group would make through a newly-organized Holland & Portugal Trading Company in which they would share equally. The
offices would be in The Hague in line with the recently adopted
tactic of placing more and more of their investment control outside of Lisbon. Among them they now had on deposit in banks in
England, France, Switzerland and Holland more than $750,000.

And finally there was a discussion of the planned trip to
Angola by Reis and Hennies. There they would check over investments the group had already made and would look for new
opportunities to put their money to the best use.

At 2:00 P.M. the meeting ended on a note of self-congratulation. They drank several toasts to the bank they owned, Angola &
Metropole—as well as to the Bank of Portugal which made possible their great success. The bank they soon would own.

Then to cap a very useful day there was the letter Reis had
just received from his chief lieutenant in Lisbon, Ferreira. While
their own bank was prospering mightily and doing splendidly

> . . . several banks in Portugal are on the verge of closing their
> doors . . . mostly because of withdrawals made by the govern-
> ment from them in their African branches . . . things are des-
> perate in Angola and Mozambique and these banks will blow up
> any day now unless things change drastically.

Ferreira proved a fair prophet. Five of the seven banks he
listed did close their doors within the next few months. The closing of one of them, the Bank of Minho, gave Alves Reis particular
pleasure. Some of the bank's directors had been behind his imprisonment on the Ambaca affair.

More importantly, however, the closing of these banks would

mean that the Bank of Angola & Metropole would have much less competition in buying up hard foreign currencies.

LONDON / August 29, 1925

IT HAD BEEN a wet summer with remarkably little sun, even for London. But for José it was like entering the resplendent golden capital of the world. Entering as the honored managing director of an important bank and not as the misguided youth who had stolen some trifling sums from a British shipping company in Lisbon; or the fearful fellow jailed by British police in South Africa for some ridiculously petty crimes. He was entering as a proud member of a syndicate about to acquire some $9,500,000 worth of beautifully printed banknotes. A Monte Cristo couldn't have a more fitting vindication.

From their suite at the Carlton, Marang phoned Waterlow's to tell Springall they would be coming over for the first batch of notes in an hour. Springall said everything was ready for them and that he had ordered even stronger valises this time since Marang had complained about the locks on the others breaking open in transit. Then he added:

"Oh, by the way, we have a visitor from the Bank of Portugal here today."

Marang's heart skidded but he managed to ask casually who the visitor was. It was José Armando Pedroso, Technical Head of the Bank of Portugal's Printing Office and its leading expert on counterfeits.

"Yes," Springall went on, "he's taken in our Pavilion at the British Empire Exhibition at Wembley and he's going through the plant to see our automatic numbering machines."

Marang quickly decided that perhaps this was not the best day to introduce José to the Waterlow executives. The chances were good that Pedroso would not come to the directors' offices on Great Winchester Street and would probably remain at the Scrutton Street factory in Finsbury, one of the eight Waterlow plants in the area. But since Marang also got the notes at the factory the possibility of a confrontation existed. Why risk it?

He told José of the change in plans.

"Pedroso doesn't know me at all but he might recognize you and we certainly don't want him to connect the managing director of the Bank of Angola & Metropole with Waterlow & Sons."

José agreed, reluctantly. Even if Pedroso didn't recognize him he would still spot him as a fellow countryman. José bore the unmistakable stamp of a Portuguese: short, thin-faced, dark-visaged.

Waterlow's was particularly proud of the work at the Scrutton Street factory. The author of the company souvenir book, "Under Six Reigns," described it as being erected

> . . . for all things connected with the production of bank notes, postage stamps, share warrants. . . . Millions of bank notes are passed through this Department in the course of a year for a great many Foreign Countries and for many of the Scottish banks and for the Colonies.* The precautions necessary to be taken during the process of manufacture are of the strictest and most perfect kind . . . Watchmen patrol the buildings, and a rota of Managers is formed, whose duty it is to visit the factories during the night and take the "all well" report to the Chairman. . . .

Senhor Pedroso's mission was slightly indelicate: he was there as a patriotic industrial spy.

Before World War I, the Bank of Portugal had printed its own banknotes but had not been able to continue doing so, under Senhor Pedroso's supervision, because the numbering equipment had broken down and new ones could not be obtained. He was now in London to inspect Waterlow's numbering equipment more closely to see if, somehow, it could be duplicated so that the Bank of Portugal could return to the manufacture of its own notes.

* Five Scottish banks: Bank of Scotland, Royal Bank of Scotland, British Linen Bank, the National & Commercial Bank and the Clydesdale Bank—still have the right to issue their own banknotes. These circulate in Scotland just as Bank of England notes do. But Scottish nationalists naturally prefer their own.

Roland Springall who had arranged the tour for Pedroso had a fair notion of the purpose of the visit but it would have been too impolite to turn away the representative of such a good customer.

Pedroso watched the numbering machines for hours imprinting numbers on some of Marang's order of the 500-escudos notes. But since Pedroso knew that Waterlow's was still printing the 500-escudos notes for the Bank of Portugal under the continuing contract signed in 1922—Romer's great coup—he had no reason to ask when *these* notes would be reaching the Bank of Portugal.

It was fortunate for Springall. The terrible thought had occurred to him and he had not decided what he would say if asked.

Nor did Pedroso meet Marang. After his 50,000 notes—weighing some 250 pounds—were packed into two strong tan leather suitcases Marang was accompanied to the now-familiar Liverpool Street Station Cloakroom by Springall and George U. Rose, Jr.

Rose, then 60, was manager of the Waterlow banknote factory in Scrutton Street. He was Waterlow's sole American employe. After working for the U. S. Bureau of Engraving & Printing in Washington on U. S. banknotes for many years, he went to the American Bank Note Company, helping run the firm's great banknote printing plant in the Bronx, New York City. Sir William who had an enormous respect for the U. S. firm's technical competence lured Rose away with a fat seven-year contract.

In the cab going to the station Marang said to Rose, "What a terrible responsibility I have in the safe transportation of these notes."

George Rose was reassuring. "The safest way," he said, "is often the simplest way but I quite agree you do not like the responsibility of this thing. I believe I can claim to have carried more notes as personal luggage than any man living." It was some time before World War I and he had to bring several million dollars worth of banknotes from the Bureau of Engraving to San Francisco.

After checking in the bags with some $1,250,000 worth of banknotes in them, Marang, fully reassured by George Rose's experiences in banknote transportation, took a cab to the Carlton.

He and José returned to The Hague that evening. It hadn't been an altogether wasted trip for José. In Bond Street he bought some handbags for various friends.

Upon their arrival at Marang's offices in The Hague—where Coutinho was already installed in a specially-designated "Commissioner's Office"—José wired Alves Reis.

ARRIVED SAFELY. ALL IN ORDER. WORK ON SHARES COMMENCING.

LISBON / September 14, 1925

ORIGINALLY, COUNT PLANAS-SUAREZ was to meet José, Marang and Coutinho in Paris where he was to take charge of the new banknote shipment, and escort it by Sud Express to Lisbon. But the Count broke a leg while vacationing in Dax, in southwestern France. He suggested he meet the Sud Express when it stopped there instead of coming back to Paris. Reis, who had joined the group in Paris, agreed.

For one incautious moment Reis thought of putting his seventeen trunks, one pram and two bicycles in the diplomat's charge but true to his new role as international banker and financier he scorned such cheap chicaneries. He casually paid some $225 in duties at the Portuguese frontier on the table linen and crystalware his wife bought in Czechoslovakia and Germany.

In Lisbon the banknote valises were taken first to the Venezuelan's apartment for a quick recount. Plansas-Suarez insisted. He was wise enough to volunteer a measure he knew they were bursting to suggest—if they dared. After the quick survey José and Coutinho took the bags to the Bank of Angola & Metropole.

Now out of numerical sequence, the notes were quickly poured into the Portuguese economy: real estate was purchased;

foreign currency bought up; loans made, and Bank of Portugal shares acquired.

But getting control of the Bank wasn't going to be as easy as Alves Reis had once thought.

The Statutes of the Bank of Portugal helped spell out some of the difficulties. Article 75 made it clear only holders of at least 50 shares could have a vote in either the ordinary or extraordinary stockholders' meetings. And the shares had to be paid in full.

Article 77 laid down another restriction:

> The shareholders at the meeting have a number of votes proportional to the number of shares they own but none shall be entitled to more than five votes. From 50 to 99 shares, 1 vote; 100–149, 2 votes; 150–199, 3 votes; 200–249, 4 votes; 250 and over 5 votes.

Only a "native born Portuguese or one by naturalization who owns bank shares totalling 5,000 escudos worth or more may be elected a director." * And there were restrictions against nepotism:

> Article 70. The following may not be jointly members of the General Council of the Bank:
> 1. Two or more members of a commercial corporation or two or more managers of a company.
> 2. Father and son, brothers, uncle and nephew, brothers-in-law; father and son-in-law, step-father and step-son.

In 1925 the Bank of Portugal had 97,000 shares outstanding, representing some 1,734 votes. In order to get a safe 900 votes—and control—Reis and his group would have to purchase at least 45,000 shares, preferably in groups of 250 at a time so that there was no waste of shares for voting strength. Why buy 255 shares when you could vote the five times maximum for only 250 shares?

Many of the shares, Reis knew, would never come on the market except at exorbitant prices. These were held by some leading Portuguese families almost in perpetuity, their permanent stake in the power structure of the land. Governments might come and go—and in Portugal between 1910 and 1925 govern-

---

* This was enacted in 1910 when the escudo was worth more than a dollar.

ment had become a revolving door affair—but the Bank of Portugal endured.

An additional difficulty: the purchases could not be done altogether in the dark. Long before Reis could get control, the Bank of Portugal would know what he was up to. Inevitably, some potential stock sellers would also offer the shares to the Bank, partly out of fuzzy patriotism but mainly in the hope of getting the share price bid up. *Na agua envolta pesca o pescador.* (The fisherman catches fish in troubled waters.)

They would then learn, as Reis had from Article 21 of the Bank's statutes, that the Bank is "expressly prohibited from buying up its shares on its own account."

Still, that could be gotten around without too much trouble. The Bank could not buy the shares but friends of the Bank could—other private bankers; brokers who were able to discount their notes at the Bank. There were many friends.

When Reis first started buying the Bank of Portugal shares the price had been about $40. It rose steadily and now it was $68 to $70.

On this day Reis took stock of where they stood. They had in hand, registered in "safe" names some 7,100 shares representing about 140 votes. There was still a long way to go. Too long, perhaps.

He wished that he had stayed in Lisbon through the summer instead of going on to Carlsbad where he had been fairly miserable. He would, henceforth, stay patriotically devoted to the Portuguese spas.

Before he left for Carlsbad he impressed José with the arch importance of the Bank of Portugal stock purchases. He also stressed that while he didn't want José throwing money around wildly, neither should he haggle: they weren't buying rugs in a bazaar. In order to win control of Portugal it would be necessary to overpay occasionally for the Bank shares.

Of course, he could not lecture José *too* much on the subject. Now that he was managing director of their bank his *amour propre* had risen proportionately. He had become sensitive about shortcomings brought to his attention.

José, he knew, had spent much time trying to ferret out *who* held the Bank shares. These were not publicly listed and the

Bank did not disclose the list of shareholders. If he pressed José the latter would inevitably turn on Reis with the sensible demand:

"Why don't you ask your friends at the Bank for the list? It would make my job much easier."

Twice now Alves Reis had been tempted to take José aside after an intimate little dinner and end the continuing deception. He had even rehearsed a little talk:

> *Meu caro José*, we have been through much together in the past eight months and we have profited enormously from our association. Now the time has come for me to speak more frankly than I have dared to you or any of our other colleagues.
>
> Surely by this time you know that the "contracts" with the Bank of Portugal and Alves Reis are forged; that the only way I could get Camacho's signature while I was in Carlsbad was to forge it. We have both been in jail and we surely do not have to pretend to one another as we have to that hypocrite partner of ours, Marang.
>
> Now that we understand one another I must tell you firmly that unless you apply yourself with every energy and resource to the business of buying the Bank of Portugal stock we will be defeated—and jailed, of course. We have no in-between choice: we must become masters of the Bank, or jailbirds—with the keys thrown away.
>
> While I am in Africa with Hennies I must rely on you to carry this through at the expense of *everything* else. And I must speak firmly again, almost as a father, even though you are older. It's delightful to watch your boyish pleasures in women, in gambling, in cavorting in nightclubs—but the time has come to put such joys aside until we are safely in control.

How would José react to such a man-to-man talk? Alves Reis had to admit he was no longer sure. José had become too wealthy, too powerful, too soon. Such a frank confession might serve to get him to buckle down to the number one task but it could just as easily frighten him to death. He simply might transfer every asset abroad and flee—with a brief stop in The Hague to tell his brother.

Not only was Alves Reis unsure of the reaction he would engender but he still had too much pride in his clever planning and cunning to take anyone into his great secret. He had become somewhat like that curious self-contained mathematical vessel he read about. The great German mathematician, Felix Klein, had just died and in one of the papers there was a feature about the Klein bottle, whose spout curves back into its mouth so that it became "a one-sided surface which is closed and has no boundary."

No, the little talk with José would not be forthcoming. Instead he would instruct Ferreira to take a more active hand in the purchase of Bank of Portugal stock. Ferreira would do it wisely and would understand that he and José must not compete secretly and thus drive up the prices ruinously.

He hadn't forgotten the devotion and long hours some of his "loyal and true friends" had put in for him. Ferreira had received bonuses totaling $20,000; Silva some $15,000—enormous sums in Lisbon then, when good office managers were glad to earn $1200 a year. The loyalty was genuine, not merely goldplated. Shortly before Alves Reis was to leave for Angola, Silva wrote his brother from Lisbon where he had gone from Oporto

> . . . for the sole purpose of saying goodbye to my biggest friend, Engineer Alves Reis. My interests are linked to his by a trust similar to that I place in you, a pure and intimate brotherly feeling. Alves Reis is my other self, on a larger, grander scale. . . .

Reis' loyalty to Angola was responsible for some major investments and loans by the Bank of Angola & Metropole. On August 14th the Bank signed a contract with Aboim Company of Angola which had large palm oil plantations and a railroad.

The Bank would lend the firm $50,000 on signing, another $50,000 on September 1st and October 1st and finally, $20,000 the rest of the year as the company required the money. The money was lent cheaply: Amboim agreed to pay 10% on repayments in 1925 and 12% on later repayments. In addition the Bank got options on 90,000 shares of the company's stock and could at any time buy the company's largest palm oil factory for $200,000.

The interest rate was modest for Angola. But the fact that the Bank was making the loan, not in depreciated Angolan escudos but in hard British pounds, made a mere 10% interest rate extraordinarily generous to the borrower.

A somewhat similar deal was made with the Compania das Minas de Cobre of Bembe which operated several copper mines.

The Bank was going to help Bembe finance a railroad from the mines to the port of Luanda. Controlling interest was purchased in a leading Angolan newspaper, *The Graphic.* A large loan and option-to-purchase deal was also made with Quissama Agriculture Ltd., a huge copra plantation. And they bought a controlling interest in the large colonial trading firm, the Mercantile Company of Portugal and Angola.

In September the Bank of Angola & Metropole opened branches in the principal cities of Angola. At a press conference in mid-September Alves Reis announced that he was heading a party of technical and development experts who would go to Angola in October to undertake a survey of Angola's problems. High on the group's agenda would be the possibility of settling 1,000 Portuguese families in the plateaus of Benguela and Moçamedes. The Minister of Colonies promised every possible aid to the visiting experts.

The coming of Alves Reis was heralded in all Angolan papers and one editorially praised the new bank as "the highly conscious instrument for the development of Angola."

In Oporto and Lisbon the Bank's agents were quickly converting the new 500-escudos notes into hard foreign currency which in turn was transferred to various British and Dutch banks. In October, 1925, the Westminster Bank in London alone held more than $400,000 for the Bank of Angola & Metropole.

With its many investments in Portugal itself the new bank brought about a considerable improvement in the economy. Tomé Vieria now an editor of the Lisbon *Diario de Noticias,* was a reporter in Lisbon during the last half of 1925. He recalls, that suddenly

> there was a lot of money around. Loans were easier to get. There were more jobs around. Buildings were going up. The department store sales rose. Everything was booming. I think if Alves Reis stood for the Chamber of Deputies he would have been elected easily. He was being hailed as a great financial genius who was taking Portugal out of the economic doldrums.

There were many personal benefactions. An acquaintance approached Reis tearfully at the Bank. Unless 75,000 escudos could be raised he would go to jail for embezzlement from the government department he worked for . . . A wife and three children.

Reis got up from his desk, put his arm around the man and ordered him to stop crying. He called to a teller: "Give the man 75,000 escudos" (about $3,700).

A Lisbon businessman who knew Reis well in those days recalled that

> when he came into the room he immediately took charge. . . . He always seemed to know what you were going to say before you said it. He listened carefully as if he was really interested in what you were saying. And because he was great at remembering faces and names he was quite popular. He would have made a successful politician. And if he ran for the Chamber of Deputies you could be sure that he would have become a cabinet minister in no time.

Even while he was riding a great wave of popularity and working out deals involving millions of escudos, Alves Reis found time to buttress the underpinnings of his great crime. He learned that a distant relative owed a small personal debt of 600 escudos (about $30) to Camacho Rodrigues, the governor of the Bank of Portugal.

He easily persuaded his kin that it might be embarrassing for Alves Reis, a leading banker, to have a blood relative in debt to the head of the Bank of Portugal. Even for only 600 escudos. It was a rather silly pretext but who doesn't like to have debts paid painlessly?

Reis wrote Camacho Rodrigues that he wanted to pay the old debt owed the governor by Luis Filippe Fernandes Alves. If the governor would send someone to the Reis office, with a receipt signed by the governor, the money would be paid.

Repayment of old, forgotten debts is particularly welcome, found money. The governor was earning $3,000 a year as Portugal's most important banker and even $27 was useful.

On his own personal Bank of Portugal stationery—Governor's Office—he wrote Alves Reis:

> I acknowledge receipt of your letter of the 23rd inst. in which you authorize me to send to your office for the arrears of an account that my friend Fernando Alves has placed at my dis-

posal through your good selves. The bearer is carrying the respec-
tive receipt.

> With my highest regard, Yours etc.
> I. Camacho Rodrigues

Reis was naturally fascinated to see how his concept of the
governor's stationery—used so successfully with Waterlow—
differed from the actual. With the Portuguese crest, Reis' version
was far fancier than the governor's real stationery. Reis was also
shocked—and amused—to see several small points of difference
in the governor's actual signature, compared to the ones *he* had
been forging.*

He started practicing the governor's newer signature but decided a change was dangerous at this stage: why tamper with
success? He put the governor's letter in his safe. Who knows
when acknowledgement of a debt by the governor of the Bank of
Portugal to Alves Reis might not be most useful?

They had obtained more Bank of Portugal shares but they
still had only 9,000.

ANGOLA / October 8, 1925

THE TRIUMPHS IN Lisbon were interrupted only by the voyage to
Luanda. There the Reis party—Mrs. Reis; Hennies; Albano
Teixeira da Silva, a department head at the Bank of Angola &
Metropole, and Jaime Mendoça, Reis' private secretary—were
greeted with viceregal warmth and welcoming speeches. Reis
didn't exaggerate much when he later recalled

> I was received by the authorities with the love that would be
> given to a messiah backed by a pot of gold. I had a lot of friends
> in Angola and even my enemies felt the strength of will of a man

---

* Mainly, the Reis version had thicker letters which were more regular
than than the original.

who wanted to develop the wealth of the nation. Nobody considered my plans as those of a dreamer.

A Provinica de Angola—a paper he didn't own—spoke for the colony when it said that there

> is no need to introduce Engineer Alves Reis. Angola has, for long, owed him signal service, whether as a competent public servant with a great record, whether as an enterprising colonialist, having set up among others, the South Angola Mining Company to exploit the rich gold and copper deposits in the Mossamedes interior. . . . He is a man of action, with unusual vision, full of decision and initiative. . . . He has unshakable faith in the great future that is in store for Angola, provided that the vast resources it contains are fully exploited.

Everywhere Reis was greeted as "the great hope of Angola." And in many ways he was just that. Angola was then, as it had often been in the past, in a hellish mess.

❂   ❂   ❂   ❂   ❂

Today Angola finds its way to the front page because it is frequently discussed at the UN by African and Asian delegates determined to end all colonialism. In 1925 Angola was just an underdeveloped, economically-stricken Portuguese colony that almost never interested the foreign press.

Most of the Portuguese colonization efforts hadn't gotten underway seriously until the 19th century and even then the occupation was limited mainly to the coastal regions. In the interior were hostile tribes, every known tropical disease and no roads. As recently as 1908 the Portuguese were still trying to quell guerrilla warfare of the natives. But by 1917 all eleven tribal groups were brought under control.

Long before that the Angolan system of contract labor had become the cruelest perpetuation of slavery in the 20th century. An Inspector of the Portuguese Overseas Ministry called the system even worse

> than simple slavery. Under slavery, after all, the Native is bought as an animal: his owner prefers him to remain as fit as a horse or an ox. Yet here the Native is not bought—he is hired from the State, although he is called a free man. And his em-

ployer cares little if he sickens or dies, once he is working, because when he sickens or dies, his employer will simply ask for
another.

All African natives except the so-called *assimilado* or "Euro-
peanized" native, are subject to contract labor unless gainfully
employed. And subsistence farming, which most villagers practiced, is not considered "gainful employment." The employer
agrees to pay the contract laborer a very small salary and to provide lodging, food and clothing.

When Alves Reis and his party arrived in Luanda, Angola, in
October he soon found contract labor abuses still the rule—as
they had been when he was last in the colony in 1921. But contract labor meant that his group's investments in several large
plantations were likely to prove profitable. Large employers
could usually get contract labor at even less overall cost from the
government.

Among the Portuguese in Angola there was considerable dis-
satisfaction with Lisbon's policies. The Pro-Angola Party which
had been formed recently, plumped for much greater autonomy
to satisfy the economic and political aspirations of Angolans.
Many of Reis' friends belonged to the new party.

Some of their complaints were political but by far the most
important were economic. S. C. Spouse, who then was the only
British trader in Angola, recalled later how bad business was in
the colony:

> The local bank [Banco Ultramarino] could offer absolutely
> no facilities for transferring money abroad, or even to Portugal,
> and it was a common occurrence for Government officials and
> other Portuguese to beg of me a cheque in sterling at practically
> any exchange rate in order that they might be able to remit money
> to their families in Portugal who, they stated, were starving.

When word got around that Engineer Alves Reis and his
Bank were interested in buying local properties for hard foreign
currencies, long lines of desperate businessmen and plantation
owners besieged him in the hotels. Reis had to stress repeatedly
in interviews that little buying would be done during this trip:
this was primarily a tour of inspection. His group already had a
$1,500,000 stake in Angola.

In Moçamedes where Alves Reis' first son had been born in 1918 the great benefactor from Lisbon received a hero's welcome. According to the local paper:

> The distinguished colonial and great friend of ours finally arrived in this city by special train accompanied by his wife and M. Adolf Hennies.

> The train arrived at 8 A.M. and even at this hour the station was crowded with people, major traders, official individualities and many of Engineer Alves Reis' personal friends who flocked there to embrace him.

> An exchange of views with the illustrious visitors leads us to state that we cannot advance anything definite beyond the objectives set by them in several interviews they were kind enough to give us. . . . One must give time for the splendid goals to be achieved, as it has to be carried out with a great deal of method and prudence.

Reis kept the cables between Angola and Lisbon and The Hague busier than they had been for years.

The news was all good.

LONDON / October 9, 1925

JOSÉ CAME to London with Marang for the delivery of the 150,000 notes worth some $3,750,000. Again they had a suite at the Carlton. But this time Marang got around the possibility of running into any Bank of Portugal personnel at Waterlow's by arranging a luncheon at the hotel for Springall to meet José.

He had written Springall and again complained about the trunks and valises used for previous shipments. This time he requested Waterlow to

kindly order seven trunks for me with safe locks, as the locks
of the trunks you formerly supplied were very bad. Perhaps the
factory can make the trunks this time extra solid.

Marang and Springall took the three filled pieces of baggage
to the Liverpool Street Station where they were checked as before. Marang introduced José Bandeira as the managing director
of the Bank of Angola & Metropole.

Marang was ebullient, Springall later recalled, because

> he was soon to become a director of the Bank of Portugal.
> He said he and his friends were buying up the shares of the Bank
> and before long he expected that he and his friends would have
> control. . . . He assured me that only Waterlow's would print the
> Bank's notes thereafter. . . . He mentioned the possibility of the
> Bank issuing new notes for 2500 [$125] and even for 5000 escu-
> dos [$250]. . . . You may take it from me, he said, that I will
> see to it that you get these orders.

José discussed some changes in the share certificates he
wanted for the Bank of Angola & Metropole. It was a very useful
luncheon, Springall told his boss, Frederick Goodman, later that
day. "Yes," he said, "Mr. Marang is a very nice man, indeed."

It was good to see virtue and hard work rewarded, he added.
Mr. Bandeira had been only a secretary to Mr. Marang and now
he's become managing director of their new bank.

Springall wasn't commenting idly. At 53, he was still but an
assistant to Frederick Goodman after having lost his department
managership when the two Waterlow firms merged in 1921.
Originally he assumed that Goodman, in his 70's, would stay on
for only a year at most. But he was still there.

On the Channel boat José felt inordinately pleased with
himself. He hadn't said anything when Marang talked about becoming a director of the Bank of Portugal. Marang was a clever
businessman but he had neglected to do something José had
done several times: study the statutes of the Bank of Portugal. It
specifically stipulated that the Bank's directors had to be born
Portuguese or naturalized citizens. Of course, the group could
change the statutes once they were in control but why raise a
touchy issue in so nationalistic a country as Portugal. No, it would
be far easier for José dos Santos Bandeira, son of an ancient Por-

tuguese family. Before Alves Reis left for Angola José had extracted a promise from him: José *would* be a director of the Bank of Portugal.

THE HAGUE / October 10, 1925

EVEN WITH the great advances in the fortunes of the Bandeira brothers in the past seven months, life hadn't changed too much in the four-story Portuguese Ministry. José no longer lived there as he had for the past three years—Antonio's new wife didn't like her husband's younger brother—but otherwise life in the Ministry was much the same.

Frau Bertha Leuchtner, the Bandeiras' German housekeeper, ran the house with the help of a Portuguese couple, Manoel and Maria. Frau Leuchtner thoroughly approved of the new Senhora Bandeira. They were alike in many ways: the Minister's wife daily checked shopping expenses and was always on the lookout for cheaper supplies for the table. She did her own sewing and her dresses were made by a seamstress who made simple, sturdy clothes rather than stylish affairs.

But Antonio, now that his brother's financial coups had made him comparatively prosperous too, did insist on replacing the simple Portuguese wines they served when entertaining with the more expensive French *crus*. Now he was able to entertain more even though his "representation" allowance from Lisbon was shamefully meager. The fete they had given in honor of Prince Henry of Holland—and paid for by José—had been a notable evening in the diplomatic colony's social season. Marang and his wife had been among the guests and he never tired of telling how he had been mistaken for Prince Henry by the Lisbon press in the spring. And, really, there was no resemblance at all. Marang, of course, refrained from pointing out that he was much handsomer than the Prince Consort.

This evening José dined alone with his brother. Fie was playing in Sutton Vane's play *Outward Bound,* a great hit in The Hague and Amsterdam. She was still youthful enough to play the ingénue. José had seen her in the role several times and Antonio wanted a quiet talk together. His wife was in Lisbon.

During dinner they exchanged family gossip and José filled his older brother in on his luncheon in London with the Waterlow official. Then with the coffee Antonio grew somber:

"Is it possible that your Hennies is not what he seems?"

José was startled into a *non sequitur.* "He's in Angola."

Antonio continued. Two weeks ago he learned from an old friend in the Portuguese Embassy in Paris that the Minister of Colonial Affairs in Lisbon had asked the Military Attaché at the Embassy in Paris to contact his best source in the French Deuxième Bureau (Counter-intelligence) to see what they had on Adolf Hennies.

José broke in quickly: "Adolf a *spy?*"

Antonio sometimes wondered how his younger brother, so shrewd and cunning usually, could be so dense.

"You knew he had been a German spy here during the War, didn't you?"

José shrugged. "Everybody knew. But that was during the War. Now—now he's a rich businessman. My partner."

Antonio was patient. "José, you're not listening. I told you that the investigation was requested by the Ministry of *Colonial* Affairs—not the Army or Navy."

José finally caught it. "Oh. The Germans are trying to get our colonies in Africa . . ."

"Exactly."

The Deuxième Bureau's report was fairly accurate, although Hennies would have been pleased to see that even the French Secret Service had not been able to uncover his real identity:

> He is a Brazilian of German origin; father Swiss. Is a great Germanophile. Was born in Berne, Nov. 21, 1884. . . . During the War worked closely with head of German espionage in Holland. One of his pre-war business associates, Robert Haag de Lima, was sent to U.S. to spy for the Germans. . . . Was in arms

and securities traffic for the Germans after the war. . . . Was in touch with Soviet government soon after the war. . . . Lady friend is a German. Frau Dr. A. Angold whom he lived with in Paris and Palace Hotel, Scheveningen. . . . Has an account at the Rotterdamsche Bank with some 500,000 florins [about $150,000]. . . . Recently told an acquaintance in The Hague that he soon expected to be as well known as Hugo Stinnes [a prominent and wealthy German industrialist].

José smiled. "So what. What's all that got to do with Portuguese colonies?"

"There are, unfortunately, certain influential ministers and officials in Lisbon who are convinced that Hennies is a secret German agent *now*," Antonio went on. "That his job is to get a big foothold in Angola by buying companies and plantations there through your Bank of Angola & Metropole. If Alves Reis had asked *me* I would certainly have advised him against giving Hennies' enemies more ammunition."

José explained that all the investments the group made and was going to make in Angola were made *together*—and they were being made solely for business reasons and not in the furtherance of an international plot. "Why should Alves Reis or I want to *give* Angola to the Germans? And who says they would *want* it—even as a gift? The damn place is nearly bankrupt and most Portuguese down there would love to get back to Portugal— if they could only get out their investments. We're putting money into Angola because there are a lot of bargains to be had."

Antonio, anxious to be convinced, accepted his brother's explanation of Hennies' role. But he was much more disturbed that the Ministry of Colonial Affairs hadn't asked *him* for a report on Hennies as they had Paris. Obviously, someone in Lisbon realized that the brother of the Minister to The Hague was closely allied with suspect Adolf Hennies, that his report might not be unbiased.

Later, in his apartment, José mentally composed a letter to Alves Reis in Angola giving him the gist of his brother's disclosures. Then he remembered: Reis had told him several times that the big investments in Angola had been *ordered* by "the Men" at the Bank of Portugal, the powers who had made possible the secret emissions of banknotes. And he knew how much Alves

Reis respected Hennies' business judgment and acumen. After getting such a letter from José, Reis might easily decide José had become a nervous tattle-tale—certainly not the kind of man one would want as a fellow director in the reorganized Bank of Portugal. He didn't write.

*   *   *   *   *

At Marang's offices, Coutinho was counting and reassembling the second batch of 150,000 banknotes out of sequence. He wasn't happy. Occasionally he would dine with José but the necessary secrecy of his work at Marang's office—none of Marang's clerks were allowed in the "Commissioner's" Office—and his inability to speak Dutch or French limited his social contacts greatly. Worse, Marang was paying him spasmodically and insufficiently. Marang insisted that it had really been up to Alves Reis to pay Coutinho. Only loans from José enabled Coutinho to pay his own expenses in The Hague.

The notes were repacked in the extra-strong valises and this time Planas-Suarez escorted the 150,000 notes straight from The Hague down to Lisbon where they were stored in his apartment until they were needed at the Bank of Angola & Metropole.

LISBON / November 12, 1925

BEFORE JOSÉ LEFT The Hague for Lisbon he had a long talk with Marang.

The news his brother had given him—that Hennies was suspected as a German agent by the Portuguese Ministry of Colonial Affairs—had begun to worry José. He *knew* Hennies wasn't a German agent trying to buy Angola for political reasons; but stranger things happened. Since he didn't dare write Alves Reis about this growing concern, José decided to share it with Marang.

Marang's reaction was reassuring: Nonsense! He would vouch for Adolf Hennies—a man he had worked with more than a decade! An international businessman of vast acumen and considerable resources. Not only was Hennies his partner in Marang & Collignon but he was a *friend*. The whole business was bureaucratic nonsense. José had been wise not to write Alves Reis in Angola about it.

Perhaps Marang had been *too* reassuring. Josè decided it would not hurt to acquire a little insurance. From his brother's safe in the Portuguese Ministry—long ago his brother had entrusted the combination to him—he took the two original contracts between Reis and the Bank of Portugal authorizing the issue of banknotes and placed them in a thick manila envelope which he asked Fie Carelsen to hold for him.

Marang still didn't think that his associate had been a German agent all along in their collaboration but the fact that some higher Portuguese officials *thought so* might be dangerous. He decided to hold 100,000 banknotes of the last shipment from Waterlow. He'd keep these in The Hague until Reis returned from Angola and talked to "the Men" at the Bank of Portugal to find out what was behind the campaign against Adolf Hennies.

In Lisbon, José tried to put the vague fears out of mind by a lot of work—and some new love affairs. He didn't forget Reis' emphatic instruction to get all the Bank of Portugal shares that he could find. But it wasn't easy. The price kept going up and some speculators smelling something afoot helped bid the price up by buying all they could in the hope of unloading the shares later at a still higher price. Obviously, someone wanted the shares badly and would pay.

Meanwhile, he supervised the Bank's various aides in converting the new bills into foreign currency in Oporto—where the Angola & Metropole Bank had an impressive branch—and in Lisbon. Things were picking up all over Portugal and several financial writers on the local dailies predicted that the coming Christmas would be the most prosperous one Portugal had had in a long time. The obvious prosperity and increased employment somehow managed to impress foreign exchange dealers abroad.

The escudo rose slowly in value vis-à-vis the pound and florin.

One morning José had a fearful thought: so far he had been making the Bank of Portugal stock purchases through dummies, friends, relatives and even employees of the Bank of Angola. The stock would be duly registered in their names in the Bank of Portugal's roll of stockholders. But now that a secret investigation was underway of Hennies, was it likely that the affairs of the Bank of Angola would remain immune to the secret ferrets of the government? Surely they would pierce the flimsy veils of the Bank stock ownership quickly.

For two weeks José stopped buying Bank of Portugal stock. But in his weekly cables to Alves Reis he resorted to some small lies so that Reis wouldn't worry:

NOW HAVE 15,000 SHARES.

And then:

SHARES TOTAL 22,000.

There was no sense worrying Reis. They could always get the shares when they wanted them. Meanwhile, they could put the 500-escudos notes to much better use. The Bank of Portugal dividend only amounted to 3%. Without trying, the Bank of Angola & Metropole could get 12% for its loans and investments.

ANGOLA / November 14, 1925

A WEEK AGO Alves Reis had gotten the first indication he had been under surveillance since he came to Angola. An old friend had become an important Angola police official. One night at dinner with Reis he told his old friend—in the greatest confidence—that two detectives under orders from the Colonial Ministry were shadowing the Reis-Hennies group in their travels; that copies of their cables were made.

Reis wasn't unduly alarmed: the cables to and from Lisbon were in code. And as for the surveillance, it must have been arduous for the detectives for they certainly weren't in the private car in which Reis and his party traveled through the tracked portions of Angola.

Obviously, his activities were simply beginning to alarm those who felt threatened by the entrance into Angola of a new financial power. Perhaps the Banco Ultramarino itself. Reis didn't say anything to Hennies. They continued their tour of inspection.

With Hennies' consent Reis committed the group to the purchase of two huge sugar plantations located on the right bank of the Quanza River, below Luanda. The price wasn't important: a mere $26,000 for 125,000 acres. (Oh, there were great bargains to be had all over Angola.) But with this new acquisition plus their heavy interests in the great empire of the Quissama plantation which adjoined the Amboim Company estate, Reis now had a lock on more than 1,250,000 acres of some of the most fertile land in Angola. Since the river was navigable they could build their own docks and not be dependent on the uncertainty of rail shipments to Luanda.

By November 17th the Reis group had concluded its inspections and purchases. What remained were a few press announcements and ceremonial farewell dinners Alves Reis' many friends and admirers begged him to attend in Luanda, the capital.

The High Commissioner of Angola, Rego Chaves, announced proudly that Alves Reis' Bank, the enterprising Bank of Angola & Metropole, had made a firm proposal to construct a railroad between Bembe and Luanda so that the copper mines of Bembe could be exploited to their fullest. "This enterprise," said the High Commissioner, "is worthy of the greatest praise as a token of the high confidence the Bank has in Angola and the nation."

At a dinner in his honor Alves Reis drew an inspiring picture of the Angola of Tomorrow which he and his associates would help build:

> New railroads will be built, communities created. Well-equipped ports will receive the ships that now despise and flee from Angolan waters . . . modern railroads will cut through

virgin territory, bringing wealth to the interior of this vast land
. . . jungles will be tamed to allow settlers to draw the maximum
wealth from the rich land where healthy children would come
with their parents to strengthen the name of Portugal in Angola.

The applause echoed long after.

The following day the local paper praised the great, bold
vision of Artur Alves Reis: "At last Portugal has found its own
Cecil Rhodes. Here is a man to give solid substance to our old,
old dreams."

On the morning of November 22, 1925, Reis and his wife,
Hennies and the rest of their party, boarded the German steamer
Adolf Woerman for the return voyage to Lisbon. The crowds at
the deck were the largest Luanda had ever seen. Before they
boarded the ship Reis got another cable from José Bandeira. The
group now had 31,000 shares of the Bank of Portugal stock. Another 14,000 shares and they were masters of Portugal—as well as
Angola. He returned the hand-waving of his many friends on
shore with greater vigor.

LISBON / November 23, 1925

ONE OF LISBON's livelier morning dailies was—and still is—*O
Seculo (The Century)*. It's fare then included scandalmongering
and exposés of government chicanery, particularly by ministers
of parties it was opposed to.

The paper was owned by Pereira da Rosa who was inti-
mately associated with several leading Portuguese banks and
industrialists.* One of the latter was Alfredo da Silva, the coun-

---

* In 1496, King Manoel I (The Fortunate) ordered a choice for the
Jews of Portugal: expulsion or conversion to Christianity. Most of the Jews
left and those who remained became the New Christians. They adopted new
names, mainly those of flowers and fruit trees, such as Pereira, pear tree.

try's leading vegetable oils magnate. Da Silva had become alarmed at the growing acquisition of Angola plantations by companies controlled by the new and growing Bank of Angola & Metropole. Early in November he had persuaded publisher da Rosa to assign two of his best reporters to look into the affairs of this dangerous new bank. Now on this morning the first of a series of articles on the Bank appeared in *Seculo*.

It was headed, right across page one,

WHAT'S GOING ON?

We are told that persons connected with a certain banking house which was greatly discussed even before its creation, are seeking to acquire various businesses in Angola and Mozambique. . . . Various landowners have refused to sell without first getting clear information about the object of the proposed deal . . . to be certain that such sales would not mean immediate or remote danger to national sovereignty.

It is known that the group, through various intermediaries, has already purchased 10,000 shares of the Bank of Portugal and that the shares have risen greatly in value as a result. . . . Persons, some of them in official places, have been acquiring buildings, some in the name of close relatives and others only weeks before they had no visible means of fortune. The expenditures in these acquisitions is believed to have attained over £700,000 [about $3,500,000].

It even appears there are friends in the government who are interested in the organization of the mystery bank. In its Board of Directors are persons who, if well known as some of them are, it is in circles other than banking. . . . There is talk of their acquiring great newspapers and launching new papers in the market. . . . All this is suspicious and alarming, in a country such as ours with a vast and coveted colonial domain.

What's going on? The nation must be told.

Their first *banderilla* had been thrust. *Seculo* deliberately planned to skip a day in the series to see how much blood would be drawn on the first attack; who would emerge to defend the new bank.

On November 23rd two other Lisbon papers joined the attack against the still unnamed bank.* The attacks had at least one immediate official effect. Several days before, the Minister of Finance had decided to do something about the mass purchase of Bank of Portugal stock by the new Bank of Angola & Metropole. He called in the Inspector of Banking Commerce, Luis Viegas, and asked him to conduct a discreet investigation.

Viegas had intended to proceed slowly and quietly but the press campaign, he said later,

> forced me, much against my will, to begin my inquiry, although I then thought, as I still do, that it would have been preferable to have let it develop gradually.
>
> I accordingly presented myself at the head office of the Bank in the Rua do Crucifixo on November 24th at 3 P.M. I was received by the Managing Director, José dos Santos Bandeira, to whom I read my instructions which cloaked and hid my real object. . . . In my presence orders were given that everything should be put at my disposal so that there should be no doubts about the aims and objects of the Bank. Having exchanged compliments, I left. . . .

José wasn't too worried about Viegas. After all, he had approved the charter granted to the Bank and one of his relatives was a director of the Bank. But there were other, more powerful forces at work.

José reacted the way very rich men have always reacted when a newspaper attacks: if you can't join them, buy them. In a long telegram to Marang in The Hague he asked him to make inquiries—through any of his Dutch bank correspondents in Lisbon—to find out if *Seculo* was in financial trouble; whether the owners were interested in selling.

Ferreira asked José if they were getting their attorney to institute a libel suit. José shrugged. "They haven't named names yet. Let's see how far they go."

His conscience had been bothering him about the false cables to Alves Reis about the stock purchases and the two-week

---

* A recent International Press Institute survey of the press in authoritarian countries points out that in 1925 the press of Portugal "enjoyed unlimited freedom. . . . Impartial historians admit that the [Portuguese] press must bear a heavy responsibility for disorders that preceded the advent of the dictatorship [in 1926]."

moratorium he had declared on additional purchases. Now, of course, it would be much too dangerous to buy any more shares. It would only confirm the dangerous charges made in *Seculo*.

On November 25th, the series continued. This time with a name:

> The notorious Bank of Angola & Metropole has begun its maneuvering. Where does it get its money from? Where has it obtained the millions with which it is flooding the country? Nobody knows. From Holland, say some. . . . From German banks, assure yet others. . . . None of the persons in the new organization is known in the financial world. But the public at large knows them, suspects them and has begun murmuring in protest. There is talk of Portuguese diplomats who have been intermediaries in the deal and there is talk of the purchase of buildings for millions of escudos in the name of relatives. . . . Names are being mentioned and everything makes us believe that Portugal has fallen prey to a gang that is getting ready to devour the nation's heart.
>
> The A&M Bank is not wasting its time. It is maneuvering, intriguing and corrupting. . . . It has made a tiger's leap on colonial companies and seized some of them. . . . It has turned on the Bank of Portugal and is harpooning its shares. . . . It wants to lead us first to the loss of our colonies and then to that of our own independence.
>
> Another instance. Someone came to the *Seculo* the other day to obtain information on the paper's financial situation which, we were told, was requested by an Amsterdam firm. What they wanted to know was whether we were in financial difficulties, if we wanted to issue stock or even if we were willing to give up our position as shareholders. Who was the instigator of this démarche? The Bank of A&M . . there is a band of vultures hovering over the land coveting every position of leadership and control of finance and of politics. And control of the press. It buys up everything that is for sale and that may be useful to it.

Ferreira was far more worried than José. He sent a long radio message to Alves Reis aboard ship and he got in touch with the Lisbon offices of the various Angola firms the Bank now controlled or in which they held important interests. He drafted a statement to be signed by all indicating their faith in the solidity and patriotism of the Bank of Angola & Metropole.

That afternoon Ferreira got a break. Into his office came a

reporter from *Imprensa Nova,* another Lisbon daily. He bore a message from the editor: for a payment of 50,000 escudos ($2500) that paper would *not* join in the campaign against the Bank. Ferreira had the reporter repeat the bribe request. This time it was heard by Inspector Viegas who was in an adjoining office, going through some of the Bank's records. The Inspector arrested the reporter on the spot. Word got out immediately and all the other Lisbon dailies stopped their attacks on the Bank. Portuguese journalism being what it was, everyone would assume a continuation of the attack simply meant they were waiting to be bought off.

Only *Seculo* continued. On November 26th it fulminated:

> The plan of the A&M capitalists is obvious. Angola is on the brink of ruin. . . . There could be no better time for a peaceful penetration. What was worth ten thousand 2 or 3 years ago can now be bought for four or five thousand. . . .
>
> Germany will be entering the League of Nations soon. It will certainly want colonies. Those she had before the war will not be restored to her. International public opinion is being prepared so that Germany may be quieted down and not be a spoilsport in the international concert—at the expense of Portuguese colonial dominion.

The next day the peculiar lack of normal activity at the Bank engaged the *Seculo* writer:

> It makes no discounts, receives no deposits and does not engage in operations peculiar to all banks. . . . Money here cost 12, 15, even 18% yet a bank that seeks our market spurns this interest but uses 12 million escudos [$600,000] to buy and immobilize Bank of Portugal shares that fetch 3%. . . .

In fact almost *every* major nation was somehow involved in the conspiracy against Portugal:

> The foreigners covet Angola, the Germans want to settle there. . . . Some American called Ross,* wearing the cloak of philanthropy, charges us with slavery. British delegate Mr. Cecil

---

* Dr. Edward Alsworth Ross, an American sociologist, visited Angola in 1925 and wrote a damning report on the brutal conditions involved in the contract labor scheme.

discreetly applauds the slander. The Dutch Consul in Lisbon has issued a good conduct certificate to the A&M Bank saying that no German capital is involved in it. The Consul lost an excellent opportunity to play dead. Is it in his jurisdiction to interfere in a discussion in which our patriotism is involved?

Ferreira sensibly wanted the Bank to stop its foreign exchange operations for a time—until the present furor blew over or until they could buy *O Seculo*. But José Bandeira, anxious to show that the attacks hadn't fazed him, insisted on business as usual: convert the 500-escudos notes as quickly as possible into pounds, florins and francs.

He knew the dangerous crisis was approaching rapidly on the afternoon of November 29th. He received a wire from his brother, Antonio, in The Hague: the Ministry of Foreign Affairs had recalled him urgently to Lisbon for "consultation."

Throughout the *Seculo* campaign there had been many insinuations about a once-penniless Portuguese diplomat who now sported new cars and gave elaborate receptions abroad—even though only a year before he had written a bitter letter to a Lisbon daily complaining about the inadequate pay Portugal gave its Ministers abroad.

The description fitted only Antonio Bandeira. On November 29th the Ministry of Foreign Affairs ordered Antonio Bandeira recalled.

On the Sud Express to Lisbon Antonio weighed his position carefully. How closely could he be tied to his brother's associates? There were the diplomatic courier passes he had signed for Marang. Surely the clever fellow had destroyed those long ago. The many telegrams sent to Portuguese Ministry in The Hague by the others? Why, those were only to the Minister's brother who was living there occasionally. And finally, the contracts—the magic documents that made possible the entire banknote emission. Fortunately he had insisted José keep them and they were now in Fie Carelsen's safekeeping.

All considered, Antonio concluded, his position was still strong. Obviously what was called for was not the bowed head but the outraged heart. On December 3rd when he was resting in one of his brother's estates outside Lisbon he wrote the Minister of Foreign Affairs:

When I received your telegram recalling me to Lisbon I was in bed with a relapse of the influenza I had suffered shortly before. As this relapse was quite serious my doctor let me travel lying down if I took medicine every hour. Although the state of my health prevents my going to the Ministry, I am at your entire disposal. . . .

The campaign in *O Seculo* is even more scandalous in that it has brought in my name, too. Although the campaign is anonymous and does not cite a single charge, fact or document I demand a complete inquiry into my activities in Holland, an inquiry designed to discover if I directly or indirectly . . . ever intervened, informed or influenced no matter whom regarding the acquisition abroad of the capital for the A&M Bank or any other act related to that Bank. . . .

He closed with the standard official greeting of the time:

"S. e F." (Saude e fraternidade, or Health and Fraternity, the slogan of the Republic. Later changed by the Salazar Administration to "A bem da Naçio"—For the Good of the Nation.)

OPORTO, PORTUGAL /
December 4, 1925

THERE ARE FOUR kinds of readers, Samuel Taylor Coleridge wrote early in the 19th century when most of his countrymen couldn't read. The first kind is

> like the hour-glass; and their reading being as the sand, it runs in and out, and leaves not a vestige behind. A second is like the sponge, which imbibes everything, and returns it in nearly the same state, only a little dirtier. A third is like a jelly-bag, allowing all that is pure to pass away, retaining only the refuse and dregs. And the fourth is like the slaves in the diamond mines of Golconda, who, casting aside all that is worthless, retain only pure gems.

There was a fifth kind Coleridge had not yet encountered. It was the semi-literate reader who read as he ran and jumped to wrong conclusions. Such a reader was Manoel Lutero de Sousa of Oporto.

In Portugal today a man is considered literate by the authorities if he can *trace* his name onto a document.* De Sousa was far more literate. He could read *and* write and fancied that he had even developed a higher form of literacy: reading between the lines.

On his daily walks from his small apartment across the metal bridge spanning the Douro River—the first important work of that French engineer, Eiffel,—he read newspapers. Walking as he read he absorbed the allegations made against the Bank of Angola & Metropole: its mysterious wealth, its broad, dangerous plans.

On the Iberian peninsula the division between Spain and Portugal is not just geographical. The difference in temperament is far more important: the Spaniards have a sense of drama, the Portuguese have common sense.

On this morning's walk to work as a teller for the money-changer, A. P. da Cunha, de Sousa suddenly knew that the newspapers were missing the whole point of the Bank of Angola & Metropole operations: their notes were counterfeit. That had to be the secret, the source of its great wealth.

At work he carefully studied several of the 500-escudos notes that his employer got from the local branch of the A&M Bank. Alfred Pinto da Cunha, the owner of the shop, had an arrangement with the Bank to be on the lookout for foreign exchange. They would buy it at a premium. Since such operations were illegal, da Cunha would remove the ledger sheets for these deals as soon as he paid out the 500-escudos notes to customers who came in with dollars or pounds.

The more de Sousa studied the notes the more convinced he was they were counterfeits. Admittedly, it was very hard to tell the difference between the A&M Bank's notes and those he knew

* In the newspapers I often read this pitiful sentence: "The people must be taught to read" and I say to myself, What shall they read? It is education and undesirable literature, these are our enemies.
—Antonio de Oliveira Salazar.

came direct from the Bank of Portugal but he was sure there were distinctions. These must be *expert* counterfeits. And that, of course would explain why his boss destroyed the ledger sheets so furtively.

He excused himself and left the store to go to the Bank of Portugal branch where a friend worked. He told of his suspicions and the destroyed ledger sheets. The friend took him into the branch's manager and de Sousa told it again.

Ordinarily the manager would have simply asked for the suspicious notes and sent them on to Lisbon for study if they weren't obvious counterfeits such that he could detect them. But these weren't ordinary times. Everyone knew the Bank of A&M was up to *something*. Could counterfeit notes be the answer? It didn't seem likely and he remembered how the Bank of Portugal had laid to rest rumors about these 500-escudos notes in May. Still, there was the business of the destroyed ledger sheets. Even if the notes weren't counterfeit there was probably an illegal foreign exchange racket going on in da Cunha's shop.

So on this Friday in December the branch manager put in a phone call to the Bank of Portugal in Lisbon. He spoke to Assis Camilo, a director, who had fought bitterly in the summer to prevent the Banking Council from granting a bank permit to the Bank of Angola & Metropole.

The telephone connection was a normal one which meant every other word uttered in Oporto was heard in Lisbon. And some of those heard were misinterpreted by Camilo, who heard only what he wanted to.

What he heard was that there were *dozens* of counterfeit 500-escudos notes in Oporto; they had come from the branch of the A&M Bank. He heard that the Bank was financing many money-changers in illegal schemes to get foreign currency. He heard that the records of such deals were carefully destroyed every day. He heard enough. He took the news to another Bank of Portugal director, Dr. Ruy Ennes Ulrich. In the excited re-telling there were now *hundreds* of counterfeit bills coming from the suspect bank.

By that afternoon the governor and vice governor of the Bank of Portugal heard the story. They called in Dr. Teixeira Direito, who was both Judge of criminal investigation and an Inspector of Commercial Banking. Later that afternoon Dr. Direito and several key employes of the Bank of Portugal—including the Bank's great expert on counterfeits, José Pedroso—took the overnight train to Oporto.

When de Sousa learned that his warning had been heeded, that his suspicions were being investigated by leading officials of the Bank of Portugal itself, he remembered one of his favorite stories. It was "The Mandarin" by Portugal's great 19th century novelist, José de Eça de Queiroz.

Like Manoel da Sousa, Teodoro, the hero of "The Mandarin" was also a poor Portuguese clerk. Then the devil tempted him: just by touching a certain hand-bell he could kill an old mandarin in China and acquire his splendid fortune of $114,000,000. The clerk touches the bell, the mandarin dies and Teodoro becomes the troubled Croesus of Lisbon.

Now Manoel de Sousa had touched another kind of bell and soon mandarin Alves Reis would die. Of course, things are not as well-ordered in life as in fiction so there was no chance Manoel would come into a fortune. But surely, a grateful Bank of Portugal would reward him generously for his warning.

On Saturday morning, December 5th, the Bank of Portugal squad first sought further reinforcements from the Oporto police. Then, as one of the Bank officials, Campos e Sa, later recalled, a guard was put around the Bank of Angola & Metropole; Adriano Silva, the branch manager, was arrested in the street and sent to prison. Then

> . . . we presented ourselves at the money changer's, da Cunha. We asked for the books of account for purposes of verification. . . . We made a rapid search on the first floor and observed new notes of 500 escudos. Then our technical official, Pedroso, stated that these notes were genuine, that is, of the same plate issued by the Bank, without the least doubt, which moreover all of us observed.

The Bank of Portugal reconnaissance force was suddenly aware that they had worked themselves into a somewhat embarrassing position. Without warrant or evidence they had consigned an innocent branch bank manager to prison and ransacked a reputable moneychanger's premises. The looks cast in the direction of Manoel de Sousa, the original informant, grew less friendly as the day wore on.

Casting around more desperately, the searchers went next door to the jewelry shop of David Pinto da Cunha, a brother of the suspect moneychanger. They found more of the new 500-escudos notes there. These were also examined by Pedroso and

> were found to be of the same plate as issued by the Bank, Pedroso stating that it is absolutely impossible to engrave a forged plate with the same perfection and evenness, which led to his conviction that these notes were good.

In their increasing frustration the Bank of Portugal officials consigned the jewelry store's manager and bookkeeper to prison and confiscated all the account books. Several in the party began to wish they hadn't been so eager to go to Oporto. Soon, each began eyeing the other covertly to see who could be blamed with safety. The Bank of Angola & Metropole had powerful friends. There would be much invective oratory in the Chamber of Deputies and thundering editorials about the dictatorial iniquities of the Bank of Portugal and its police minions. Every now and then, one of the Bank's raiding party would ask the counterfeit expert, Pedroso, "You're *sure?*" He would nod glumly. A distressed Campos e Sa continues:

> The three individuals having been sent to prison, we went on to the branch of the Banco Angole e Metropole, which had since morning been guarded by the police with instructions not to permit the outgoing of money, nor the opening of safes and there we ordered the safe in the private office of the director to be opened. . . . All the notes were of the 500 escudos type and arranged in packets of 20 notes folded in two but completely new. On examining them Pedroso said they were genuine, without the smallest doubt, which as a matter of fact all of us felt compelled to confirm.

It was the blackest moment of the cold, wet day and several members of the party inwardly began framing excuses and apologies to the unjustly imprisoned men. More than once de Sousa was asked with increasing hostility just where were the *forged* notes he had mentioned. Quite frightened, he now remembered that Teodoro, the clerk in "The Mandarin" had a great many desperate troubles, too, after he touched the bell that killed the Chinese millionaire.

Although the escudos notes had been pronounced genuine again and again, Campos e Sa, kept studying the packets they were in and

> noted that the numbering of the notes was *not* consecutive nor the series the same, which would not be the case if they had come directly from the Bank of Portugal to this Bank, which their condition of absolutely new banknotes appeared to demonstrate, . . . then seeing the hope of coming across forged notes vanish . . . and being already convinced of their having been made from the original plate stolen from the factory from which the genuine notes came, I asked the Inspector to seize all the contents of this safe in order that a minute examination of the said banknotes should be made. . . .

Pedroso was in the unhappy position of having to disabuse his colleagues of a popular notion of criminal fiction.

Stealing the plates alone would *not* solve all the criminal's problems. He would have to have the proper and very expensive kind of press to handle the engraved plates; he would need exactly the same paper; an expensive and intricate numbering system—so rare that even the Bank of Portugal hadn't beeen able to obtain such a device at any price.

Campos e Sa was beyond logic by now. The plates *had* to be stolen. Pedroso simply didn't know what enormous ingenuities clever criminals were capable of. To *prove* the plate had been stolen Campos e Sa ordered the 500-escudos notes taken to the Bank of Portugal where they would be compared with genuine banknotes.

Meanwhile, the Bank of Portugal crew became increasingly aware that their high-handed methods and almost total lack of hard evidence was going to make their stay in Oporto quite difficult. Campos e Sa got a hint of just *how* difficult on Saturday evening when the manager of the Bank of Angola branch, Moura Coutinha, was

> interrogated by Dr. Teixeira Direito and the Chief of the Police, Pereira dos Santos, who thereupon set him at liberty and then communicated to me by the said Chief of Police his suspicions regarding the technical official Pedroso, from which I inferred similar suspicions regarding myself, as his opinion was that

the notes, though forged, had issued from the Bank of Portugal.

I had confirmation of these suspicions when on the next day he hindered us from being present at the interrogation of Adriano Silva, owing to his making, it was said, accusations against the employes of the Bank of Portugal.

The Bank of Portugal men spent a miserable, haunted night at their hotel in Oporto. The police in the lobby, they had been assured by the Police Chief, were for *their* protection but they had no illusions. The Chief, they knew, was half-convinced all of them were in on some enormous conspiracy and given *any* kind of proof would thrust them into jail, too.

Then at approximately 11:30 on Sunday morning, December 6, 1925, the long, incredible run of Alves Reis' luck ended. Ended because one of the bank investigators may have read Nietzsche's warning:

> One seldom rushes into a single error. Rushing into the first one, one always does too much. Hence one usually commits another; and this time does too little.

The end came because one—Luis Alberto de Campos e Sa of the Bank of Portugal—did too much. The second time.

On this Sunday morning, Campos e Sa later recalled,

> as a result of the work of separation of the banknotes which I had ordered to be carried out at the Bank of Portugal branch office, there appeared the first duplication of numbers and series, which was an undoubted proof of forgery and I immediately telephoned the governor of the Bank of Portugal in Lisbon. I resolved to go to Lisbon immediately in order that on Monday the branch office could be authorized with instructions or money, in anticipation of the panic which the news of the forgery would provoke.

❋   ❋   ❋   ❋   ❋

THE HAGUE / December 5, 1925

OSCAR ZENHA, José's secretary and gambling companion, arrived at Marang's home late in the afternoon after a weary train trip from Lisbon. José sent him to get a power of attorney so that the Bank's lawyers in Lisbon could institute suit for libel against *Seculo*. It had been José's idea that Marang should sue. Antonio, who had also been named, felt it was beneath the dignity of a foreign service official. Besides, as a former newspaperman he knew how dangerous it was to sue. The old journalistic adage had the same bite all over the world—don't sue: the paper might prove it.

> The power of attorney was ready, [Zenha recalled], and . . . during a conversation with Marang the phone rang. He answered. It was the Havas News Agency. They had just gotten word that the Angola & Metropole Bank in Oporto had been raided by the police who had seized many false notes in its vaults. Marang fainted.

Oscar, a calm fellow, didn't. He got the next train to Paris where he knew some girls. He didn't return to Lisbon for four months—not until the girls, his money, and zest, ran out.

✿   ✿   ✿   ✿   ✿

ABOARD THE S.S. ADOLF WOERMAN / December 6, 1925

THE RETURN VOYAGE had been relatively tranquil. There had been the wireless message from Ferreira about the attacks in *O Seculo*

175

but Alves Reis who knew how easily Portuguese papers were bribed didn't worry about that too much. Obviously his acquisitions in Angola had begun to alarm certain entrenched interests but that was to be expected.

> I was returning to Lisbon by sea for the eighth time. It was a sad and rainy winter morning . . . the boat was anchored in the bay near Cascais awaiting the pilot boat. Suddenly a speedboat came alongside and I heard my name called out. Some friends had come to warn me—that handcuffs awaited me in Lisbon. They suggested I flee.

Jail awaited him, his friends warned, because of the results of an investigation into the affairs of the Bank of Angola's branch office in Oporto. The Bank had counterfeit banknotes in its vaults. There was also a warrant for Herr Hennies.

Hennies came up on deck when the speedboat approached. His Portuguese was fluent as a result of his long stay in Brazil and he understood the shouted warnings.

After the speedboat left Hennies had a talk with his partner.

"You are not going to let yourself be arrested, are you?"

"I haven't committed any crime. I won't let myself become the sacrificial goat just because my friends in the Bank of Portugal lost to the other faction."

Surely, Hennies insisted, it would be easier to continue the fight—and help his friends in the Bank—by going abroad. There he would have access to various deposits and documents or whatever would be needed.

No, I must stay and fight, Reis went on. I have photographic copies of the contracts and all the evidence I need to prove that I was *ordered* to carry out the banknote issues by the governor and vice governor of the Bank of Portugal.

Hennies countered: Why handicap yourself by having to prove these things from a jail cell? Surely you would be far more effective out of Portugal. Believe me, I will see to it that we both get away safely. If it's a matter of money . . .

It wasn't money. Reis pulled out a readily negotiable bearer bond for 300,000 escudos ($15,000) that had been entrusted to him by the manager of an Angola plantation for delivery to Lisbon.

Hennies tried another gambit. Admiralty lawyers had an expression: peril point. This was when you passed the point at which you cannot recover from your own peril. If Alves Reis stayed on the ship to be arrested he would be well past the peril point. But he could avoid the peril simply by leaving the ship now as Hennies was going to do.

Reis was adamant, hardened by the vanity of villainy. He would stay—and fight! The odds against him weren't as bad as Hennies thought. Reis recalled the many other great financial scandals Portugal had endured in the past five years. All of them involved corruption in high places. Invariably the guilty were not convicted—and the great profits were kept by the rascals. Everyone had powerful friends happy to share in the illicit profits.

For a wild moment Reis was tempted to ask Hennies: Did *he* think the contracts were genuine? Did he know that Artur Alves Reis, the Lisbon businessman they had scorned when he was thrust into the Oporto jail, had taken in Marang and Hennies, those shrewd international businessmen?

But Reis resisted the childish query his pride tempted him to pose. He could still use Hennies and Marang—but only if they believed that their partner was the tool of a great inner conspiracy in the Bank of Portugal itself. If he had rigged all this by himself—and hoped to get away with it—why he was clearly a madman. And who would want anything to do with him in that case?

Hennies took stock of his own position. He had befriended the German ship captain. It wouldn't be difficult for him to leave the ship with the pilot boat coming at 7:00 A.M. He had with him a considerable cash reserve plus some letters of credit and the link to his first life, the old passport. It was time to molt the Adolf Hennies identity, to become the other self he had been until 1914.

At 6 A.M. Reis took his farewells of his wife. It wasn't tearful and sentimental. Reis coached her in several things she would have to say at different times; lies she would have to utter with conviction.

The police came on board at 9 A.M. and served the arrest

order on Artur Alves Reis, chairman of the Bank of Angola & Metropole. On shore, inconspicuous in a waterside cafe, Adolf Hennies saw his brilliant partner led away in a police car. He quickly walked to the quay and got into a boat he had arranged to take him back to the *Adolf Woerman*. The Captain wouldn't sail until his wealthy compatriot had returned to the ship.

LISBON / December 6, 1925

THE CITY'S SUNDAY calm was interrupted by more than just the street shoe-shine boys who gave Europe's noisiest shine. The Bank of Portugal had key employes in the building and special police squads were running to different parts of the city. They traveled almost as fast as the rumors about the Bank of Angola & Metropole. As for Alves Reis,

> after arrest aboard ship I was taken to the civil governor of Lisbon and then by order of Dr. Crispiniano da Fonseca, the head of the Criminal Investigation Department I was now transferred to the questioning cell of the Pampulaha precinct where I would be questioned by Dr. Fonseca tomorrow.

For a man who had been in jail before Reis took this incarceration hard.

> The horrible hole I was thrust in poisoned every decent instinct in my heart. The damp, infected and morbid atmosphere of a cell with no air and no light and a strict incommunicability to which I was subjected showed me the inhumanity of the so-called elites of the Republic. If such methods were to be used to wrench my secret from me . . . I would be stupid to surrender to my executioners. That was when I began to commit my greatest crime— I would not give up. Scandal would be my revenge and I coolly, calmly planned to attack innocent people—the Governor and Vice

Governor of the Bank of Portugal, the High Commissioner of Angola, politicians. I wanted to drag them all down in my cursed wake. I began planning my attack against them during the hours I lay on my jail cot.

Late that afternoon Campos e Sa phoned from Oporto to give the terrible news to the governor of the Bank. There were so far four or five genuine banknotes of the 500-escudos type with duplicated numbers and series. He suspected there might be "tens and tens" if not thousands.* There was absolutely no way to tell the notes apart. Much worse was the final news Campos e Sa gave. It looked as if a director of the Bank of Portugal, Dr. Lobo D'Avila Lima, may have had a hand in the great conspiracy.

Two of the key employes of the Bank of Angola & Metropole in Oporto said they believed the notes they handled were genuine because they had often seen Dr. Avila Lima in intimate conversation with José Bandeira in the Angola Bank's main office in Lisbon.

When the Bank of Portugal's directors were rounded up by phone for an emergency meeting at 8:00 that evening Dr. Avila Lima was not called.

At the meeting Bank Governor Camacho gave his fellow directors the details of the awful news from Oporto. Then the Board decided

to immediately withdraw from circulation the notes of the said plate and to have notices published in the papers of Lisbon and Oporto, advising the public that the cashing of said notes will be effected at once at the chief office of the Bank and at all its branches.

The directors reluctantly concluded there was no other choice. Since the duplicated notes could not be told from the legitimate originals they could not expect innocent holders of the notes to bear the burden. The Bank would have to issue notes of other denominations to all.

Another emergency meeting was called for noon on Monday, December 7th, and this time Dr. Avila Lima showed up. He was furious he wasn't notified of the Sunday meeting and at the slur

---

* The Portuguese equivalent of "dozens and dozens."

cast on his name. When he insisted on attending the noon meeting his colleagues

> urged him to absent himself, owing to the delicacy of the present circumstances. The fact that he had relations with one or more of the heads of the Bank of Angola & Metropole . . . might become public and the knowledge of these facts would create a really difficult situation for the Bank and the management.

Dr. Avila Lima refused to budge from his chair in the Director Room. The whole truth, he said, was that he had conversed with José Bandeira, whom he knew slightly, two or three times. This he had done only at the request of a friendly banker who had a large block of shares in the newspaper *O Seculo* which the Bank of Angola was interested in acquiring. Nothing more.

His fellow directors stonily refused to let him attend the meeting. The miasma of suspicion had begun to spread—even before Alves Reis' campaign had begun. Notes made from the same plates the Bank itself used could only mean that Bank officials must have been involved. Who else besides Avila Lima was in the plot?

The telegraphed notice to the Bank of Portugal branches ordering the exchange of notes stressed that all holders of twenty or more notes of the 500-escudos Vasco da Gama type, would have to identify themselves very carefully and sign a receipt for the new notes.

At 2:25 in the afternoon of December 7th Camacho Rodrigues telegraphed Waterlow in London:

> GREAT FALSIFICATION NOTES OF FIVE HUNDRED ESCUDOS. SEND EXPERT LISBON URGENTLY TO EXAMINE. MAKE INVESTIGATIONS ON YOUR SIDE.

The wire arrived after Sir William had left for the day and it wasn't until noon the following day, December 8th, that Waterlow replied:

> ARRANGING FOR EXPERT TO LEAVE LONDON IMMEDIATELY. WILL WIRE YOU ACTUAL TIME AND DEPARTURE. WRITE FULLY AND SEND SPECIMENS.

All over Portugal long lines formed in front of the branches of the Bank of Portugal to exchange the 500-escudos notes. The exchanges took time, and men on the lines had lots of time to exchange the latest news: the Bank of Portugal itself was involved; several directors were already on their way to prison; it had been a German plot—didn't they have so much experience making billions of their own inflated currency?—in order to acquire Portuguese colonies. With each telling the rumors grew. So did the riots in Lisbon and Oporto near the banks.

❋   ❋   ❋   ❋   ❋

LONDON / December 9, 1925

THIS MORNING'S ISSUE of *The Telegraph* which Sir William read as he was driven to the Waterlow office in the City carried a short item on page one:

PORTUGAL FORGED NOTES
MANUFACTURED IN RUSSIA

Lisbon. Dec. 8. Sensational developments are anticipated as a result of the discovery of the issue by a newly established banking concern of forged notes amounting to £600,000 [$3,000,000] or more. The notes which are being withdrawn from circulation were, it is alleged, made in Russia, and the police believe that they are duplicates of those manufactured by an English firm of note engravers to the order of the Portuguese Government. The banking establishment was opened some time ago with a high sounding Colonial title, but the moving spirit was a Dutchman of dubious financial stability who obtained credentials from the Portuguese Minister in Holland who has since been recalled by the Portuguese Government.

Now for the first time Sir William knew that the notes his firm had run off for Marang and his group were the ones being recalled by the Bank of Portugal. There had been no overprinting of ANGOLA on them, apparently.

He wasn't surprised to find that Colonel José Auguste dos Santos Lucas of the Portuguese Embassy in London was most anxious to talk to him. He also found a memo from the bookkeeping department: Marang still hadn't paid his bill of £458 4s. 6d. for his trunks and personal printing.

The Colonel, a Portuguese Army veteran, had been assigned to the matter the day before. The Ambassador received a wire from Lisbon about the forged notes and the likelihood that several directors of the closed Bank of Angola & Metropole probably had sizeable accounts with London banks.

Colonel Lucas went to the foreign branches of the Midland Bank and the Westminster Bank. At the latter the Colonel was told the Banco de Angola had deposited as much as £76,000 (about $380,000) but that the great part had been withdrawn. At the Midland Bank he found a deposit of more than £20,000 in the name of José Santos Bandeira. The Bank refused to stop payment on any checks that might be presented by Bandeira unless so ordered by a British court or unless the Portuguese Ambassador or the Bank of Portugal would agree to compensate them if Bandeira sued them. But they agreed to postpone payments for 24 hours if any checks did come through.

With a Scotland Yard Inspector he knew, F. J. Eveleigh, Colonel Lucas now called on Sir William Waterlow. There were certain careful amenities to be observed. Sir William was, after all, an alderman of the City of London which has its own police force and Scotland Yard could only come into the City with permission.

At the meeting with Sir William, Colonel Lucas later recalled,

> I explained to Sir William the purpose of our visit, then asked him to give me every assistance. Sir William told me at the beginning that he divined what the purpose of our visit was by reason of the notice published in *The Telegraph* of this morning. I asked him to whom he had delivered the notes. He replied, without any hesitation, that it was to Marang, and that the notes were not false because his firm had manufactured them under the conviction that it was fulfilling orders and instructions of Senhor I.

Camacho Rodrigues. Sir William with good will acceded to the
request to show me these orders and instructions, giving us various documents for inspection . . . I asked Sir William to furnish
me with copies of these two documents . . . Sir William asked
what my opinion was as regards the authenticity of the Contracts
and also of the letters from Senhor Camacho. I replied that I considered such documents to be forgeries.

At the Embassy, Colonel Lucas was up until 2:30 A.M. en-
coding his long telegram to the Foreign Affairs Office, telling
about the contracts.

After the Colonel left, Sir William's cousin, fellow director
and great enemy—Edgar L. Waterlow—came to his office. He
had learned enough of the details to understand that Sir William
had, with the knowledge of only two other Waterlow directors,
entered into an extraordinarily strange banknote printing contract
with a Dutch stranger. Edgar wanted a Board meeting called the
first thing on Thursday morning, December 10th.

At the meeting that morning Sir William gave his fellow directors some of the background of the Marang order and left the
impression that Waterlow's was now caught in a cross fire between two factions of the Bank of Portugal. But Sir William also
sensed a resentment by many of his directors that they had not
known of the Marang contracts and orders.

Later that morning Colonel Lucas came for the serial numbers on the second batch of banknotes delivered to Marang in the
summer and fall of 1925. These he wired to Lisbon. Then on the
evening of December 11th his certainty that the contracts were
forged was shattered. He found two wires from Lisbon: Camacho Rodrigues, the governor, and Mota Gomes, the vice governor of the Bank of Portugal had been arrested as accomplices in
the banknote case on the order of the Examining Magistrate in
charge.

He woke the Ambassador to discuss the terrible news of the
arrests in Lisbon. *If* they were indeed involved and with them the
Bank of Portugal itself, there would be incredible financial difficulties ahead for Portugal. They must fight for time to get further
details from Lisbon. As long as the news didn't get out, Portugal's
credit would be preserved for a while. Desperate measures were
called for and Colonel Lucas, the Embassy's special fix-it man for

security, police, intelligence and press matters, was the very one to do it. As he remembered it later, he had

> a conference with a senior official of Reuter's Agency in order to request him that in the event of his having received or receiving any news—relating to the arrests—not to send same to the newspapers. This official promised to satisfy the wishes of the Ambassador. In this way publication of the news was prevented.

That evening Lucas had another coded wire from Lisbon. This one ordered him to ask for the help of Scotland Yard in the arrest and extradition of a key Waterlow employe who was criminally involved in the conspiracy. Someone named Henry Gerard Wolfgang Romer. Similar wires were being sent to the police of the other European capitals.

*   *   *   *   *

LISBON / December 12, 1925

UNDER THE LAWS of the Portuguese Republic no citizen could be detained under suspicion for more than eight days. And no one could be held incommunicado for more than 48 hours. But these were clearly extraordinary times and many laws of the Republic were cast aside. Alves Reis was going to be held incommunicado for 108 days. Later, he wrote:

> I was so indignant at this high-handed treatment I decided to fight them their own way: I falsified documents and letters such as receipts allegedly signed by Camacho Rodrigues and others. . . . Some I had smuggled to Holland to convince Marang that the documents were genuine. . . . I wanted to revenge myself on a justice that sought severe punishment at all costs . . . the voice

of conscience urged me to confess my crimes but my indignation
at these illegal methods forced me to fight. . . .

In his cell he created a small but quite effective plant for the
manufacture of incriminating letters and documents. He was, a
friend recalled, like a fire hose, obtaining accuracy and velocity
from confinement.

Another law, this one international, was also shattered. The
inviolability of an embassy was disregarded and on December
10th investigators entered the Venezuelan Ministry—actually the
apartment of Count Planas-Suarez—where they found 85,000 of
the 500-escudos notes. On December 11th the Papal Count was
allowed to leave the country. He went to Paris.

Investigation of the great crime halted for two days when
Dr. Costa Santos, Attorney General of the Republic who was
given charge of the investigation was suddenly dropped. There
was a receipt from Alves Reis to show Dr. Costa Santos had once
received a 500,000-escudos gift (some $25,000) from Alves Reis.
This was one of many forgeries Reis concocted.

Appointed to replace Costa Santos was Dr. José Pinto da
Magalhães. He talked to Alves Reis for many hours and emerged
from the cell certain that high officers of the Bank of Portugal
had authorized Reis to get the notes printed and circulated.

As Chief Investigator he had unusual powers and used them
quickly. Just how, the *Diario de Noticias*, a leading Lisbon daily,
described on December 13th:

ACT OF INSANITY?

A serious occurrence took place yesterday which can only be
attributed to a sudden disturbance in the mind of the Chief Investigating Judge, Dr. Pinto de Magalhães. During an exchange
of conversation with a Foreign Ministry Official, the latter asked
the Judge what he believed was the consensus of opinion in the
Bank of Portugal regarding the counterfeit note case. The Judge
grew suddenly excited, walked around the room violently, and
with wild gestures shouted to the Foreign Office official that he
had naturally come to make insinuations on behalf of the Government.

"I am working hard to do my duty, and if I am not doing any
more it's because I cannot." He then shouted very loud that he
couldn't stand it any more. A crowd of people flocked into the

room. . . . The Judge then dashed over to Dr. Camacho Rodrigues and Dr. Mota Gomes who were also present and grabbing
them by their coat lapels cried out in a voice that was heard all
over the building:

"You are under arrest! At my orders! You are under arrest in
the name of the law!" Then addressing a policeman who was
there, the Judge said:

"Take them to a Police Station. Right away."

The two Bank officials were taken to a room next to the Civil
Governor's office.

This rapid and unexpected scene left everyone astounded and
the Judge's excitement continued. Questioned by some present
who pointed out the gravity of his order, the Judge said:

"You are right! This is really serious. If there is nothing in the
investigation that is against these men, I'll put a bullet in my
brain."

Meanwhile the two Bank of Portugal Governors were detained
and the Prime Minister was apprised of the fact. He informed the
President and ordered the Judge to call at the Prime Minister's
office for a conference. Until 3 A.M. there were no signs of the
Judge and the Prime Minister ordered the release of the two Bank
of Portugal Governors.

But Judge Pinto Magalhães continued to be the Chief Investigator of the case. He had long ago ordered the prisoner,
Alves Reis to have certain amenities. *O Seculo* complained in a
long front page article:

> It is strange that the Judge should have authorized Alves Reis
> to furnish in princely fashion the jail at the Lapa Police Station
> in which he is and which already contains sofas, a dressing table,
> mirrors, rugs, etc. The mastermind criminal has converted his cell
> into a kind of Thousand and One Nights cave. We don't know
> whether he installed central heating but it seems nothing is miss-
> ing for one who is used to the social amenities and receives fre-
> quent visitors. He enjoys a special status that softens imprison-
> ment and encourages him to stand up to adversity and all en-
> deavors to force him to speak the truth. Despite his incommu-
> nicability Reis knows all that goes on outside, reads the papers
> and receives the visits of his wife who is in touch with his lawyer.
> In the Chief Investigator, Reis has found the ideal lawyer for his
> defense and his great protector. Were it not for him, the mystery
> of the A and M Bank would have been unravelled long ago. . . .

Things were even worse than *Seculo* suspected. Reis had won the investigating Judge almost completely. The Judge made it a point of addressing Reis as "Your Excellency" and let him confer with the other prisoners such as José Bandeira and Francisco Ferreira. To show his great trust in Reis, the Judge would leave the room during these useful conferences.

Shortly after the Judge ordered the arrest of the governor and vice governor of the Bank of Portugal he called on Reis in his cell and informed him of the arrest. He asked Reis not to "let him down." Reis replied that the good Judge had done well in arresting the two men and that he could be at ease. In a few days he would have more evidence of their complicity. Irrefutable evidence.

The Judge wasn't the only man in Lisbon who firmly believed Reis and the other prisoners were merely the tools of an incredible but real plot by the governor and vice governor of the Bank of Portugal.

Meanwhile the Bank of Portugal at its head office and in the 34 branches had exchanged more than 500,000 of the suspect 500-escudos notes for notes of different denominations.

In the midst of the sensational press stories of the great banknote case, most readers missed a minor item: The Bank of Portugal had voted a reward of 3,000 escudos ($150) to Manoel E. de Sousa of Oporto "for services given early in December by providing this Bank with information respecting the forging of notes of the 500-escudos type." The man who had helped collapse the splendid edifice of chicanery by his timely call—even if his information was somewhat inaccurate—was voted the reward conditionally. Manoel would get only 500 escudos a month for six months. The Bank wasn't *that* hard up. There were reports Manoel was a compulsive lottery player. They didn't want him splurging all the money on tickets—and then coming to them for still more.

*   *   *   *   *

LONDON / December 12, 1925

THERE HAD BEEN another directors' meeting at Waterlow's on Friday morning, December 11th. As Sir William later recalled,

> at my request my directors agreed that I should go personally to Lisbon with Mr. Vivian Goodman, another director who is the son of director Frederick Goodman, and Mr. George U. Rose, the Manager of our Bank Note Department, in order to give the Bank of Portugal and the Portuguese Government any assistance that we could. We left that afternoon by the 4 o'clock train from Paris.
>
> The directors heard several discordant items:
>
> —The Governor and Vice Governor of the Bank of Portugal had been arrested—and then ordered released by the Prime Minister.
> —The Portuguese Ambassador in London had refused to receive Sir William.
> —The Bank of Portugal was encountering a shortage of banknotes. They would like Waterlow's to print more banknotes for them of denominations other than the Vasco da Gama 500-escudos note. But these new notes must *not* bear the insignia of Waterlow & Sons.
> —Waterlow's solicitor suggested that the party going to Lisbon first get a safe-conduct from the Portuguese Government. When this was not forthcoming immediately Sir William decided that the group must go anyway.

Edgar Waterlow was busy this Saturday morning, December 12th. He had a long talk with Henry Romer who told of his warnings to Sir William a year ago on the Marang contracts. Romer was particularly vexed Sir William had not chosen him to go along with the group visiting Lisbon. He told Edgar Waterlow:

> You know I could have been a great help to them in Lisbon . . . create a more pleasant atmosphere for the party and help them in many ways.

He still didn't know that orders for his arrest had been sent all over Europe; that the Bank of Portugal was convinced he was an important part of the huge conspiracy. How else could the

188

plotters have gotten the secret series and numbers key to the banknotes?

Roland Springall who was also interviewed this Saturday morning provided some useful but quite dangerous material for the dossier Edgar Waterlow was accumulating against his cousin. Used wisely, the dossier would help topple Sir William from the chairmanship of Waterlow's. And this time Edgar Waterlow would get the post he should have obtained in 1923 when the unfortunate scandal about his father and the de la Rue rebates deprived him of the chairmanship.

Springall told Edgar that when Marang called on the firm in July, 1925, to discuss the second issue of banknotes:

> Marang asked me for a list of the numbers and signatures already used on the banknotes supplied the Bank of Portugal in the 500-escudos notes. After being told by Frederick Goodman to supply this information to Marang, I got it from the books and gave it to Marang.

Edgar listened with horrified fascination. Not only had his firm supplied the plotters with the banknotes—he refused to believe the Bank of Portugal was in on the plot—but Waterlow's had even helped the criminals greatly by giving them the pattern of serial numbers and directors' names. Extremely useful, secret information, handed out like the time of day.

The data, Edgar knew, was quite dangerous. It did give him a weapon against one of Sir William's friendly directors, Frederick Goodman, but the information could be used with deadly effect against Waterlow & Sons if a damage suit materialized—as it probably would. This would have to be handled with great caution. He kept the dossier in a safe at home, where he also kept many of the more valuable items of his considerable postage stamp collection.

LISBON / December 14, 1925

THE WATERLOW PARTY arrived in Lisbon on Sunday evening, December 13th—with Lady Waterlow. She insisted. When they got out of the Sud Express there were hundreds in the station. "A very unpleasant experience," Sir William recalled. They had rooms awaiting them in the nearby Avenida Palace and there Sir William got the first of many shocks. In the lobby he spotted George T. Foxon, the special representative of Bradbury, Wilkinson, the rival banknote firm. The jackals were gathering, he observed bitterly to Goodman.

A *Daily Mail* correspondent sought out Sir William. Yes, things were terribly confused, he told the reporter. Waterlow's was anxious to do everything possible to help but it would have to proceed cautiously. For example, it had been asked to help the Bank of Portugal by furnishing new banknotes during the current exchange of the suspect 500-escudos banknotes. But, of course, he went on, "Waterlow's would not undertake the printing of new banknote orders except on proper authority." Communication being a terribly inexact art, the reporter heard Sir William say that he wouldn't give the Bank of Portugal a single banknote until he knew who in the Bank was *really* authorized to give such an order. After all, there was the strange business of two top officers of the Bank being arrested.

Early the next morning, Monday, Sir William

accompanied by Mr. Rose and Mr. Walker (our Resident Agent in Lisbon) proceeded to the Bank where the Board of Directors were at that time in session. We asked to see the Directors but were informed they could not see us as the matter was in the hands of the Police and we must go to the Office of the Civil Governor of the town. This we demurred from doing. They also took exception to a statement I was reported to have made to the correspondent of the *Daily Mail* the night before. . . . On our pressing for an interview with the Directors, Mr. Ruy Ulrich, who speaks English, came out from the Board and confirmed that they could not see us but that they would send for the Judge who was investigating the case to come and see us. Mr. Ulrich at first declining to shake hands with Mr. Rose, believing him to be Mr. Romer, but shook hands with Mr. Rose directly his mistake was pointed out. The Judge having been sent for, we thought it advisable to telephone for the British Consul and he came at once . . . the excitement at the Bank was very high . . . I was not surprised but they all lost their heads and one could not discuss anything with them. We endeavored to keep our heads.

It was not easy to do so, when you are being treated as a criminal. As Sir William was to say, later,

. . . and for all practical purposes we were under arrest. I had to resent the conduct and treatment of us more than I can say, but I was so anxious to be of assistance that I swallowed my pride. . . .

Judge Pinto Magalhães questioned the Waterlow men all week, sometimes up to 9:00 P.M. During one very long interrogation, reports appeared in the afternoon papers that Sir William had been arrested. A reporter went to Lady Waterlow at the hotel to tell her of her husband's arrest. Fortunately, Sir William appeared 30 minutes later to end that false account.

The Judge was friendly and once even volunteered to the Britons "that there were no honest trade practices in Portugal."

On two occasions the Judge, Sir William recalled,

produced the prisoner Reis and he asserted in front of us that the Contract on which we acted was a genuine Contract and had been given him by the Governor of the Bank of Portugal.

Sir William was asked by the Judge about the opinion he had formed of Romer, Rose, Walker and Goodman. Sir William was forthright:

Romer was a very excitable person but honest; Rose and Goodman are persons of highly proved honesty; and that Walker whom he had known for sixteen years is also most honest.

Again and again the Judge came back to (1) the letter of January 7, 1924, which Sir William had *mailed* to Camacho Rodrigues but had never been delivered and (2) how the plotters had obtained the key to the banknote numbers and accompanying directors' signatures.

Everything that happened at the Criminal Investigation Department got into the Press the next day and the atmosphere was
exceedingly bad, as bad as it could possibly be, and I had come a
great many miles to endeavor to try to clear things up, whatever
had gone wrong, so far as one could, to put it right, and one was
met with this keeping you absolutely at arm's length. So I said to
Mr. Goodman, Junior, Well, we have got a lot of work in hand
for the Bank of Portugal. It's no good going on like this; we must
try to re-establish confidence with them.

The way to do that, the proper British way, was to stop all
this talk of suits and counter-suits and show faith in one another.
Walker was sent to the Bank as an emissary. He was received
and told the directors of his

profound regret regarding the matters that had occurred
which had caused great displeasure, both to the firm of Waterlow
and to himself . . . and to propose to the Bank as indemnifica-
tion to replace the notes of 500 escudos and to pay all the extraordinary expenses incurred by the Bank with respect to the banknote matter and being desirious of making a deposit with the Bank
of £ 50,000 as a token of confidence and esteem . . . Sir William
was convinced that after all this disagreeable matter was cleared
up, the Bank and the firm of Waterlow would become greater
friends than ever before.

Later in an interview with Dr. Ruy Ulrich, Sir William
repeated the deposit offer "as an earnest of our good will." But
Ulrich wanted to consider the money a partial "indemnity,"
which Sir William could not accept. He said

we could admit no liability but I agreed with him that when
the whole facts were known the matter should be carefully considered between us. He told me it was the intention of the Bank to
honour their contracts with us and they had shown this by the current invoice they had just paid . . . the amount of 500 escudos
notes paid out to date over and above the legitimate issue was
£ 170,000 [$850,000], and against that they had the assets of the
Angola Bank and certain balances at various Banks abroad which
they had attached.

On December 21st the Waterlow party arranged to leave
Lisbon. But the atmosphere during their stay had become in Sir
William's words "highly charged; electric" and Judge Pinto Mag-

alhães thought it wise for them to leave under assumed names. The police certificates said that the British subjects named

> Sir William Alfred Waterlow, Lady Waterlow, George Rose and V. Goodman may travel in the respective names of William Smith, Mrs. Smith, George Cooper and Jack Jones and in those names they may leave the territory of Portugal.

For the first time since his ancestor came to England in 1625 a Waterlow had to drop the proud name. Sir William was to be "William Smith." But the deception was quite pointless. The erratic Judge and some of his investigators came to the station to see the Waterlow party off. Since everybody knew the much-photographed Judge the Britons were readily recognizable. Still, they got off without any riots or outcries from the bystanders.

Only *Seculo* was still calling all good Portuguese to outrage, if not to arms. It's latest editorial, translated for the Waterlow party before they left, ran:

> We shall say it again: the Angola & Metropole scandal could only be possible in a country such as ours, where misery prevails. In another country of sound morality, or even a less venal morality, the Reis,' Marangs, Bandeiras and their ilk could never put into practice such a large-scale plan. This could only happen in a country where rottenness has corrupted all the fibres that make up the honor, the dignity and the prestige of a nation. We are living in the midst of social decay. All of the collective virtues have vanished. All the basic qualities of the Race, maintained by tradition through the centuries, through every calamity and sacrifice, have been throttled and despised by political gangs, greedy for money, no matter how acquired. Then there appeared Marang, a diplomat from a republic of blacks; Bandeira, the South African convict and then the Oporto thief, and then their trunks of 500 escudos notes. That was enough. Everyone bowed low before them. The gang's success was complete.

One of the Portuguese who read the editorial with fervent approval was a 36-year-old professor of economics at the University of Coimbra named Antonio de Oliveira Salazar. He was particularly interested in the case of the false banknotes. His doctoral thesis had been on the evolution of Portuguese currency.

✿   ✿   ✿   ✿   ✿

LISBON / December 24, 1925

THE DIRECTOR OF the Bank of Portugal finally decided to take the unprecedented step several of them had been threatening for the past two weeks: they would resign. Enough of the aspersions and accusations by Judge Pinto Magalhães!

They gathered at noon in the Directors' Room of the Bank to draw up a statement defending their previous actions and to explain their resignations.

> Was the manufacture of the duplicate notes to the benefit of the Bank of Portugal?
>
> Obviously, no.
>
> The Bank only profits by notes which, within its potential of circulation, it applies to its productive operations. And everybody knows by the perusal of the weekly reports, that the amount of such operation is decided below that potential. Obviously the notes which were wrongly placed in circulation, did not benefit it.
>
> On the other hand, is it not known to all that the culprits made heavy purchases of the shares of the Bank with the evident intention of conquering the administrative posts and thus assuring that at the feared moment when the notes were cancelled, . . . a complacent Board of Directors would not allow the compromising proof to appear . . .

The statement went on to relate how the Bank's officials had uncovered the crime, doing this "by itself voluntarily, determinedly, persistently, . . ."

And what was *really* behind the plot?

> We are face to face with a vast plan of social subversion with many ramifications, the purpose of which, with communistic tendency, was precisely the destruction of the Banks of Issue, with the intention of making them fall through their own means. Banknotes having to kill Banknotes and credits as a consequence being wrecked in the desired catastrophe.[*]

[*] All through the Twenties any major counterfeiting of European currencies was sure to bring the charge that Communists were behind it. It wasn't all baseless Bolshevik-baiting. In 1928, Stalin, desperate for foreign

194

Then came the real purpose of the statement—an attack on Judge Pinto Magalhães:

> A public calamity (almost as serious as the fraud itself) so decreed that at the head of the police investigations . . . was the inconceivable incompetency of a man whose actions call for explanations from the realms of pathology . . . a Police Magistrate, acting under the evident influence of a criminal from whom he cannot flee, and confusing autocratically all the threads of a skein which his own hands are decidedly unfit to unravel.
>
> As victims of the fraud . . . we energetically protest against the disastrous confusion with which the arrival of truth has been delayed, and before the country we demand that the guilty shall be punished, be they where they may, and that full and complete justice be done. . . .

Two days later, on December 26th, a special meeting of the Bank's stockholders was convened. The shares purchased by the Bank of Angola & Metropole were now in the custody of the Liquidating Commission and would not be voted.

The most dramatic meeting in the Bank's history got underway with Vice Governor Mota Gomes crying as he told how under the influence of the insane Judge

> there gradually appeared in the Press and in the streets a campaign of discredit against this institution; they accuse it of a crime of which it was the sole immediate victim . . . Not only in our country, but also abroad, newspapers with wide circulation had no hesitation in presenting the Bank of Portugal as swindlers. This was the result of a gesture by a magistrate absolutely unworthy of occupying such a position. [Hearty applause.]

When Governor Innocencio Camacho Rodrigues—short, heavy set, with bulging eyes—came into the room there was prolonged applause. He cried, too. He asked his fellow directors to

> . . . pardon me for not displaying the serenity to be desired at this moment . . . it was due to the violent commotion, the tremendous vexations to which I have been subjected by all the madness of some people and the malice of others or of all.

exchange, approved a scheme to counterfeit German marks and U.S. $100 bills through a secretly purchased Berlin private bank, Sass & Martini. But the plot was uncovered when less than $100,000 of the forged notes had been distributed.

This morning I said in my house: this is Passion Week. On Thursday [Dec. 21st] the representatives of all the Lisbon banks came here and I had the pleasure of seeing them and of embracing them. I passed the day yesterday as one dead, but today I am resuscitated. Hallelujah! Hallelujah!

Was it Alves Reis who engineered all? No. It was not his head that directed the whole of this wicked plan against the Nation. Some days ago when the accused was presented to me for identification . . . this man whom I did not know as an adult stated that he had been a pupil of mine and that being so, he could not avoid the influence which the former master exercises over the pupil forever after. He did not dare look me in the eyes because he knew very well he was face to face with an honorable man whom he accused unjustly. Reis was so crushed that he asked to leave the room because he was ill.

In spite of everything, you my friends, were not convinced that I was to blame! [Voices: "No one was convinced! You are an honorable man!"]

Thank you, gentlemen, thank you. [Much clapping of hands cut short the last words of the speaker who was heartily congratulated and embraced.]

Somehow the meeting managed to get a motion passed that its attorney should present to the nation's Superior Judicial Council a complaint against the investigating Judge.

Only the irreverent afternoon daily, *ABC*, thought there was a bright side to the terrible mess.

> In the final analysis the new notes are of as excellent a quality as those issued by the Bank of Portugal . . . the Bank has even gained because it keeps the issue for free, as well as all the assets of the authors of this fantastic feat . . . an adventure born in the highly fertile imagination of one man but carried out rather badly at times, like certain plays in which the actors are not up to the author's work.

LONDON / December 28, 1925

DURING SIR WILLIAM's absence, Edgar Waterlow had been filling-in his fellow directors on a few of the more startling items he had uncovered as a result of his talks with some of the staff. When the special board meeting was called for this Monday he was ready to make his first overt move against his cousin, William.

The chairman reported at length on the visit he and two other directors had made to Lisbon; of his talks with the Bank of Portugal directors and the offer to deposit £50,000 with the Bank as a token of their good-will.

There was another money report: more than 200,000 of the Marang notes had been exchanged by the Bank of Portugal. As well-printed paper the discarded currency represented a loss of £1500 ($7500) but as negotiable currency some $5,000,000 was involved. The galactic gap made the Waterlow directors increasingly conscious of the firm's vulnerability. If a deposit of £50,000 in the Bank of Portugal could somehow soften the Bank's claims for damages it would be money well-lent. The letter to the Bank that Sir William drafted for his fellow directors' approval made it clear the money was a deposit—at the prevailing rate of interest and that it was a "sterling deposit and repayment, when made, would be in sterling." No escudos, please.

With these preliminaries out of the way the stage manager of the quiet revolt was ready to move. As recorded in the minutes of the board meeting, the scene developed this way:

> Mr. [Russell] Palmer proposed and Mr. [F.R.] Muir seconded the following Resolution:
> "That a Committee consisting of R. Palmer, W. Flemming, F. R. Muir and R. T. J. Smyth is hereby appointed to investigate and report to the Board upon all facts and circumstances to date relating to the Company's transactions with Marang, and all matters incidental thereto and that the Directors immediately responsible for these transactions give to the Committee every assistance and all the information within their knowledge."

Sir William objected. The clear implication was he had *not* given his fellow directors all the "facts and circumstances." He

197

suggested that the offending resolution be withdrawn and he would furnish "all the Directors with a statement of all the circumstances known to himself, Mr. F. W. Goodman and Mr. [Thomas W.] Goldsack. The matter would then be considered by the whole Board."

Palmer and Muir who had anticipated this objection in their pre-meeting caucus with Edgar Waterlow, refused to withdraw their resolution. Sir William tried a delaying tactic: "that consideration of this Resolution be adjourned for ten days during which time the Chairman will furnish all the Members of the Board with a complete statement of all the circumstances surrounding the matter, including all the correspondence."

"The amendment on being put was lost by five votes to four. The original Resolution was then put and carried."

It was Sir William's first major defeat at Waterlow's. When he was driven home that evening he knew that his hopes of having another Waterlow, his son James, carry on at the firm after he completed his years at Cambridge, was ended. Edgar Waterlow, his bitter enemy, was now in effective command of the family firm.

The year 1925 was closing, said *The Times,* with great floods at home and abroad.

1926-1932

THE HAGUE / January 11, 1926

MARANG HAD BEEN arrested on December 30th at the request of the Public Prosecutor and was brought before the Rechter-Commissaris whose function was to examine the criminal charges, in the fashion of the Continental systems of criminal justice. In the records of the District Court of Justice of The Hague, Karel Marang "calling himself Marang van Ysselveere" was still the "Verdachte" or "the suspected," a term used for the preliminary proceedings. Only at his trial would he become the "Beklaagde" or "the accused."

He told the Rechter-Commissaris he had

> no doubts as to the signatures on the contracts given him by Reis because Waterlow himself, a man not easily fooled, was sure of their genuineness. . . . When he read the reports of the scandal in Portugal he wanted to turn over the many escudo banknotes he still had to the Police but was dissuaded by his attorneys who felt he should consult Reis first. . . . When he was asked by the Portuguese Chargé d'Affaires in The Hague to hand over the contracts he said he did not have them but could furnish them to anyone going to Lisbon provided with a safe-conduct. When Antonio Bandeira came to Holland [at the request of the Lisbon investigating Judge, Pinto Magalhães] he gave the contracts to Marang and also asked him to go to Lisbon to testify. Marang had to refuse because his passport had been withdrawn and he felt that his safety in Lisbon could not be insured. He said that Adolf Hennies had been living in Berlin but that he had not seem him for some time.

Marang wasn't very truthful. He had seen Hennies the morning of his arrest at the office. Hennies suggested that his partner flee with him but Marang who had already given his predicament much thought decided to stay. His role would be that of an hon-

201

orable Dutch businessman who had been taken in by a set of contracts he believed genuine.

Hennies had transferred nearly all his funds to Germany in accounts he had set up in his old name. When he left Marang this morning—only 30 minutes before the police came—he completely resumed his old identity.

A few days later a reporter for the Lisbon daily, *ABC*, interviewed Fie Carelsen in The Hague:

> When she was in Portugal this past summer, pseudo-elegant salons opened their doors to her, articles were written about her. Then, scandal broke out, and there was talk of a mysterious locked box that she always carried about with her. A complete turnabout took place: praise became insults, admirers turned into accusers.
>
> "Tell me, what will the future hold for José? Is it true that he is being harshly treated? Will he be severely punished? *José est bien gentil, le petit José! Pauvre petit Bandeira.* Is it true that he has been speaking ill of me? They've told me what the Portuguese papers are saying about me—that I wasn't even an actress, only had walk-on parts. They called me a cocotte and say that my love for José was a calculated thing, that I burned up all his money. Is that true? When I was in Lisbon, they called me the Dutch Sarah Bernhardt! Silly praise. What did they know of my art, my class, my position? And now they insult me. But I don't care. What hurts me is not that they should doubt me as a woman but as an actress. Me, a bit player! You've seen for yourself. All Holland knows me. They all want me. In the streets, in hotel lobbies, in restaurants, wherever I go, people whisper about me: 'It's Fie, it's Fie!' For them I mean nights of emotion, tears and happiness. To think that they consider me an ambitious and wasteful women . . .
>
> "I warned Bandeira when I was in Lisbon. Too many people were living at his expense. He paid for everything. Now they slander me. All I want to know is what is to become of Bandeira."

Although Antonio had been sent by Judge Pinto Magalhães to The Hague for the specific purpose of bringing the original contracts back to Lisbon, he didn't do so. Later in testimony before the Judge he explained.

> Statement by Antonio Carlos dos Santos Bandeira, 50, married, Chief of Mission 2nd Class, on reserve status . . . who said he went to The Hague . . . in search of the original contracts

between the Bank and Reis and so proved his good faith in the entire business. These were in the custody of a very good friend of his brother, José, but having obtained them he [Antonio] gave them to Marang, for it would seem strange if he, the Minister, returned to Portugal with documents that might give the appearance of his being involved in anything . . . whereas Marang had major interest in the documents proving his own good faith in his dealings with Waterlow. He had made Marang pledge to deliver the documents to the Portuguese authorities which he said he would do after consulting with his lawyer as to the best method. He then did notify the Dutch and Portuguese authorities that the two contracts were at their disposal at his lawyer's office. . . .

Antonio turned over the contracts only after Marang pledged solemnly he would pay for the attorneys representing José and Antonio. Now that José had, perhaps foolishly, turned over his foreign holdings to the Liquidation Commission he had no resources. Only Marang still had his money. Hennies did, too, of course, but he wouldn't show up again, Antonio knew.

When Marang was arrested the Dutch police also took in a young man named Reis, a student. He was Alves Reis' 17-year-old brother, Alvara, who had been sent to Holland to learn business methods and languages. The Portuguese were taking no chances. He might have learned some other skills from his brother.

LISBON / January 13, 1926

THE PRESSURE of the Bank of Portugal, backed by the nation's bankers and leading merchants, finally had effect. On January 3rd Chief Investigator Pinto da Magalhães resigned. He was replaced by Dr. Joaquim Auguste Alves Ferreira, an Inspector of the Courts, a Judge of the Supreme Court—and no relation of Alves Reis' aide, Francisco Ferreira.

The outgoing Investigator left with a threat. In an interview he said that since

> he was called insane he would really do something crazy—he would reveal the truth to the Nation. He had received consideration only from abroad. . . . He considered Marang a fine man and that what the papers said about him was not true. Marang's letters to him were full of praise. His involvement in the affair was due only to good faith. . . .

With the new Investigator at work the evidence of Alves Reis' plotting and machinations started to become clear. When Reis was shown a letter he had written ordering the stationery for the governor of the Bank of Portugal he admitted the letter had been written by him. But nothing more.

> He absolutely refused to say another word until he went on trial. No matter who his Judge was and whatever violence was used on him or even if they killed him. . . . Reminded that perhaps innocent people were now languishing in jail on his account he insisted that not a word would leave his lips. But then he burst forth: "On my wife's honor, I swear that all that I have said has always been the truth."

Police Chief José Xavier told Reis his wife was jailed in a filthy, rat-filled cell. (She had been imprisoned as an accomplice in lieu of 5,000,000-escudos bail.)

> Reis who loved his wife dearly, grew indignant and began to pour insults and protestations and finally broke down with sobs. He then said he was the only one guilty and didn't care whether he got 30 years for it.

An hour later he retracted the confession.

Seculo carried an item about one of the plotters who had departed Lisbon in hot haste:

> The furniture and furnishings at the Planas-Suarez residence at 157 Ave. de Liberdade, a dingy second-floor apartment, were auctioned off today. Planas had lived in Portugal ten years. All the domestic effects in the apartment were shoddy and in bad taste . . . bourgeois furniture, cheap oil paintings, much champagne and lots of bedrooms. . . . The Count's gray topper

fetched 27 escudos. . . . He is said to be in Paris where the investigators have found he has large deposits in banks there. . . .

On January 11th Sir William and his wife, and one of his fellow directors, Francis R. Muir, arrived in Lisbon. Muir, of course, represented the majority on the Waterlow Board. A somewhat dour Scottish solicitor who had also been trained as an accountant, he handled the firm's legal and financial problems. He felt the entire situation would not have arisen if Sir William had consulted him about the Marang contracts instead of taking them to his personal solicitor. At Oxford, Muir won honors in mathematics; he believed formulas could be worked out to solve most problems, even this one. He had another advantage, too: he could read Portuguese.

Waterlow came to Lisbon because he had been asked to give further testimony by the new Chief Investigator, Dr. Alves Ferreira. He also brought from London copies of Romer's telegrams and letters warning against acceptance of the Marang contracts. Dr. Ferreira was impressed and immediately decreed the Romer arrest order rescinded.[*]

Sir William also sounded out the Bank of Portugal about settling the awful mess.

"An arrangement satisfactory to both parties," were his words.

The trouble was both parties saw "different *animals*," a contemporary put it. "Waterlow saw only a skunk, small, not too dangerous but potentially awfully smelly. The Bank? They looked about fearfully and saw only an enormous monster, so big and dangerous they hadn't even been able to establish its measurements. They suspected that it might be getting bigger and more destructive all the time."

Sir William was not depressed. Maintaining a business-as-usual air he and Robert Walker called upon the Minister of Commerce to express his regret that the order for a special issue of stamps for Madeira had not been placed with his firm. He was told that by government decision the Post Office had been in-

[*] By this time several Bank officers realized Reis could have worked out the serial numbers–directors' names sequences without assistance from Romer or even a corrupt Bank official.

structed not to place any orders with Waterlow until the case had been settled.

Before he left Lisbon, Sir William, according to *Seculo,*

> called on several Ministries to leave cards. He finally received reporters at the Avenida Palace Hotel. . . . Asked about Romer, Sir William said he was very honest, somewhat irritable but a worthy man. The Portuguese papers, he said cast doubts on Romer's honor but will render him the justice he deserves. . . . He said he did not feel the case of the notes involved any international Bolshevik plot but anything might be possible. . . .

When the Waterlow party returned to London they reported to the other directors on their fruitless attempts to get the matter settled. It might be well to assume that legal battle was impending.

Clearly, 1926 was going to be a terrible year for banknote printers. Thomas de la Rue & Company, an important competitor was having great difficulties, too. Through no fault of its own it lost its primary customer—India. That subcontinent and British possession had decided finally to print its own banknotes. Since Sir William had taken away several de la Rue customers in the past five years, de la Rue was really hit hard. There were rumors that the firm might have to declare bankruptcy.

❊   ❊   ❊   ❊   ❊

THE HAGUE / March, 1926

MARANG HIRED several of Holland's leading lawyers when he was jailed in January. They saw him often in jail and he was questioned regularly by the examining judge. Now, in March, a new element had been introduced when the Bank of Portugal through its Dutch attorney, Jan Tobias Asser, applied for and secured a sequestration writ, *saisis arrets,* on "the goods and moneys belonging to the five criminals in the Netherlands." Accordingly, all the banks in the country were asked to report how much they were holding for Marang, the two Bandeira brothers, Hennies and Alves Reis. Under such an order the banks are forbidden to deliver goods or money to the named parties. The banks reported a total of some $70,000 of which about $66,000 was in José Bandeira's name.

Although both Marang and Reis were in jails hundreds of miles apart they were able to arrange for secret couriers to keep them in touch. The main courier was Carlos Chavez, an old crony of Reis'. Marang's curious loyalty to a man who had now been exposed as the author of the key false contracts was commented on by Antonio Horta Osorio, the attorney for the Bank of Portugal:

> How strange it all is: here is Marang, the honest Dutch businessman whom Alves Reis "took advantage of" and pushed "unknowingly" into a criminal adventure. Sees his name ruined but does he break with his partner, betray him openly and offer the Court all the data at his disposal? Not a bit. His first act is to write to the man who fooled him, putting himself at his disposal and offering all the money Alves Reis might need for his defense. They keep in close contact, their defenses are pre-arranged, letters and couriers follow one another.
>
> What about the money? Did he turn it back to the law and open his books so that people could see he wasn't keeping a single penny? No, he guarded his money carefully and no one knows where it is. The fact is, he still has it.

In spite of the best efforts of the Official Liquidation Commission that had sought out every asset of the gang and the Bank of Angola & Metropole, Osorio felt, as did the Bank of Portugal, that too much was still uncovered. The criminals still had too many secret accounts out of which they could draw to prepare new attacks against the Bank's officers, make new forgeries to confuse the public. Osorio worked it out this way:

> About 105 million escudos [about $5,250,000] were circulated. Adding up all the known expenses, the financing of the African companies, the purchase of buildings, securities, loans, prom-

issory notes, furniture, cars, etc., we still get slightly over 40,000,-
000 escudos [$2,000,000] for "expenses." To this we may add
the money turned over by José Bandeira [$300,000] to the Liq-
uidating Commission and we get 46 million escudos. If we suppose
that in non-documented expenses, including bonuses to the small
fry—estimated at 10 million escudos [$500,000] we have a total
expenditure of 50 millions. By deducting foreign currency deposits and securities in other countries we get about 32 million escudos
[$1,600,000] left. This was divided equally among the four asso-
ciates because we know the four always balance their books from
time to time. . . .

I estimate that Alves Reis has under assumed names in foreign currencies and securities from 15 to 20 million escudos
[$750,000 to $1,000,000].

Yet the secret Reis-Marang letters often touched on Reis'
need for more money. In them Reis often asks for *quese veja*,
something discernible, as, "I have such an awful lot of expense
here."

Osorio wouldn't be taken in by these poor-mouth cries:

There are two reasons Alves Reis was interested in getting
Marang's money. First the less he spends of his own, the more he
will have left. Also part of what Marang has is his. Secondly Alves
Reis has ever desired to pretend to be poor not only for the general public but to his own accomplices.

Marang sent considerable sums to Alves Reis as long as he
thought it possible that (a) Reis might turn up documents proving Marang's complete lack of knowledge that it was a criminal
conspiracy or that (b) it really was a plot by the Bank of Portugal directors in which case Alves Reis was only carrying out
orders and Marang got involved innocently.

The letters were conducted in French. Marang's quite fluent,
grammatically correct; Reis in a schoolboy variety with frequent
solecisms. In the letters, Reis always refers to Marang in the third
person, no *tu* or *vous:* "Marang ought to be convinced I am not
lying."

One of the letters Marang got from Reis in March was about
Hennies:

The international police are after Hennies. They know he is
in Berlin. They're in touch with a woman named Angold whom

they consider Hennies' friend . . . the Bank of Portugal is sending an agent to Berlin to look for Hennies. . . . It is essential that Hennies not be arrested. . . . I am rather broke.

By now Marang's attorney, J. Rolandus Hagedoorn, had made it clear he thought his client's case would be hurt if there was going to be dependence on any further Reis forgeries. But Marang didn't interrupt the secret correspondence or refuse to keep sending Reis money. However he did cut down the amount. He knew if Reis decided to turn on him he could be hurt.

Alves Reis provided reassurance from time to time:

> Tell Marang to be patient. I'm working day and night for him . . . I'll give him everything to prove his innocence. If I make a pledge I'll fulfill it.*

Once, Reis, the family man, urged the courier to stop off in Paris for a little shopping for his wife who was still in the Ajube Women's Prison:

> From Paris I need six brassieres and matching vests in good crepe de chine embroidered in pink. You'll find them at Galeries Lafayette. . . . But something good, size 45 . . . also six boxes of face powder, Doge, and 12 pairs of silk stockings. You can get all this for £ 100. Try and get £ 200 from Marang. . . . Cook up some story and you'll get £ 300 from Marang. . . . Marang is a skinflint and that's the only way we can get some pounds off him. It's only fair considering all I've done for him.

Alves Reis' attorney, José Soares da Cunha e Costa, spent considerable time trying to get Senhora Reis out of prison.

Her release was opposed vehemently by the Bank of Portugal which believed she was their only hope of getting a confession from Alves Reis. The knowledge that his wife was being subjected to the continuing indignities of prison might do it. Osorio, the Bank's attorney, soared in opposing her release:

> Look among the women you know and to whom all bow their heads in respect. There are still many in Portugal. Pick any one of them . . . Your own mother . . . Ask her what she would

---

* The Supreme Court removed the "incommunicado" status from Alves Reis on March 19th. He was now in "preventive detention" which meant he could wear his own clothes, receive visitors and food from the outside. He ate well for the next three years.

have done on the day she knew the father of her children was bringing stolen money home! This woman could tell you that from the time she knew her destinies were linked to that of a thief, that she would have no other thought but to divert from the path he was treading and that she would touch the stolen money only when all other resources had been exhausted, and only to avoid letting her children die of hunger. I tell you that from the cursed instant the dishonor was revealed to her, her heart would only know tears. Her first reaction would certainly not be to go to Paris, loaded with the stolen money to spend it in the company of an actress who was the mistress of an accomplice in the robbery. Millions of escudos in dresses covered with valuable jewels—all stolen from the people of Portugal. Tender souls might say the poor thing didn't know a thing about it. Ha!

The Bank was vindictive for another reason: Senhora Reis persisted for months in repeating a story her husband had given her before he was arrested on board ship in December: that she often saw the bank governor and vice governor at her home in secret conference with her husband; that Vice Governor Mota Gomes had contacted her husband several times at the Claridge Hotel in Paris. Only late in March, 1926, did she admit that these were terrible lies. In his thundering denunciation, Osorio exulted that:

> God's justice is watchful. So today she is where she wanted to put those two innocent men who had reached the age of sixty without scandal. . . . Alves Reis himself taught her what she must say if he was jailed. . . . Therefore she knew he had done something which might land him in jail . . . when she wore her fabulous necklaces and fur coat . . . which could have supported six honest Portuguese families for life . . . she must have known all was stolen.

She remained in prison.

LISBON / May 28, 1926

TODAY PORTUGAL was offered two paths to tomorrow. The first was offered by a general backed by the Portuguese Army. The other by a minor novelist who purported to show the country's glorious future if only bungling politicians and police hadn't interfered with Artur Alves Reis.

In Braga, in northeast Portugal, General Gomes da Costa issued a proclamation and appealed to his fellow countrymen to enter the struggle for national dignity and honor by ridding the country of the incumbent Democratic Party.

Between May 28th and 31st the country rose in arms—or at least most of the army garrisons did—and the central government in Lisbon capitulated. There was hardly a casualty. As one historian marvelled:

> The astonishing thing is that in the course of the five days there appeared nowhere the slightest appreciable support for the regime against which the revolution had risen. . . . The government in power lacked all will to survive. . . . The wonder was that someone had not pushed it over long before that.

The new government was installed on June 4th. Professor Antonio de Oliveira Salazar of Coimbra University was asked to take over the Finance Ministry but he didn't last long. Neither did this revolution:

> The country lived in a state of chronic deficit. . . . Inflation was increased by a constant flow of paper money. . . . By 1928 living costs were about 30 times what they had been in 1914.

A far more attractive revolution was offered by novelist Eugenio Battaglia. You didn't need an army or generals or the shots fired in anger. All you needed was Artur Alves Reis.

The book was called *The Fantastic Bank: Fraud or Patriotic Action?—A Social Novel*. It was a nervous best seller for several months. Almost certainly Alves Reis had not paid to have it written; rather unlikely he even knew it was being written.

Thanks to Alves Reis' iron will he was now Prime Minister
after having been Minister of Finance & Industry. . . . Led by
his dream he had gone from Governor of the Bank of Portugal to
Finance Minister to Prime Minister leading the country to its maximum prosperity even though the Chamber of Deputies ungrate-
fully pretended to ignore the origins of the country's prosperity.

It had begun, of course, with the Bank of Angola & Metropole:

Lisbon had become aware of a new banking house with almost inexhaustible capital and almost spendthrift philanthropy.
It's branch offices were scattered throughout the country and it
placed much capital in the colonies.

There were many visible improvements in Lisbon:

The Eduardo VII Park was levelled and beautified. [This
was not done until 1954] . . . Plans for a huge power station
near Leiria to link the Sado River to the Guadiana River were un-
dertaken to combat lack of water in the south—the granary of
Portugal. [Such a project was begun only in 1963.]

The new Bank tried to buy up *O Seculo* which attacked it.
Under pressure the Government ordered an investigation but
Alves Reis was not afraid.

. . . Alves Reis has a mistress, Maria de Lourdes, a sophis-
ticated woman with firm and succulent breasts . . . of limited
intelligence, no morals and no affectations . . . But he respected his wife, a saint, and kept everything from her . . .

Camacho Rodrigues and Ulrich of the Banco Ultramarino
rush over to Alves Reis: what the hell are you doing, they ask.
"I'm saving the country, that's what." They call him vile names.
Reis pulls out a gun and tells them to shut up. "My notes are worth
more than yours . . . The day is near when the Chamber of Deputies will make my notes legal . . ."

Under Alves Reis' threat and gun they both sign a letter calling off the investigation of the Bank of Angola & Metropole. They
go to the Prime Minister and ask him to call off the inquiry. He
asks, why? And they tell him as long as they keep it quiet there
won't be any danger to national stability. He resists: "Must I bow
down and be a lackey to this outrageous swindler and even praise
him for his patriotic moves?" He must; and does so.

Alves Reis builds great housing projects providing quarters
for 10,000 poor families. He merges the Bank of Portugal, the

Ultramarino Bank and the Bank of Angola & Metropole into one, called the Bank of Issue for Portugal & Colonies. The escudo rises in value daily.

> Dazzled by all this the Prime Minister resigned and offered his post to the great banker. . . . The entire bureaucracy was extinguished immediately . . . taxes reduced . . . soon the state was marching in giant steps towards anarchy in its most beautiful and ideal form . . . Without being a politician or even a dictator Alves Reis was leading the country to the summit of social ideology . . .

Complications ensue. Alves Reis' mistress turns on him because he won't marry her. The ex-Prime Minister rises in the Chamber of Deputies to denounce Alves Reis as a traitor. Alves Reis rises to reply:

> Yes, I will answer . . . I will not lie. Alves Reis is the only one who brought this country to prosperity . . . What did you have before I came: a decadent, hungry nation without industry, or trade . . . and now I've given you homes, bread and invigorated the colonies . . . the irrigation scheme is a reality . . . all taxes have been reduced and we shall be back on the gold standard shortly . . . The Army has been disbanded and the people have their own militia . . . They say I'm an agent of Moscow but I don't need them for anything . . . I'm against all dictatorships including Mussolini's . . . I'm against the Yankee civilization and I'm against the British Laborites who stink of racial imperialism . . .
>
> They say my notes are false? What about the Government's? Could anyone in 1925 exchange 20 escudos in paper for 20 in gold? What I did was create credit . . . I didn't steal from anyone or ask anyone's permission to do this . . . With a few well-drawn contracts I saved the country and did no one any harm . . . All this money was created and spent without expense to the taxpayer . . .

At the end of the parliamentary meeting and Alves Reis' speech he is carried out on the shoulders of the cheering Deputies. He's taken to the waterfront and shown the Island of Bugio in the Tagus where they promise to raise a statue to him so that foreigners would know what Alves Reis had done for his country.

In the evening a bearded philosopher was telling the crowds what Alves Reis had done . . . like a farmer who had a fallow field and stole one million escudos from his neighbor and with it cultivated his own land, paid the neighbor back with the profits . . . But, someone shouted, wouldn't the neighbor suffer? Ah, said the speaker, but there was no money missing from Portugal and no one complained it was missing.

In prison, Alves Reis read the novel and thought a long time about ordering several hundred copies sent to key figures throughout Portugal. But he didn't like the part about the mistress. It wasn't the "firm and succulent breasts" aspect. He rather liked that, in fact. But that she had "restricted intelligence and no morals" was ridiculous. The ideal mistress, he thought in his lonely cell, was tall, slender, *intelligent.* In fact, rather like Fie Carelsen. Did she still have the car he had given her?

* * * * *

The Chamber of Deputies agreed with novelist Battaglia on one point. Alves Reis was not an ordinary criminal who could be tried in the ordinary fashion. On April 16th the Chamber passed a law by which the accused in the Angola & Metropole case would be tried by a panel of judges rather than an ordinary jury. The justification, said an editorial in *Seculo,*

> was clear. This is an abnormal case that if not discovered in time would have imperilled national integrity. The crime to be punished is not one for which sanctions have been set down in the Criminal Code. It is beyond the scope of the present laws in force. Exceptional measures have to be taken.

In short, if the state was going to convict Alves Reis and his band it would have to be done with unconstitutional *ex post facto* laws.

* * * * *

THE HAGUE / November 26, 1926

THE TRIAL OF Karel Marang began this day in the District Court of Justice at The Hague. There was no jury, as there seldom is in most of western Europe. Instead, three judges sat. The witnesses against the accused included Sir William, Frederick Goodman, Roland Springall, Camacho Rodrigues; the High Commissioner of Angola (Rego Chavez); several Customs Inspectors; J. J. Quitems, Marang's chauffeur; E. H. Van Helten, Marang's book-keeper and J. E. T. H. de Jong, Marang's secretary. And Fie Carelsen. A reporter noted:

> She was dressed in black through the trial.
> She whispered her replies to the questions put to her. She seemed surprised by all the curious glances thrown at her, that each gesture of hers was observed with fascination.

She told about giving the Angola contracts to Antonio:

> Once when José was going to Portugal he came to my house with a little package and said: "If something happens to me I don't want this found at the Embassy." I thought they were old love letters and just put them in a drawer. . . . Then late one night in December Marang phoned: did I know where José had the contracts. I said no, what contracts, but I would look. Then I phoned Antonio and told him I had a package for him.

Shortly after José was jailed in Lisbon she got a telegram: "ALL WELL DON'T WORRY. FLAGGIE. It took me some time to figure out that 'FLAGGIE' was a kind of code translation for Bandeira," she said.

Several police officials testified on how they found valises with Portuguese banknotes in the offices of Marang's personal attorney, Fritz van Raalte; in the storeroom of a Rotterdam shipping concern, Brasch & Rothenstein; and another yellow leather valise in the Rotterdamsche Bank.

Dr. W. F. Hesselink, the prosecution's official expert on the documents and signatures involved, told how Alves Reis had prepared the forgeries. Later he volunteered that

215

the whole crime was handled with a shrewdness, almost worthy of a genius. It is astonishing that such a plan could originate in one man's brain. . . . It was so ripe in its careful details that one could foresee every step of its execution. . . .

Marang's defense went along two lines:

He had acted in good faith throughout; he believed the contracts were genuine and was certain of their validity after Sir William accepted them.

In addition, he claimed that *the Bank of Portugal had no right to issue the 500-escudo banknotes.* This curious defense stemmed from information Alves Reis had dug up. The Bank "did not exist legally in terms of Portuguese law and could not legally issue banknotes."

> The Portuguese Commercial Code prescribes in Article 49 that a Limited Company in order to have legal existence must have its statutes registered in a Special Register. This the Bank had not done.

Reis was quite right. The Bank of Portugal had neglected this prescribed step and, in fact, didn't get around to correcting the oversight until late in 1926.

The trial lasted six days. On December 10, 1926, the three judges found Marang guilty and sentenced him to prison for eleven months on the sole charge of receiving stolen property. It also ruled that

> all counterfeit banknotes of Banco de Portugal contained in the four trunks which appeared in the hearing and which served as full proofs in the present case, be destroyed within eight days after the sentence was passed.

Since Marang had already spent a little over eleven months in jail awaiting trial—bail is not ordinarily granted in Holland—he was ordered released.

The Prosecutor, influenced perhaps by the vehement protests of the Bank of Portugal and the Portuguese Minister to The Hague, carried the case to a higher court. He felt the sentence had been too lenient.

But before the case could come before the Court of Appeal Marang took his wife and four children to Brussels. In absentia, on June 15, 1927, the Court of Appeal sentenced him to two years' imprisonment. But under Belgian law no extradition of criminals was possible for sentences of less than four years. He was safe there. In 1928 the Marangs moved to Paris to begin a new life.

The Bank of Portugal persisted in its efforts to get the Marang and Hennies assets. In April, 1930, the civil case was supposed to commence in The Hague but none of the defendants showed up, although they were represented by attorneys. Hennies' lawyer, Dr. J. H. W. Peter Spill, said his client's whereabouts were then unknown but he had been paid to represent him. The Court found for the Bank of Portugal in its claim for 12 million guilders (about $5,000,000) but by then there wasn't much point to the case. Hennies and Marang had long ago moved their major assets out of Holland.

*   *   *   *   *

HELSA, GERMANY / May, 1927

IT WAS NOT a decision to make casually. After weighing all the risks carefully, Adolf Hennies decided it would be safe to surface. His Berlin attorney found that in the Weimar Republic, extradition could almost never be granted to another country against a German citizen.

Hennies was now 46, wealthy and lonely. It is an age when many men yearn for the sweet, uncomplicated days of their childhood. Or were they really that good?

Philosophers haven't resolved the issue, either. As Charles Pierre Peguy, the French Catholic Socialist, saw it, those of us

> who escape from destitution do not escape from the memory of their destitution. Either by dwelling upon it or by reacting

against it, all their future life is affected by it. The majority of the once destitute take refuge in voluntary amnesia.

An arguable point. For many an old German proverb was really nearer the mark: What was hard to endure is sweet to recall.

For Hennies in the past 16 months it was far easier to take refuge in a voluntary amnesia of Lisbon, The Hague and Paris. But Friedrichsbrück and Helsa—ah, how sweet to recall the good days of his youth. So he returned to the towns of his childhood and youth. And his shameful cowardice.

On November 20, 1881, he was born in the village of Friedrichsbrück, 14 miles southeast of Kassel, and not far from the present boundary between the Bonn Republic and East Germany. He was the fifth of seven children born to a German peasant family and was named Johann Georg Adolf Döring. Döring's father, Hans, was a farmer, a competent carpenter and self-taught veterinarian.

The Dörings were Huguenots—just as Sir William Waterlow's ancestors had been. In 1777 the Hessian Landgrave, Frederic II, founded the village as a colony for some French Huguenots. He built them ten farmhouses in the typical style of lower Saxony: the living quarters, stable and barn were all under one roof so that in winter everything could be done without leaving the building.

Döring's grandfather built his own farmhouse in 1850. (The house on the property he bought had burned down in 1840.) Döring's father added a wing to it, doing all the planning and work himself.

The boy attended a single-room elementary school in the village like the other lads but he was clearly a loner. His slightly stunted right leg marked him but he helped to set himself apart with his voracious reading. He was the top boy in class and when he was ten the schoolmaster, Kehl, told Döring's father that he didn't know what to teach him anymore. There wasn't much to read in Friedrichsbrück but by that age Johann Döring had read it all. The mother of the village's present Burgomaster—who was a fellow student—recalls that he would even read torn pieces of newspaper which he straightened out and put together. Most of the pieces came from the walls of privies.

He developed a flair for declamation and acting. No local wedding was celebrated until little Johann gave one of his set declamations from Schiller. Johann's olive-brown complexion and his black hair added to the impression he was a traveling entertainer who had come from the Mediterranean littoral instead of central Germany.

In the odd mores of this Huguenot colony, the art of being a good actor rated highly. Recently a former resident of Friedrichsbrück explained:

> In the old days when we used to go to our nearest big city, Kassel, which wasn't very often, we'd pretend to be engineers, agricultural experts and the like. And the "colony people" played their roles so well they passed. They'd save money before the trip so they could dress for the part even.
>
> The tradition is come by honestly. Just to survive a century of persecution and ten wars fought for religious liberty, the Huguenots had to learn the art of disguise and pretense. They'd be forced to go to Catholic Mass but only after they said their Huguenot prayers before. As they were forbidden to leave France during persecutions they had to disguise themselves as Italian or Spanish merchants or even jugglers and play-act their way out of France to safety. And even in the safety abroad, in their colonies, they did not let their highly developed art of deception rust—just in case. But they didn't have to *act* their stiff-necked non-submissiveness. The Huguenots always talked "man to man" to their Margraves and Electors. They were Europe's most zealous practitioners of equality. Still, we Huguenots thought ourselves very special.

Since Johann's older brother would inherit the farm, the boy's father didn't worry much about his non-agricultural interests. In time he would find his son an apprenticeship as a cigarmaker.

When Döring was 19, he moved to the slightly larger village of Helsa, six miles from Friedrichsbrück. There he worked for a cigarmaker. In 1905 he married a local girl, Anna Elizabeth Schminke, and on July 7, 1906, their first child, Anna Elizabeth, was born.

Using his wife's modest dowry, Döring took his family to Kassel where he opened a small tobacco shop. He didn't do well and rented a tobacco kiosk near the railway station.

In May, 1909, Döring knew his wife was pregnant again. At 28 he could see the spectre of eternal family imprisonment ahead. More children, more responsibilities and an ever-decreasing chance to break out, to go into the greater world he yearned for. Frankfurt, at least.

From the owner of a small food store in Kassel, Döring was able to borrow $400 to buy a tobacco shop in Frankfurt. On May 13, 1909, the Kassel Registration Office recorded that Döring "moved to an unknown location." He had become a family deserter.

He went to Frankfurt and found a tobacco shop for sale. During the negotiations the owner was called out of his tiny office for a few minutes. Döring took the opportunity: he had spotted a letter of credit for 2500 marks (about $600). He pocketed it and continued the desultory negotiations for an hour. He would return, he said, in three days to conclude the sale.

He went to Hamburg, caught a steamer to New York. There he made cigars for a year, saved more money, and secured an agency from the Singer Sewing Machine Company to operate a sales branch in Manaos, Brazil.

It was a prosperous period, for Singer machines had no competitors in Brazil. Sometime in 1910 Döring concocted a story. Through an attorney his deserted wife—she was living in Helsa with her family—was told her husband discovered she was to inherit some money from a distant relative who just died in America. In order to get the money she would have to send her husband a power of attorney and her birth certificate. (I have been unable to find out why Döring needed these documents but, in any case, they were sent to him.) His wife did not hear from him again.

In 1914 he sold his Singer Agency and left for Rio de Janeiro. He traveled through South America selling everything from toothbrushes to locomotives. Then came the war and his return to Germany, his assignment to the German Purchasing Commission in Holland and the beginning of his association with Marang.

In 1922 when he was a flourishing import-export dealer in The Hague and Berlin he heard that his wife had died. He sent an aide to Helsa to give his two daughters—the second, Anna Katharina, had been born in October, 1909—10,000 marks (about

$2500). The messenger was under firm instructions not to disclose where their father was—or whom he had become.

Now in May 1927, Döring returned to Helsa. He first sought out an old friend, Siebert Magersuppe, a butcher and owner of the "Goldener Anker." On the floor above the tavern had been the cigar factory where Döring once worked.

It was a joyful reunion, oiled by many drinks—and wealth. As soon as Döring learned his old friend was in financial trouble he gave him 10,000 marks. His generosity didn't end there. He gave a local carpenter who had taken in his younger daughter, Anna Katharina, on her mother's death, another 10,000 marks—to enlarge his workshop.

It wasn't easy to recognize in this distinguished, expensively clothed white-haired newcomer the cigar-maker's apprentice. There were reunions and dinners and drinks for all. But he didn't talk much about where he had been or what he had done. All that was certain was that little Johann Döring had become a very wealthy man. During the next few years he was to return sporadically to Helsa.

For his permanent quarters Döring took a suite in the first-class Hotel Schirmer in Kassel. On Sundays he invited his daughters and his old friends to come and have dinner with him in the hotel.

As the Portuguese business receded deeper into his memory he became restless for more business opportunities. Not that he needed the money but just to keep his hand in, to negotiate, to make deals. His old associate, Marang, had opened an office in Paris and had written Hennies. He was on to something promising: an opportunity to acquire arms for shipment to China.

LONDON / July, 1927

AS IT BECAME clear there was not going to be a quiet out-of-court compromise with the Bank of Portugal, Edgar Waterlow's position at the firm grew correspondingly stronger. In July, 1927, he was able to force his cousin, Sir William, out of the post as chairman and back into the co-equal "joint managing director" role.

The Bank insisted that only $5,000,000 would assuage their financial hurts. Waterlow's talked of $100,000, perhaps even $150,000 and that was all. They were clearly much too far apart for compromise.

When his son, James, came down from Cambridge in June with his degree, father and son had a talk. James, who resembled his father physically, had long thought he would go into the family firm after the university. But Sir William discouraged him. "He didn't think there'd be much opportunity for me there," his son recalled later. Instead, James Waterlow went to work for Amalgamated Press which published several women's magazines and children's books.

Edgar Waterlow didn't dare be too abrupt in ending his cousin's role in the firm. It was clear long, expensive litigation was ahead. Unfortunately, Sir William would have to be a vital witness for the defense. But Edgar made it clear his cousin should start looking around for something else to do. He expected to recommend to the Board of Directors that Sir William's role in Waterlow's be ended completely by November, 1928, when he would be dropped even as a director. All of Waterlow's directors were active managers of the firm and since Sir William would no longer be active in management . . .

The dismissal to come was particularly ironic for Sir William. Great honors—but quite expensive honors—lay on the horizon. Unfortunately, he could not say: "Gentlemen, you will have to excuse me. In view of my changing circumstances I don't think I can afford to be Lord Mayor of London." It just wasn't done.

He made a commitment back in 1922 when he had stepped on the invisible ladder of accession by becoming an alderman, one of 25 select men. Almost from the start he knew he would be asked to be Lord Mayor before the decade was out. In fact, when he gave depositions in Lisbon in 1926 he would say that not only was he an alderman of the City of London but that "he could reasonably expect to be Lord Mayor in five or six years."

The succession was always worked out quietly among the aldermen to avoid the messiness of electioneering and politics. The honor was a great one but not all men could afford it, could take a year out of their businesses to be Lord Mayor. Still, few eligible men wouldn't *try*.

The Lord Mayor got £15,000 from the City towards his expenses but it was never enough. There were almost endless rounds of dinner and luncheons, gala balls and handsome gifts to many charities. The average out-of-pocket costs were about £10,000 ($50,000). Because the honor was so great, much—and sometimes, all—of the extra costs were quietly absorbed by the Lord Mayor's firm. Since he was usually the owner or at least a senior partner it wasn't too difficult to arrange. But Sir William wasn't going to be an owner or partner or even a director of Waterlow's when his turn at the Lord Mayoralty came up. He suspected, with some reason, that Edgar was anxious to get him out of the firm before the Lord Mayoralty was imminent, so that there wouldn't be any discussion *at all* of Waterlow's picking up part of Sir William's expenses. Edgar remembered the bitter fight when his cousin became an alderman and had to give the City a portion of his time.

*   *   *   *   *

LISBON / April 27, 1928

WHEN GENERAL OSCAR CARMONA was proclaimed President of the Republic on April 15th he announced that the nation's "Perma-

nent Secretary of Finance" would be a man of the highest competence in whom the whole nation could have confidence. Obviously, it could not be any of the men at the Bank of Portugal who
had been libeled by Alves Reis, false as his accusations had been.
On this day the General appointed Salazar, the 41-year-old bachelor professor of economics. When Salazar took his oath he was
dressed in the conventional black, the uniform of Portugal's more
serious business and professional men. He was so thin and pallid
that some unkind critics thought he looked like an "underpaid
funeral parlor assistant who would bury Portugal's finances for
good."

Like Alves Reis, and other men too conscious of their destinies Salazar preferred to talk of himself in the third person:

> The new Minister of Finance is a modest person. His health
> is somewhat precarious although he is never ill. He has a limited
> capacity for work, but labors tirelessly.

Although Carmona held the presidency from 1928 until his
death in 1951 it was clear almost from the beginning of their relationship that Salazar was the new, dictatorial ruler of Portugal.

Still in preventive detention and awaiting trial, Alves Reis
labored tirelessly to prove the iniquities of the Bank of Portugal.
But he had fewer and fewer listeners—or readers. He wrote and
had published a thin volume while in prison. It was called *The
National Cancer,* by which he meant, of course, the Bank of Portugal. He still maintained the fiction that the banknote issue his
group had engineered had been with the consent of the Bank's
top officials.

The book didn't sell nearly as well as Eugenio Battaglia's "if-
only" book, *The Fantastic Bank.*

Reis still had access to various bank accounts and through his
attorneys he kept delaying his trial. The criminal always values
delay: witnesses die or disappear; passions wane; officials lose
office; prosecutors are kicked upstairs. As long as he could postpone trial he still had hope.

Of course, it meant staying in jail in "preventive detention"
but it wasn't too uncomfortable. He could still have frequent visitors and good food sent in from the outside. Almost as important
he could still get his daily quota of 100 cigarettes.

LISBON / May 31, 1928

ALVES REIS HAD BEEN transferred to the battlemented Cadeia Penitenciaria de Lisboa on the hill overlooking the Edward VII Park. Since it was just where Avenue Libertad ends, the inevitable local joke was that if you follow Liberty you end in jail. It was Alves Reis' lowest point.

> I was exhausted, abandoned by all and misery knocking at the door of my home. I had lost all hope and confidence in myself. . . . I knew I had failed and life had become a burden. . . . Suicide was all I could think of. With my death my unhappy wife would receive 200,000 escudos [$10,000] in life insurance.
>
> For months I had been carrying an extremely active poison [probably atropine] and when the cell doors were closed at 11 P.M. I dissolved the bitter poison in a glass and lay back on my cot to think of my life and family. When the prison clock struck 4 A.M. I gathered my courage, picked up the cup and I had made up my mind to destroy myself.

(It was one of the few unoriginal thoughts he ever had.)

> I wrote a brief confession of my crimes for the Attorney General. I placed it in an envelope in the drawer of the pine table next to my cot. I drank the potion and went to the washstand to wash the cup so as to remove all traces of the poison. I got back on the cot and fell into a deep sleep. . .
>
> Only the healthy body of a man of 32 had been able to wrench me from the arms of death. I awoke on the afternoon of June 10. I had no memory of my attempted suicide. My wife told me that on June 1 at 8 A.M. when they opened the door to my cell I was stretched out on the floor wrapped in my bedsheet. . . . They called the prison doctor and my own doctor came at 10 A.M. . . . the diagnosis was belladonna or a brain disease. My condition grew worse and only the great zeal of my doctor and the nursing staff in the penitentiary saved me from death. . . .
>
> As I listened to my wife's account I was suddenly glad that no one realized it was a suicide attempt and ascribed it all to some mysterious brain disease. . . . When I was able, I got the confession out of the drawer and tore it into bits. By the middle of July I recovered fully but my sight was impaired.

In the meantime my lawyer died, just before the case was
to go to the Court of Appeals, yet new hope filled my heart. I
managed to get 30,000 escudos in loans and once again I tried a
devilish plan to prove my innocence. I collected all the scattered
data I had in my cell and organized another full scale attack on
the Bank of Portugal.

I only wanted a full scandal and nothing else. I no longer
cared about the fates of my accomplices.

*   *   *   *   *

LONDON / November 29, 1928

TODAY THE GRADUAL break with Waterlow & Sons Ltd. became
final for Sir William. The firm's secretary was a little more detailed than the bare announcement that appeared in the press. In
a letter, the Bank of Portugal was told:

> Sir William A. Waterlow, K.B.E., has resigned his position
> as a Director of this Company, and has, therefore, no longer au-
> thority to sign and endorse cheques or any other documents on
> behalf of this Company.

The Bank had to be told with almost brutal specifics because
it was now officially an opponent in law. On March 27, 1928, the
Bank's London solicitors, Travers-Smith, Braithwaite & Company,
informed Waterlow's that it had been instructed by the Bank

> to institute legal proceedings against you claiming damages
> sustained by the Banco arising from the printing and delivery by
> you of 500-escudos Banco de Portugal notes to one Marang.

Before he left Waterlow's Sir William had assured his associates there that he would, of course, give them every possible help
in preparation and at the trial itself.

Nor would he be idle until the trial. He was elected a director of Universal Printers, a smaller firm than Waterlow's. More importantly, he was elected one of the two Sheriffs of the City of London. Their main function is to attend the Lord Mayor and sessions at the Central Criminal Court. One of them must be present each day during the sessions and both have to be in court when a capital sentence is passed. In the old days the Sheriffs were responsible for carrying out executions at Tyburn but now they played no active part in any of the court procedures.

The Sheriff's other main function was to act as a glorified messenger if the City of London wanted to deliver a petition to the House of Commons or if the Corporation of the City wanted to present an address to the King.

In many ways the business of being Sheriff for a year would be a useful preliminary for the job that lay ahead. The succession had been worked out smoothly and quietly as always and the choice had been made: Sir William Alfred Waterlow would become Lord Mayor of London in 1929. It was much too late to get out of a commitment he had, in effect, made in 1922. But he didn't try *too* hard. Cost what it would, he wanted to be Lord Mayor. Not only would it discomfit his cousin, Edgar, but the honor would help overcome the impending indignities in the Bank of Portugal trial.

PARIS / January, 1929

MARANG HAD BEEN living in a large, comfortable middle-class apartment house at 96 Boulevard Richard Lenoir, in the 11th *arrondisement*, with his wife and four children. There were his three sons, Karel, Jr., Florent and Ido, and his daughter, Jannet Wilhelmina. At 45, Marang had come to a firm decision.

Now that he was reasonably certain he would not have to

stand trial again—as long as he stayed out of Holland—he began to look ahead. This meant, of course, long unsettling looks at his past. Even after paying expensive legal counsel; after sending large sums to Alves Reis in jail, he still had a comfortable fortune, probably in excess of $200,000. He could have lived as a *rentier*, letting the money work for him, but he knew himself well enough to know that an active occupation was called for. Besides, as a father he had to think of his sons' future.

Originally he had been fairly enthusiastic about the plan to obtain arms and sell them to warring factions in China. But his ardor waned as he realized what a tricky business it would be, at best. No, Hennies could have it all. For himself, he now wanted a quiet, steady business requiring little or no travel; to lose himself in middle-class Paris as a solid bourgeois.

Early in January he had learned of a small electric chandelier manufacturing business that needed capital. He bought the business and soon had a modest plant going at 34 rue Bréguet, not far from his apartment. His contacts with Hennies became fewer and fewer. And he gave his lawyers in The Hague orders not to forward mail from Alves Reis. He was finished with that part of his past.

On December 16, 1928, he happened to glance at the obituary of Baron Rudolf August Louis Lehmann, the Ambassador of Liberia to France. It took a while before he remembered the shameful manner in which the Baron had resolutely refused to renew his diplomatic passport as an attaché of the Liberian government. In his present role of honest bourgeois such affectations were ridiculous. From his office safe he took the old Liberian passport and burned it.

The Portuguese government had long since rescinded the honors it had awarded him. Even the Royal Automobile Club had "suggested" that it would be best for all if he didn't try to renew his membership.

These petty vengeances didn't vex him too much. There was still a greater and more honorable organization that was forgiving and understanding. In March, 1929, M. and Mme. Karel Marang became members of the Dutch Reformed Church of Paris.

*   *   *   *   *

NICE / April, 1929

LATE IN 1928, Hennies-Döring ran a classified ad in the *Berliner Tageblatt*. He was trying to contact people who exported to Far Eastern countries. One of the men who answered was Karl Lampe, a native of Kassel who was running an import-export business in Nice, France.

Lampe was in Kassel when the ad appeared, visiting his mother. Döring wrote Lampe and a meeting was arranged in Kassel where Döring was then living.

Lampe who is now a very vigorous 80, lives in a cozy house on the outskirts of Bad Wildungen. He prides himself, rightly, on his memory. Recently Lampe, a heavily-built Hessian with a round, bald head, recalled his first meeting with Döring.

In Döring's suite at the Hotel Schirmer, Lampe quickly learned what Döring really wanted: contacts with "war matériel" exporters. He already had a market contact in Paris who was in with some warring groups in China. Only later did he speak openly of guns and other weapons. Lampe said he knew nothing of that kind of business but he did have some acquaintances in Nice who knew Basil Zaharoff, the legendary arms dealer. Zaharoff lived in splendor at the Hotel de Paris in Monte Carlo.

Döring did get in to see Zaharoff but the old Merchant of Death was retired and no longer interested. He casually suggested Döring go to England to see his original supplier, Vickers-Armstrong. But Döring didn't think it wise to go to London. The Bank of Portugal–Waterlow business was still in the courts there.

In April, 1929, back in Nice, Lampe spotted Döring seated at a sidewalk cafe.

"I said to him: 'What are you doing here?'

"'Just watching the people pass by.' So I said, 'I've got my car there, do you care for a ride?'"

It was the beginning of an acquaintanceship that would endure for several years. Lampe was fascinated by Döring and the stories of his past adventures. "You didn't meet a man like him every day," Lampe says.

Soon Lampe invited Döring to share his house in Nice.

Lampe recalls: "He was no burden at all. But he was restless. Time and again he grabbed the phone to call Paris on this arms deal and other things. He was still looking for new deals, for something to bring in more money. I got the impression he had invested quite a lot in the arms deal and somehow it was not paying off as well as he expected."

But Döring continued to spend money freely. He used to send a messenger over to Cairo once a month to bring back certain cigarettes in soldered tins containing 500. Lampe estimated that the cigarettes must have cost Döring about a dollar each. Döring would shrug: "I agree, but there is simply no such cigarette available in France today so I must get it in my own way."

One day Lampe got another insight into some of Döring's odd extravagances:

"Suddenly he felt like having liverwurst, baked potatoes and beer. But it had to be a special brew from Kassel. So what did he do? He took a train to Marseilles, got on a plane and flew to Stuttgart. There he hired a car and was driven to Kassel and about 6 P.M. he sat down to his liverwurst, baked potatoes and the beer for which he had come such a long distance."

From time to time Döring would reminisce about his experiences. Yet Lampe recalls him as "very reserved and never said more than was necessary. . . . He kept himself under control at all times. He never drank more than he could stand, never one too much. . . . As I began to enjoy his confidences he would talk of his successful adventures which somehow always worked out to his benefit . . . but I think he was proudest of the fact that somehow he always managed to get out of trouble five minutes before it was too late."

He occasionally talked about the Portuguese banknote affair:

"Such big plans they had for Angola! Three Zeppelins were on order for tourist traffic and those Zeppelins would supply off-season fruits to London, Paris and Berlin."

As time passed he spoke rather disparagingly of Marang in Paris. Although he visited Marang fairly often he said that Marang never once invited him to his factory. "Imagine," Döring laughed scornfully, "he is now making *lampshades* or something."

Once Döring impressed Lampe with how much power he

had when he was with the German Purchasing Commission in Holland during the war:

"I came to Warnemünde and had to get on the ferry to get across to Denmark to clear up some orders. But the Commandant of Warnemünde wouldn't let me on the ferry until he saw my official passport. So I said, 'All right, mister. Let me use that telephone.' I called Berlin and one hour later the Commandant got an official call from the War Office: he was transferred immediately to another post and I was allowed to use the ferry even if I was the only passenger."

Lampe added: "He had a lot of influence. I could see."

But in all his confidences Döring never talked of his days before Brazil. Somehow his life seemed to have begun full-blown when he arrived on the upper Amazon to take over a Singer Sewing Machine Agency.

Partly, the subject was too painful for Döring. In Kassel several members of his dead wife's family had accused him of a swindle and through a court order had sequestered some $10,000 of his locally-held funds. They based their claim on the letter Döring had written his wife in 1914 from Brazil in which he spoke of an inheritance due her. Döring defended the suit successfully and the court found that no crime had been committed; that there had not been any inheritance. The $10,000 was later returned to Döring.

His great luck at avoiding serious entanglements with the law was still holding out. But it was getting more and more expensive.

*   *   *   *   *

LONDON / November 9, 1929

ON THIS SATURDAY the new Lord Mayor of London was "shown" to the people of his mile-square domain, wedged between the Tower of London and Temple Bar. As usual, thousands from all over Greater London came to see the Lord Mayor's show.

Sir William Waterlow, now the 602nd Lord Mayor, rode in state from Guildhall to the Law Courts to present himself to the Judges for the King's approval.

The centuries-old ceremony began when the Lord Mayor and his Lady drove up to his Mansion House to take the salute. There was a trumpeting of sound down the wet City canyon, flashes of scarlet and gold and then the colorful parade of cavalry and coaches.

The parading military were led by officers proffering, as one reporter later told it, "their special trembling British salute." The bells of St. Paul's and all the City churches rang out steadily.

In honor of the new Lord Mayor's background the traditional pageant's theme was the printing trade. There was the first English printer, William Caxton, in his 15th century costume standing by his own press. On another float was a mason carving letters in stone; on still others linotypers were setting type on their tall machines but, of course, no engravers preparing banknotes. At Ludgate Circus the procession paused while the president of the Federation of Master Printers handed the Lord Mayor a casket containing an address of congratulations which also recalled his services to the printing trade.

In the cars and carriages in the parade were aldermen, the masters of the City's traditional livery companies, the Sheriffs, lawyers in their full-bottomed wigs. All were laughing and waving to the crowds on the sidewalks. A great day.

The office of Lord Mayor, Sir William knew, was no sinecure. The Lord Mayor is the leading citizen of Great Britain and in the City he takes precedence over everyone except the King.

He is also London's Chief Magistrate and presides at the opening session of Old Bailey, the Central Criminal Court. And,

232

of course, he heads the City Corporation which controls the wealthiest square mile in the Empire.

Another important function is dispenser of hospitality to distinguished visitors. After the visit to Buckingham Palace, the most important part of a state visit was the ceremonial luncheon at Guildhall presided over by the Lord Mayor. When the Lord Mayor entered the Guildhall for one of these many luncheons he would be preceded by his Marshall in plumed hat and red cutaway coat. Then come the Lord Mayor's Sheriffs and his sword bearer carrying the sword given to an earlier Lord Mayor by Queen Elizabeth. Wherever he went in the City, whatever function he graced, the Lord Mayor brought with him all the authority of a long past and confidence in its continuity in the future.

The Lord Mayor's daily routine is geared only for very healthy, indefatigible men. He usually has to make some three speeches a day, and attend, on the average, four functions. As someone once put it, "He will work like a slave and have a chance to eat like a horse." In many ways he is almost the equivalent of Britain's "Vice President."

There were congratulatory wires and messages from old friends and associates. Even George U. Rose who had left Waterlow's to return to Washington, D.C., sent a cheering cable. Only his cousin, Edgar Waterlow, wasn't heard from. Sir William was not surprised. Edgar had always been small-minded, even vindictive.

The staff of the Mansion House, the official residence of the Lord Mayor,* took particular care to make sure there were no untoward reminders of that still-unresolved business, the Portuguese banknote case. For the Children's Fancy Dress Ball which the Lord Mayor and Lady Mayoress give each Christmas, the word went out quietly that it would be unsuitable for any child to come costumed as a Portuguese native.

From the Lord Mayor's Room, the beautiful Venetian Parlour, Sir William had to handle occasional correspondence re-

---

* Whyte Ways, the splendid 18-room Waterlow home at Harrow Weald was sold in the summer of 1929. The house in which Sir William's family had lived 12 years was later bought by the County Council as a possible county nursing home. But the plan fell through and now the house is a ruined, windowless derelict.

garding the case. The letters were typed by his old Waterlow secretary, Alice Shaw, who had now become the Lord Mayor's private secretary.

The first private task the new Lord Mayor had was to postpone the forthcoming trial until he had concluded his one-year term of office. The Bank of Portugal saw no reason why the trial should be delayed. But diplomatic pressures were brought to bear and finally the Bank, through its solicitors, acceded:

> In spite of the inconvenience to the Bank and its witnesses, we have been instructed to consent to your request and we feel you must look upon this consent as an act of courtesy to the office held by Sir William and so that such office might not suffer embarrassment by its holder having to devote his time and attention to the Defendant's case. We are instructed to ask that the new date for trial be fixed for the earliest available day in November.

Sir William had been surprised to discover that he was, after all, going to be the chief witness for the defense. That the firm's counsel had advised them to

> rely on my evidence alone and not on that of the other directors concerned. I am not questioning the wisdom of this decision but if counsel had been fully instructed with regard to the part taken by the other directors I am sure. . . .

Sir William was firm. "They will not make me the scapegoat," he told friends.

LISBON / December, 1929

ALVES REIS WAS preparing his last attack against the Bank of Portugal. With the help of Manoel dos Santos, he would launch a new series of documents and letters against the directors of the Bank.

Manoel had once been a Bank messenger but was fired when he tried to get the proceeds of a winning lottery ticket that the owner had sent in to be collected. (A common procedure in most Latin countries where canny lottery winners know how wise it is to remain anonymous.)

Manoel visited Alves Reis in prison and offered his services.

> He wasn't even 20 but his cynical offer shocked me. I gave him some fatherly advice but I lost the sympathy which I first felt for him as I saw in him all the hallmarks of a born criminal who commits crimes for the sake of pleasure. . . . I tried to dissuade him but he took out his wallet which had a sheet on which were the signatures of several Bank of Portugal directors which he said he had forged.
>
> I was astounded at the perfection of the work. I let him have my pen and asked him to reproduce the same signatures. He put the sheet against the door of the cell and without hesitation traced out the signatures. I decided to use him. . . . I planned a large scale forgery on real Bank of Portugal letterheads which I had obtained the year before through bribery of a clerk. . . . I promised Manoel 100,000 escudos. . . .

Alves Reis had fallen into a trap. Manoel had been sent to him as an *agent provocateur* through the connivance of a newspaperman and Antonio Horta Osorio, the Bank's attorney. When the plan was disclosed in front page stories Alves Reis wept bitterly. To have fallen for so obvious a trick! The months that followed were the darkest he ever endured.

Then in March, 1930,

> following untold internal suffering, the Spirit overcame the flesh: I wrote a priest in the Catholic Church and asked him to hear my confession. For the first time I received Holy Communion. . . .
>
> Full of new-found courage, I confessed to my unfortunate wife on April 21, 1930, what only God, my confessor, and I knew. She turned pale and did not want to believe it but then became convinced and resigned herself to the truth.

His final trial was to come on May 6, 1930. When the case would be heard before the highest special court ever constituted in Portugal.

* * * * *

LISBON / May 6, 1930

THE STRANGEST TRIAL in Portugal's history, employing a procedure never used before nor ever again after, got under way at 12:45 P.M. Because it was a special court without regular quarters of its own, the Hall of the Military Tribunal at Santa Clara was used for the hearing.

It was soon apparent there would not be enough space in the improvised courtroom. Not only would the public have to be kept out but it looked as if all the witnesses could not get in at one time.

The president of the Special Court, Dr. Simão José started with a roll-call of the fifteen attorneys representing nine defendants, eight of whom were present. Only Adolf Hennies was absent.

The counsel responded with a complaint there just weren't enough chairs. The Judge counseled patience and went out to look for more chairs. When all were finally seated he explained the special procedure that would be followed.

A jury of seven additional Judges and one alternate was to be chosen from among 39 Judges. Dr. José's 9-year-old son pulled the eight names out of a hat. The Judges were sworn in and a roll-call of the 85 witnesses ensued. Then just as the finally constituted court and jury was about to get down to the business of the trial an Army major came in and explained that the room would be needed in an hour for a court martial. The court president sighed and adjourned the trial until 4 P.M. on May 8th. He knew what he was in for and had fought bitterly against being given the assignment to this case. One of the 20 reporters present noted in his account that when the Judge announced the postponement Alves Reis went over to his wife, another defendant, and kissed her.

The charges against the nine defendants ranged from twelve —against Reis—down to one charge against his wife and Adriano Silva.

Alves Reis, the indictment read, was charged with: (a) conspiracy; (b) the falsification of spurious contracts; (c) the

236

forging of various letters purporting to be from the governor and vice governor of the Bank of Portugal; (d) the use of these forged contracts and letters; (e) the use of a forged engineering diploma and (f) the crime of forging 580,000 banknotes and of

> passing the Notes to an amount in excess of 200,000 which Notes were exchanged for foreign exchange, genuine Portuguese Notes, gold, silver, jewels, land and buildings

(g) the passing of forged notes "in concert with the manufacturer or with his complicity;" (h) the introduction of forged notes on Portuguese territory; (i) fraud in getting a charter for the Bank of Angola & Metropole; (j) violation and non-delivery of the correspondence from Waterlow to the governor of the Bank of Portugal and (k) bribery of a public official to carry out unjust or even criminal acts and (l) bribery committed by a public official.

The first eight charges were also leveled against José Bandeira. Antonio was charged with only four as was Francisco Ferreira, Reis' aide. Adriano Silva and Moura Coutinho were accused only of passing the forged notes and bringing them to Portugal. Mrs. Alves Reis was charged only as a receiver of stolen property; Manuel Roquete only with helping to forge some of the letters under Reis' direction. And Adolf Hennies had five charges against him (a, d, f, h and i).

Since Marang had already been tried and convicted in a foreign court, he was not listed among the defendants.

The prosecution was conducted on behalf of the public by a Judge named Dr. Jeronimo da Sousa and on behalf of the Bank by Antonio Osorio and Dr. Barbosa de Magalhães. The latter had long since given up trying to defend the fact that in 1925 at the time of the Portuguese Red Cross Anniversary celebration he had been among those who had recommended Marang for the Order of Christ. Naturally, he was the most vindictive prosecutor of the three.

    ❋   ❋   ❋   ❋   ❋

LISBON / May 11, 1930

TODAY ALVES REIS gave his finest performance. In a continuous five-hour peroration he accepted full responsibility for the crime, with the complicity of Marang and Hennies, and thus sought to exonerate fully all the others on trial. The best account of the moving session was written by Antonio Ferro of *Diario de Noticias*. Ferro had been a classmate of Reis' in the Lyceum and had known him again in Angola. Later Ferro was to write a popular biography of Salazar, become the mouthpiece for the Salazar regime and found the present effective Government Tourist Office. Portuguese enemies of the regime used to call him Salazar's Goebbels. But now, in 1930, Ferro wrote of his old schoolmate:

> Everyone knows Reis is a criminal, the best of all. He has confessed it with unique pride, punishing himself publicly. There is no doubt Reis succeeded in impressing the court yesterday. Perhaps he failed to convince it of his good intentions, of the sincerity of his confession, of his "full" responsibility for the crime, but he did convince it of his intelligence, his eloquence, his ability, and his admirable lawyer's temperament.
>
> There was no Defendant, no Court, no Jury. There was a free man before other free men. A Minister in the Chamber of Deputies replying to a question; an orator at a rally, a captain of industry explaining his business. There was only admiration when he began speaking and soon the Court was his. Perfect, almost respectful silence. Reis related his romance, with energy, with literary flavor at times and dazzled everyone with Articles and Clauses . . .
>
> He related how he committed the fraud, how he discovered the numbers and series of the notes, how he forged the signatures, how he found out there was no "control" of the notes in the Bank of Portugal, explaining all this as an engineer might elucidate an intricate machine. . . . Reis kept on talking until he was tired, then he asked for a glass of water. It was intermission. Then he continued with equal energy . . .
>
> The Attorney General allows himself to call Reis "Your Excellency" which he hurriedly withdraws and the presiding Judge, impartial and dignified, said that the defendant's words had been

238

"listened to with great pleasure." . . . Reis confesses fatigue at one point and everyone acknowledges his right to be tired, the prodigious effort of his memory, of his nerves, of his intelligence during five hours of struggle.

I found him sincere overall . . . Reis' truth may be filled with lies but it is truth. One cannot lie for five years without keeping the tic of lying. . . . The surprising thing was that a man who should appear beaten, timid, humiliated following his confession of a shameful crime, should appear with his head up, in a fighting mood, almost jovial, without any cynicism.

He dedicates himself with ardor to a new cause, the defense of his companions whom he tries to clear of all guilt. . . . This discredited and finished man suddenly becomes transformed into a terrible defender of his own victims. There is a certain moral beauty in his attitude to the unfortunate men: "It was I who dragged them in here! Ruined five years of their lives. . . . Now I shall do everything to free them."

When a Judge asked why he had changed his attitude so suddenly, Reis' answer was simple and moving:

"You are here to judge men, not souls!"

Yes, isn't it time to seek the human truth instead of the juridical truth? To give up the old clichés that a man who lies once is always a liar . . . 25,000 pages to find the Truth! And has it been found? The Bank of Angola Reis has been tried and will be sentenced. . . . But this Reis, the Reis who confessed yesterday and defended his victims, who always respected the sanctity of his family life, does he not deserve a minute of pity, a moment of compassion? Throw stones at him if you will. I cannot.

The reactions on the Bandeira brothers were noted by other reporters:

Antonio Bandeira, holding back his tears, turned to his brother, José, and squeezed his hand in a tender gesture. José tries his best not to cry, but he is overcome, his lips tremble and the tears course freely down his cheeks, onto the hands of Antonio, whose brotherly grasp is maintained.

Not *everyone* was absolved of responsibility. There is, thundered Alves Reis,

. . . another criminal who should be here with me in the dock, instead of on the Lord Mayor's throne in London. If this man had not been so stupid and irresponsible this crime of mine could not have gotten underway. . . .

Reis' attorney, Dr. Nobrega Quintal, pleaded mitigating circumstances that should be considered in sentencing his client:

—his previous good character
—important services he has rendered to society
—his intention of averting the economic and financial crisis which was bringing Angola into a desperate condition
—the long imprisonment he had already undergone
—his actual precarious economic circumstances.

Dr. Osorio didn't allow the last to pass without a heckling footnote. "Yes, the defendant Reis *seems* in precarious circumstances now but we know he has already spent 2,000,000 escudos ($100,000) in his defense, including 416,000 escudos to a group of desperadoes who promised to help him escape from jail . . . we are still uncovering secret bank accounts abroad in the name of Alves Reis or his wife."

Reis' attorney argued that his client had not been a counterfeiter but an "inflationist" who was merely carrying out unofficially the fixed policies of the Bank of Portugal—at no cost to the Bank. After all, Reis and his associates had *paid* Waterlow's for printing the notes. He threw in a semantic gambit that while it is against the law to imitate banknotes, the law says nothing about *duplicating* notes.

And, finally, he reminded the judges of the extraordinary measures taken by the Chamber of Deputies in passing retroactive laws especially to cover the defendants so that the crime of counterfeiting which had been punishable by a maximum of three years' imprisonment could now draw 25 years.

On June 19th the jury of judges rendered its verdict after six hours of deliberation. All, except Manuel Roquete, were guilty. As Alves Reis recalled the scene:

It is now 1 A.M. The Attorney General enters the courtroom, the clerk takes his seat. The Presiding Judge returns to his seat. The sentence is going to be read out. A sensation is caused by the withdrawal from the room of the defense lawyers, after a word of tribute to the Judge by the lawyers, one of whom says: "With all due respect, owing to the state of mind in which the defense lawyers are now, we have resolved to leave the Court during the reading of the verdict" Even the lawyer of the acquitted Manuel Roquete begs permission to leave.

The sentences were read:

Artur Virgilio Alves Reis, José dos Santos Bandeira and Adolf Hennies: each to serve eight years in prison to be followed by 12 years of exile, or they could choose 25 years of exile which meant residence in certain villages in the Colonies of Angola or Mozambique. Antonio Carlos dos Santos Bandeira, Francisco A. Ferreira, Jr., and A. A. Costa Silva, six years in jail and 10 years of exile, or 20 years' exile in all. J. Moura Coutinho, two years in jail or three years' exile. And Maria Luisa Jacobetti Alves Reis, wife of the principal defendant? She was sentenced to the time she had already spent in prison so that she was now free.

For Alves Reis the choice was not easy. Rather than go back in shame to Angola or Mozambique he would serve his time in the penitentiary in Lisbon. There he would be able to have visits from his wife and sons at least once a week. It was just as well he decided to stay in the penitentiary. The governors of Angola and Mozambique protested firmly against Reis' being sent to the colonies. They had enough troubles without him.

Mrs. Alves Reis tried to find work to help support her three sons. Jobs were scarce enough for unemployed Portuguese now that Salazar had set out on a deliberate course of deflation. But the wife of Alves Reis, understandably, faced even more difficulties. As a friend of her imprisoned husband put it: "If I give you a job everyone will say I once got money from your husband." But somehow she did find work later as a clerk in the government navy yard in Lisbon. She earned $20 a month.

Just before her husband was to begin his first three years of solitary confinement, a rumor swept the penitentiary that an elaborate escape attempt had been organized. An outside searchlight was focussed at night on Reis' high cell window. Alves Reis asked to see the Warden.

"If I wanted to escape," he said, "I would first speak to you, Mr. Warden. I'm not the type to scale walls. If I get out of here it would only be because I bribed you. So, please, can you remove the searchlight so I can sleep at night?" It was removed.

*   *   *   *   *

LONDON / November 24, 1930

THE PRELIMINARIES WERE over. The skirmishes (Statement of Claim and Defence) and the field reconnoitering (Particulars of Special Damage and Discovery) had been concluded and the modern version of Trial by Champion was ready to commence in "that gray Valhalla at the end of the Strand," the Law Courts.

The Champions, or King's Counsel, had been chosen with great care. Under the British legal system only a barrister can do trial work in the superior courts. And only the barristers who feel very sure of themselves ask for permission of the Lord Chancellor to be made a King's (or Queen's) Counsel. Not only do the fees their clerks fix jump greatly, but a K.C. also must have a junior barrister in attendance who will receive two-thirds of the K.C.'s fee. Both King's Counsel in the case of Banco de Portugal vs. Waterlow & Sons Limited had enormous self-confidence. Their assurance had good underpinning: both were Members of Parliament.

The Bank of Portugal's solicitors, Travers-Smith, Braithwaite & Company, had selected Stuart Bevan, a Conservative Member of Parliament for the Holborn constituency in London. Bevan was then 58 and at the top of his career as a barrister.

Tall, thin, almost cadaverous, Bevan had come from a lower middle-class Welsh family. As a scholarship boy he attended St. Paul's School and Trinity College, Cambridge. (A fellow-student he had known in college was Edgar Waterlow.) He took silk—became a King's Counsel—when he was 47, and in 1928 he was elected to Parliament.

He had a resonant, attractive voice, a commanding personality. Junior barristers preferred to listen to Bevan on a cross-examination than almost any other K.C. Like most K.C.'s, he had an effective little mannerism—a series of nervous, questioning grunts that almost automatically followed a question put to a hostile witness. He also affected a remarkable variety of spectacles during trial, as if to look deeper and deeper into the witness. He was married but childless, and an urbane connoisseur of food, wine, old silver and etchings.

242

His opponent in this case was an old friend, Norman Birkett, who was 11 years younger and in 1929 had earned £33,500 (about $165,000) in legal fees. One guess was that on this case he was to get £300 ($1500) for every day in court—plus two-thirds of that for his two junior barristers, H. Bensley Wells and Theodore Turner.

Like Bevan, Birkett was also a Cambridge man—Emmanuel College, noted mainly for its education of theologians, divines and John Harvard .The son of a prosperous North Country draper, Birkett entered Emmanuel at the comparatively advanced age of 24 on a scholarship. His schooling had ended at 15 and for the next seven years he worked for his father behind a counter.* The tall redhaired student soon discovered he had more of a flair for debate than theology. He later became president of the Cambridge Union, the undergraduate debating society. By then he had lost his distinctive North Country accent.

He practiced as a barrister in Birmingham until 1920 when he came to London and became a K.C. in 1924. His private enthusiasms were for fine books from private presses, and for cricket. He was elected to Parliament as a Liberal in 1923 from an East Nottingham constituency. He was married and had two children.

His long-time clerk, A. E. Bowker, later described his employer's courtroom tactics:

> A figure who rose quietly with a little hitch of the gown or perhaps a momentary raising of the wig, and addressed the witness in a gentle, insinuating manner, "I wonder if you can help me, Mr.—" . . . occasionally there would be a ringing challenge in his voice and the denunciatory pointing of a long finger . . . he would waggle his pencil and wrinkle his face as he asked a question . . . he was fond of using the word "manifestly" which he pronounced a bit oddly . . .

The Judge was Robert Alderson Wright. Mr. Justice Wright was then 61 and like Stuart Bevan, a Trinity College man. He had been a vastly successful King's Counsel with great skill in han-

---

* The great attraction of the Bar to bright sons of lower-and middle-class families in Britain was recently commented on by Roy Jenkins: "It was the principal means by which men of limited means and no elevated connections could found families of wealth, rank and influence."

dling difficult commercial cases. He was appointed to the bench in 1925 and married for the first time in 1928 when he was 59.

On the bench he occasionally displayed a vein of dry, attractive humor but he also had an irritable manner that some barristers resented secretly.

The issues had long been delineated by the warring sides. In 1928 the Bank of Portugal had listed its "Particulars of Negligence."

Waterlow was negligent in:

—printing the banknotes
—disregarding the warnings of Romer
—accepting as genuine the documents handed to them by Marang
—not taking any reasonable steps to satisfy themselves of Marang's authority and not making direct communication to the Bank
—printing and delivering to Marang banknotes that were similar in every respect to those already printed for the Bank.

The damages claimed for these combined negligences of Waterlow's amounted to £1,115,613 (about $5,420,000). The bulk of this was accounted for by the 209,718 Marang notes that had been turned in to the Bank of Portugal for conversion to other, legitimate banknotes. In addition there was an item for some £9,000 to cover the cost of printing the original Vasco da Gama notes which had to be called-in, plus the cost of the new notes which had to be put into circulation to replace them. Also included was interest at 5% from December, 1925.

The defense denied all negligence and insisted that if the Bank suffered damage it was "caused or contributed to by the negligence of the plaintiffs." They pointed to the fact that Sir William had written the Bank about the Marang order on January 7, 1925; that the Bank knew as far back as February, 1925, that there were many complaints in Portugal about the validity of the many new 500-escudos notes, and yet, it "failed to take any reasonable steps to satisfy themselves whether said notes were genuine."

Besides, the Bank "failed to take any proper or reasonable steps to check the number of Vasco da Gama notes from time to time in circulation." And finally, if the Bank suffered any loss, it was its own fault since there was a way, however minute, of distinguishing between the Marang notes and the Bank's own. Every banknote-maker puts tiny, secret marks on the notes—usually letters—and the marks on the Marang notes were different from those on the Bank of Portugal orders.*

More generally, Waterlow claimed that the Bank had suffered no *real* loss. Since its currency was not convertible into gold it had simply exchanged one set of paper notes for another. And in that case it was, perhaps, entitled to printing costs but nothing more.

The case was covered by the British as well as foreign press from the first day. The Lisbon *ABC* correspondent warned:

> Let us not forget that British laws are different from our own and all the unpleasant surprises that may come up may have satisfactory explanations. The case puts the nation to shame just as a family quarrel that has to be settled in the house of a stranger. For this case is not a private affair but a national one, involving all Portuguese.

Stuart Bevan outlined the plaintiff's case for the better part of three days, touching on the key points of the contracts, correspondence and the banknotes. He showed Justice Wright some of the legitimate Bank of Portugal 500-escudos notes and some of the Marang notes, distinguishable only by tiny secret letters, almost invisible to the unaided eye. When there was a moment's hesitation in handing up a pair of the notes to Justice Wright, he got one of the few laughs in the courtroom during those three days:

> "I am not likely to make any improper use of them. You seem very timid about what I might do."

There was no jury but the packed courtroom responded with a dutiful laugh at the first display of judicial humor.

Bevan's first witness was Dr. Ruy Ennes Ulrich who had been a director of the Bank of Portugal until 1928. Since he spoke English well it was easy for him to give the history of the Bank and how it suspended its policy of paying notes with gold in

---

* Both secret letters were on the face of the note. One was down in the lower left hand corner concealed in the curve of a fleur-de-lis. The other was hidden in one of the waves separating the two da Gama vessels.

1891. Temporarily. And, as often happens, temporarily became forever.

On cross-examination Birkett established that the Bank not only did not pay out gold for the notes, but that its legal gold reserves were far below what they should have been by law:

> Would it be right to say that the Bank of Portugal was merely a gigantic paper machine in order to meet the needs of the State?

Dr. Ulrich more or less admitted that this was so. But other central banks, alas, were in a similar unhappy position, he pointed out. He admitted that the Bank had received warnings about the surprising number of 500-escudos notes in circulation but when they were found to be genuine nothing was done.

No major London trial in the Twenties was really official until there was some amusing reference to Dickens. Birkett took care of this on November 28th with Dr. Ulrich:

> Q. The expenditure of the State until 1926 was greater than its income?
> A. Yes.
> Q. Well, in private life that leads to bankruptcy, does it not?
> A. In private life, yes, but in State life it is different.
> Q. I expect they have translated Mr. Micawber into Portuguese, have they not?
> A. What is that?

Ulrich testified that if the Bank had not exchanged all the 500-escudos notes, there would have been a revolution because if "the public was threatened to lose one-sixth of its money [the total of the Vasco da Gama issue], it is not very extraordinary that a revolution would arise."

Although he was a member of the Banking Council that finally approved the formation of the Bank of Angola & Metropole, Dr. Ulrich had not told his fellow Council members that Adriano Silva of the Bank staff had been spending suspiciously large numbers of 500-escudos notes.

Later, on cross-examination, Norman Birkett apologized for an unintended slur on Portugal. He had been asking Ulrich about how Alves Reis, an arrested embezzler could be allowed to form a new bank:

It is a pretty nice sort of thing *even for Portugal,* for a man to be asking to found a new bank when there is on his record that he has been arrested for embezzling from his own company 2,000,000 escudos.

He apologized and asked that the words "even for Portugal" be expunged from the record.

Other Bank of Portugal officials testified that the Bank had no choice but to call-in the whole issue of 500-escudos notes and exchange them since the legitimate notes were not then distinguishable from the Marang notes. Not until August, 1926, did the Bank learn from the investigators of the key to the tiny, secret letters employed in the notes. Of course, by then nearly all the Marang notes had been exchanged.

On the trial's eighth day Birkett had a fine time with Carlos de Barros Soares Branco, the Secretary General of the Bank of Portugal. Birkett established that the Bank not only had a million pound suit against Waterlow's but had a similar suit against the conspirators in Holland, to get all they had on deposit in banks. In short, there was a possibility that the Bank would be collecting twice over. Marang, apparently, had at one time £200,000 ($1,-000,000) on deposit in various Dutch banks. José Bandeira had already turned over to the Liquidation Commission $350,000 he had in the Bank of Westminster in London.

Is it supposed that there is a very large sum of £400,000 to £500,000 in the hands of Marang or Hennies?

Soares Branco admitted it was possible.

Justice Wright was properly disturbed. He had not been told of the possibility of *double* recovery.

The witness agreed that in May, 1925, the Bank of Portugal issued a report that there was no foundation to rumors of false 500-escudos notes circulating:

Q. That notice was of great value to the conspirators?
A. —That is a question which the conspirators would be able to answer better than I can. [Laughter.]

The governor of the Bank of Portugal, Innocencio Camacho Rodrigues, could throw no light on the letter that Sir William mailed on January 7, 1925. Yes, his files had been searched carefully but he was certain no such letter had ever been received. "If it had we should not be here now," he added.

Still Birkett found a way for the governor to be useful to the Waterlow case:

> Q. Portugal decorated Marang with the highest Order . . . the Order of Christ?
>
> A. No, it was not the highest . . . it was one of those things which are given, a small Order, nothing, really.
>
> Q. Is the bearer of the Portuguese Order of Christ entitled to wear a small button?
>
> A. Unfortunately there is a degree in the Order which allows the bearers to wear a little bit of ribbon to lead other people to believe they belong to the Legion of Honour. . . .

Camacho admitted that the man who had proposed Marang for the Order of Christ was later the prosecuting counsel in the case against Alves Reis. Camacho smiled and shrugged:

> Yes; that is only one of the incidents in the life of political people. [Laughter.]
>
> Q. I was putting it that Marang really was a plausible man, a plausible man who deceived high personages in Portugal?
>
> A. Yes, and he had done the same thing in Holland; he was an international one.

Marang's great plausibility would be an important part of Birkett's case when he got Sir William on the stand. This took place on December 11th after Birkett opened the defense.

Sir William told of his first and subsequent meetings with Marang, how he had the contracts checked by a notary and his personal solicitor, how he had written to Camacho on January 7th. About the Romer correspondence:

> I was very afraid of Romer, having past experience . . . unfortunately he had the gift of not being able to keep his mouth closed on anything.

Finally Stuart Bevan got his great chance to cross-examine the defense's most vulnerable witness, Sir William. He quickly elicited that Sir William not only had some doubts about Romer but had some about Andrew Walker, the Waterlow "bird dog" in Lisbon:

I have nothing whatever to say against his honesty. I think he was a perfectly honest man, but not a man I would place any confidence in, or ever did.

Q. Had you ever, before this action, concerned yourself personally in taking and executing an order for Portuguese notes?
A. If the letter had not come to me personally from the Dutch
firm of printers [Enschedé] I should never have been concerned about it.

Bevan brought out that although Sir William left the firm in 1928, Romer and Walker were still employed by Waterlow's.

One of the reasons Romer may not have been *too* put out by the secret negotiations for the banknote order with Marang and Bandeira, might have been that he got full commission on the order even though he had nothing to do with getting it.

As Sir William recalled:

Romer got the credit in his account for the Marang orders
and when this fraud came to light, his solicitors advised him that
he should not have taken it, and so he returned it.

Bevan now got to the heart of what he believed was Sir William's great culpability:

Q. You knew the responsibility which attached to your business?
A. A certain amount, but after all, we were only printers. We are
only ordinary commercial men. [Laughter.]
Q. You are putting it a great deal lower than I was prepared to
put it. You appreciated that if, through any mischance, unauthorized notes did, through your presses, get on to the
world, the consequences would be most serious.
A. Yes, but who would have thought of such a thing as this and
who would have thought that the Bank of Portugal did not
keep a register of 500-escudos notes?
Q. You attach all blame to the Bank of Portugal?
A. I would never have thought it possible that an issue of notes
could go on for months without knowing there were dupli-
cates. I would never have dreamt of such a thing . . . I dare-
say if the same thing happened again, without the experience
of this matter, I should do exactly the same again.
Q. From first to last had you ever the least uneasiness about this
transaction?
A. No.

Q. Did you ever realize that the Bank of Portugal would have to pay on the notes?

A. I do not think I did.

Q. Did you realize that when you handed the notes to Marang you were putting a liability of a million sterling on your customers, the Bank of Portugal?

A. I do not think I did.

Q. Why, if you had such confidence in Marang as a postman, did you write direct to the Governor of the Bank acknowledging his supposed letter of authority?

A. It was a wise precaution.

Q. Did you feel a little uneasy?

A. No.

Q. Did you think: "This is the oddest business I have ever been employed on. I wonder if it is all right. I will just throw out a feeler."

A. No.

Q. You had been asked to communicate with the Governor only through Marang. Are you sure that you did not stop the letter from going even after it had been stamped?

A. No.

Q. Does it occur to you that somebody must have been a little casual in not noticing that there were repeat orders for the same numbers?

A. I should be very pleased to show you the correspondence I have on that subject.

Q. I should be more pleased if you would answer my question.

A. I have never been able to understand it . . . I never got to the bottom of it.

Then there was the second order for 380,000 notes from Marang.

Q. Did you say anything to Marang about it: how comes it that with the original contract exhausted you want twice as many notes.

A. I am sure I raised the question with Marang . . .

Q. Did he give you any explanation?

A. That I cannot remember. I think he must have done.

Q. The situation demanded an explanation, did it not?

A. Well—

Q. Did it strike you as odd that the Governor of the Bank of Por-

tugal should be under such a misapprehension of the position
that he thought the 380,000 notes, 2½ million sterling, was
the remainder of the order for 200,000, for one million sterling?

A. I am afraid it did not at the time.

Q. It was a dreadful lapse of memory, was it not? . . . a singular
misapprehension, was it not?

A. Of course all we knew was that the customer who had been
well-introduced to us and for whom we had executed the
order to print banknotes, had turned up again to give us
another order. I have nothing more that I can add to it.

Q. I am sorry but you provoke me . . .

It was only a manner of speaking. Bevan was inordinately
pleased with Sir William. The former chairman of Waterlow's
had strengthened the case for the Bank of Portugal enormously.
Now Norman Birkett had to try to undo some of the damage on
his reexamination of the ex-Lord Mayor.

But Justice Wright, as he often did, got into the dialogue:

Q. I suppose the real question is whether there ought to have
been such a degree of unsuspiciousness having regard to the
peculiar position of printers of banknotes and whether something more definite ought not to have been done, where the
circumstances were rather peculiar. They were peculiar, of
course, Sir William, were they not?

A. They were, undoubtedly, my Lord.

Q. Obviously, you entirely trusted Marang.

A. I am afraid confidence was established in the first instance, my
Lord, and when confidence is once established,—

Q. Everything follows. Yes . . .

The Judge's comment, his inflections, his manner at this point
gave the defense barristers their first real intimation of the way
the Judge's mind was going. He had used "peculiar" three times.

At one point Sir William volunteered that he had given
Bevan an incorrect answer:

Mr. Bevan asked me the other day if this was the most confidential thing I had ever done and I said yes. But it was not so,
my Lord. . . . The most confidential business I have ever under-
taken was Secret Service during the War. I never told a single

colleague of mine about what was done. . . . If you want to have it I will write it down.*

Justice Wright, sensibly enough, did not want him to. It seemed to some spectators Sir William was visibly disappointed.

Birkett also took some of the sting out of Bevan's cross-examination about the second batch of banknotes which exceeded the original contract:

Q. Over six months had passed since Marang had visited you the first time?
A. Yes.
Q. Had there been anything at all anywhere of the smallest kind to indicate that there had been anything irregular in the first order?
A. Nothing whatever.
Q. Did the fact that Marang after six months came back to you give you confidence, if you needed it, or did it strike you as merely a continuation of an ordinary commercial transaction?
A. . . . If I had any idea that there was a fraud, I should not expect to see the man turn up again in my office.

The point had been nicely made when Justice Wright stepped in to undo it by pointing out that

the first order had the backing of two contracts and the power of attorney, and everything under those contracts had been exhausted by the first order. . . .

Bevan had a thoroughly fine time with Roland Springall.

Q. Had you ever seen £2,500,000 worth of notes packed in suitcases, placed in taxicabs, and deposited in a public cloakroom where there were turkeys and bicycles and all sorts of things? [Laughter.]
A. No.

Justice Wright couldn't resist:

Cloakrooms are the safest places in which to deposit stolen goods.

Birkett could top that easily:

Or sometimes dead bodies. [Laughter.]

* This was the business of helping the Secret Service by counterfeiting German postage stamps and currency.

Bevan knew that the defense would not call Romer as a witness. He could only hurt them and help the plaintiff greatly. But there was another way. Springall had some talks with Romer after the case broke:

Q. Romer felt in the letters and telegrams he had received a snub from his firm?
A. He felt it, I think.
Q. I suppose he was indignant at the treatment he had received?
A. I should say so.
Q. Between December and May [1925] he repeated his warnings and said he knew better than Sir William?
A. There was a divergence of opinion between them.
Q. Did he in effect say there is trouble ahead with this contract if it is carried through?
A. In effect, yes.

Justice Wright came back to Romer:

Q. When did Romer cease to express his view about it; perhaps he never ceased?
A. I do not think he has ever ceased to express his views; I hear it all day and every day.
Q. He must be a tiresome fellow?
A. I am afraid I have had to deal with Mr. Romer ever since he joined us, and I have a great deal of sympathy for him.

Later, Birkett helped delineate Romer's qualities:

Q. Do you think he talks too much?
A. I think he exercises a very great amount of discretion; he is a great talker, but there it is.
Q. In the Johnsonian tradition, a great talker?
A. Yes.

Like everyone else, Justice Wright was curious about another point:

Q. Did Romer ever see Marang?
A. Yes, he had been present in our office when Marang came.
Q. Did he ever talk to him?
A. He was never introduced to him . . . I believe I informed Mr. Goodman that Mr. Romer was in the office and Mr. Marang did not seem to wish, or Mr. Goodman did not desire, to bring anyone else in on . . . the secret business.

What a splendid judge, Bevan surely thought, and went on with Springall:

> Q. Did Romer, when the fraud was discovered, say anything like I told you so?
>
> A. Yes, that was more or less his view.

Now Springall had to take his lumps.

> Q. In the letter you wrote Marang you said: "In accordance with your request we send you herewith a list of directors' signatures." Do you observe, knowing what we know now, if you had not sent those signatures this order might never have been carried out?

Justice Wright, ever helpful, reminded Bevan that Springall had in his letter added "and changing with each series."

> Q. Do you see how you assisted Mr. Marang in his fraud by that courtesy on your part of giving to a layman . . . every help you could? Do you realize that you have helped him to the extent of supplying him with the signatures and selection of the signatures without information as to which he could not have had these notes printed? *
>
> A. Of course I do.
>
> Q. It is a frightful responsibility to have to carry through the rest of your life.
>
> A. Certainly. I am looking at it through the spectacles of 1930.
>
> Q. You were anxious to give him all the help you could?
>
> A. That is part of my job. We are expected, as printers, to do a lot of things which in the ordinary way we would expect our customers to do. . . . We are expected to do all kinds of things.

Frederick Goodman, the 75-year-old Waterlow director who looked like the late Edward VII, was warier of Stuart Bevan's questions. On cross-examination Bevan asked about the possibility of Bradbury & Wilkinson getting Marang's business since he had shown Waterlow's two Bradbury notes on the original contract:

> Q. It was alarming, was it not, that a gentleman who had the authority of the Bank of Portugal had expressed a desire to

---

* Birkett somehow let pass the fact that the Bank of Portugal had reluctantly acknowledged it had been possible for Alves Reis to work out the combinations of serial numbers, letters and directors' names "without any breach of secrecy."

have a Bradbury note, which only Bradbury could print?

A. I do not think it was alarming.

Q. Did it occur to you that the Bank of Portugal business which you had secured might slip away and go back to Bradbury?

A. No.

Q. If you had chosen you could have told Marang that these were Bradbury productions—and not just "American notes."

A. We could have, certainly.

Q. Why drag in America?

A. Because Bradbury's belongs to the American Bank Note Company.

Q. Are their printing works in England?

A. They have printing works here and in other places.

Q. Was it with a view to securing this business for yourself that you produced the Vasco da Gama note?

A. Well, yes.

Q. Did you appreciate that if you did not get this order there was a risk of Bradbury's getting back to the Bank of Portugal?

A. Probably we thought that they would be very willing to oblige the Governor of the Bank of Portugal.

Justice Wright was helpful here, too. Goodman told how he dictated the letter to Romer. In it he provided the safeguards of Romer getting the authority of the Bank of Portugal—after Bandeira "had fixed up everything with the Portuguese Minister of Finance and the directors of the Bank."

Q. And then you dropped your safeguard?

A. The authority came without it.

Q. You thought it came?

A. Yes.

Q. That is just the risk you ran. If you had stuck to your idea of Mr. Romer going to the Bank, you would never have had any difficulty.

A. No, my Lord. Now we can see that.

Q. Sometimes duty requires that you should see things in advance.

A. There were three of us and we were equally deceived.

Q. Do you remember any other similar transaction in which everything was conducted by or through one person?

A. It is a most unusual thing but I would not say that we have not had it.

Q. You cannot remember one?
A. No.

But Director Thomas William Goldsack did recall a vaguely analagous situation. Liberia, poor little Liberia, had made a deal with a London merchant named Hayman. With authority, he ordered and paid for an emission of Liberian postage stamps which he was able to sell to stamp collectors the world over, splitting his profits with Liberia. This was one of the beginnings of what is now common practice among many of the newer countries. (Postage stamps bought to fill spaces in albums and not used for postage are nearly all profit, of course.)

Another director, Francis Muir, was more helpful to Birkett. He said that if the Bank of Portugal in December, 1925, had cabled Waterlow's that there had been a "duplication" instead of a "falsification" of notes, the firm could have told the Bank almost immediately how to distinguish the two sets of notes through the secret markings.

But under cross-examination Muir had to admit that distinguishing the good notes from the Marangs was not simple, not when 800,000 notes were involved. Not even with the chart he had prepared:

Q. They would first have to arrange the notes by series and then take your chart and look at each?

Justice Wright was skeptical.

Q. Are there people whose unassisted eyesight is strong enough to look at a note and see whether it has an I or a P [secret letter] on it?
A. Yes, our girls do it with their eyesight alone. I reckoned 800,000 notes and you could have arranged them in their right order and sorted them out with the help of the chart at the rate of about two a minute. Now two a minute would be about . . .
Q. . . . 120 an hour . . . for eight hours a day. Do you work eight hours doing that? But supposing you found any individual strong enough to do that for eight hours a day, you would do about 1000 a day?
A. Yes. I reckoned it would take 30 people four weeks.

Birkett delivered his long, closing speech on December 18th and part of the 19th. Bevan who was far more confident by now had a much shorter summation.

On Monday, December 22nd, Justice Wright was ready with the judgment.

He was quite frank. He had no need for more time because he had already had "a definite conclusion on all material aspects of the case" which he called "a most elaborate fraud . . . unparalleled in the history of commercial fraud."

He outlined the case for the morning and by early afternoon it was quite clear where he was heading:

> I am bound to say that the Company [Waterlow's] by its Directors, did fall short of the standard of care and understanding. . . . The printer of banknotes cannot say he is merely a commercial printer . . . he is a printer of banknotes and the effect of issuing spurious and unauthorized banknotes may be enormous on the whole life of a nation and on the whole stability of an important Banking Institution. . . . There was a want of due care here. . . .

Now he began to ease the blow a trifle for Waterlow's.

> No one suggests for a minute a word of reflection on the honour or good faith of Messrs. Waterlow, or any of the Directors . . . it is merely one of those unfortunate circumstances which overtake the most eminent and distinguished and high class firms in which the wiles of the swindlers for the moment distracts the minds of those concerned. . . .

The crime was unique, he went on, and

> . . . it is not a thing which will ever happen again; it is only a series of unfortunate coincidences which has caused it to happen in this case.

The Bank of Portugal really had no alternative but to call-in the notes and exchange them.

> I cannot see what other course they could have taken because all their credit was at stake . . . as well as the national and financial position.

And as to what damage was done by exchanging the da Gama notes for others, he believed there was a loss, a great loss:

> These notes are currency in Portugal. They can purchase commodities in Portugal, including gold; they can buy foreign exchange—and they can do this because they have behind them the credit of the Bank of Portugal.

Yes, perhaps the notes could have been distinguished with great effort but

> in the early days . . . the rush was so great that as a practical matter I do not think the Bank could have put into operation these delicate though simple methods of discriminating them.

He would not grant the Bank interest on its claim. And he would not allow the Bank to claim some 16,000 notes which he thought it need not have paid out. Of course, the realizable assets of the liquidated Bank of Angola & Metropole—some £488,430 (about $2,400,000) had to be deducted, too. This left

> if my arithmetic is correct, a balance of £531,851 [about $2,600,000] for which, in my view, there ought to be judgment for the Plaintiff.

As usual, the winner also was awarded costs of the trial, estimated at about £50,000 (some $240,000).

And he expressed gratitude to Messrs. Waterlow for transcribing and printing the daily proceedings of the trial. But he did note that "there were a good many misprints."

Of course, there would be an appeal.

✿   ✿   ✿   ✿   ✿

The *Daily Telegraph* of London found that the decision was

> an occasion for pride in the impressive witness which the case bears to the traditional impartiality of British courts of justice. . . .

In Lisbon, *O Seculo* editorialized that there could have been on other conclusion:

> To have the honor of British justice, the trial ended as it should have . . . the Judge was not influenced by his national pride or the London atmosphere. Portuguese pride and sensitivity came out strengthened from the harsh ordeal. . . . Portugal won in London because it was right. . . . Let us rejoice.

And then, because the trial was in many ways a splendid drama, *O Seculo* added some capsule critiques of the performances:

Sir William: proud, contemptuous, stupid, stubborn, self-righteous, cowardly.

Camacho: honest, sound, plain-spoken, humble.

Ulrich: erudite, phlegmatic, lucid, very British.

The *Diario de Noticias* had an approving critical notice for Justice Wright:

> From the very first day he showed he had all the qualities of a great, austere and impartial judge. . . .
>
> Glory also to the Bank of Portugal which sent a mission of honest, competent men of rare intellectual worth. . . . Their testimony was a model of rectitude and sagacity in being able to avoid traps laid by a lawyer of immense resource bent on confusing them. The country should be grateful to them.

Sir William's critical comments were only made in private but in his copy of the trial's daily transcripts he penciled many bitter comments about the Judge's summation and verdict.

In the copy I have, his angular handwriting in the margin reads, randomly:

> That is wrong
> No mention of the Governor's letter being sent to Messer
> No mention of correspondence being destroyed by Dr. Ulrich
> Incorrect
> All most inaccurate
> Bankers would appear in the mind of the Judge entitled to special privileges
> Bankers ought to protect themselves
> Why should the printer have to live up to such a high criterion?
> Protecting the bankers!
> How can he say that?
> No responsibility ever seems to rest on the Bank

Of course, his comments couldn't have mattered less. The chairman of Waterlow's, Edgar L. Waterlow, announced that the firm had set aside a reserve fund to take care of the judgment—if it lost its appeals. "Whatever the ultimate outcome . . . our resources are ample to meet any eventuality."

After Judge Wright's decision the solicitors for both sides

met to discuss a compromise settlement. Waterlow's was in favor
and so was the Bank of Portugal's London representatives. But
the Bank's directors in Lisbon wouldn't settle for a shilling less.
They knew they could depend on British justice.

In his London apartment at 5 Balfour Place, off Park Lane,
Sir William A. Waterlow, Bart.* got small consolation from a letter written by a fellow Londoner, S. C. Spouse, who had been
the only British trader in Angola in 1925. No one, wrote Mr.
Spouse,

> conversant with the conditions existing, and having knowledge
> of the psychology of the Portuguese and their methods of con-
> ducting operations, would consider there was anything abnormal
> in the way the negotiations were conducted between yourselves
> and Marang . . . it is very unfortunate, Sir, that you could not
> receive the sympathy you rightly deserved. Perhaps I am unduly
> prejudiced, but I know only too well, that, had the positions
> been reversed, and an English firm sought redress in Portugal
> they would never have had a fair hearing. . . .

Sir William thanked Mr. Spouse cordially. Pity he couldn't have
been a witness.

❋　　❋　　❋　　❋　　❋

LISBON / January, 1931

THE SENTENCE IMPOSED on Alves Reis included a two-year stretch
of solitary confinement but that had not yet been implemented.
Reis was still permitted his own clothes and had permission to receive visitors and write.

* One of the rewards for being Lord Mayor is the almost automatic
award of a baronetcy, the lowest hereditary British rank. It was a considerably higher honor than the mere K.B.E. which he had.

It was some writer's conceit that a writer's real capital is his youth, but Alves Reis knew *his* only possible capital was his crime. So this month he began writing his *Secrets of My Confessions*. He had been studying the Bible with great care and from the New Testament he selected the opening theme for his book. It was from John (8:46):

"And if I say the truth, why do ye not believe me?" The volume was sarcastically dedicated to "Those who seek worldly riches." In it he detailed all the tricks he had employed in conceiving the crime and executing the various contracts, letters and documents he needed.

Like far more professional writers who employ an almost tic-like repetition of favorite words or phrases, Alves Reis had an oft-repeated favorite, too. When plotting and executing his forgeries he was always "calm and confident."

The second volume which told of his long five-hour confession in court opened with a line from Matthew (6:19):

> Lay not up for yourselves treasures upon earth where moth and rust doth corrupt and where thieves break through and steal; but lay up for yourselves treasures in Heaven. For where your treasure is, there will your heart be also.

The second volume concluded with the standard admonition:

> No man can serve two masters for either he will hate the one and love the other; or else he will hold to the one and despise the other. He cannot serve God and Mammon.

Mammon wasn't served with any vigor through the sale of the two-volume paperbacked set. About 2000 copies of each book were sold for about $1 each. Still, it was a help. Senhora Reis had great difficulty bringing up three boys on her $20 a month salary.

On one of her regular weekly visits to the penitentiary Alves Reis remembered that once in the old Angola & Metropole Bank days he had casually given an acquaintance 75,000 escudos to keep him from jail after embezzling money from a government office. Reis suggested his wife approach the man who had since risen to higher office and ask if it would now be possible to repay the sum.

The official acknowledged the gift but refused to pay it.

"Why should I repay with good money the bad money I received six years ago?"

"One sheds one's sicknesses in books," D. H. Lawrence wrote. With his *Confessions* completed, Alves Reis felt calmer in spirit. He was now ready to begin the rigorous two-years' solitary confinement.

✻   ✻   ✻   ✻   ✻

LONDON / March 26, 1931

THE APPEAL AGAINST Justice Wright's award to the Bank of Portugal opened in the Court of Appeal on February 23, 1931. The defense cast had been added to: Sir John Simon, a prominent Liberal Member of Parliament who was later to become Foreign Secretary and then Lord Chancellor—was now to lead the Appellants' team (Waterlow) against the Respondents (Bank of Portugal).

Birkett was younger and Simon the more experienced K.C., but the sense that he had been demoted stayed with Birkett. Stuart Bevan still led for the Bank. Why change a winning team?

Sir John opened with the Appellants' basic claim: that the judgment given by Justice Wright "called for a very substantial modification."

On the fourth day Sir John noted with inner warmth that Lord Justice Slesser seemed to be most understanding. In discussing that part of the original trial record dealing with the arrests in Oporto early in December, 1925, Slesser said:

> They seem to have done everything themselves calculated to produce a panic, arresting these people in public streets and so on. It was made as public as possible . . . I doubt if they thought the matter out at all. The question that occurs to me is

whether your clients [the Bank of Portugal] did not themselves produce the panic and agitation by their previous behaviour; I mean the panic would not have arisen at all if they acted otherwise.

Lord Justice Greer provided Sir John Simon with another bit of cheer:

> I was very much astounded to find that efforts were made on the part of the Defendants to get some evidence as to Portuguese law from a number of Portuguese lawyers and not one of them would assist. Some one of your witnesses said they were quite right in refusing to assist. I should not under those circumstances . . . attach very much value to the evidence of any Portuguese lawyer.

On March 26th the three-justice Court of Appeal rendered its verdict. Lord Justice Scrutton was in the minority: he felt all the Bank was entitled to "was the cost of replacing the notes or some £8,922. And nothing else.

Lord Justice Greer wasn't as harsh on the Bank but he thought it hadn't done all it could to mitigate the loss through the exchange of banknotes. He had come to the conclusion—and wisely didn't try to explain *how*—that Waterlow

> . . . could and would have ascertained by Dec. 9th from their printing office the existence of I to P [secret letter] test if they had received full information from the Bank and that the Bank would have had the information by wire at latest in time to apply the test on and after the 10th. . . .
>
> It is impossible to arrive at an exactly accurate figure representing what the loss would have been if they had made reasonable efforts on the early morning of Dec. 7th to discover how the false notes came on the market . . . but I have arrived at a round figure of £300,000 as the best estimate of damages.

The new magic figure also was approved by Lord Justice Slesser but for a somewhat different reason. He thought that

> . . . the date on which the Bank in all circumstances might properly have refused to issue good notes in exchange for the Marang notes was 10th Dec. and not 16th Dec.

, A kind of victory for Waterlow, but it wasn't enough. The case would be appealed to the highest court in the Empire: the House of Lords.

*   *   *   *   *

LONDON / July 6, 1931

SIR WILLIAM WAS naturally pleased that the Court of Appeal had reduced the verdict against Waterlow considerably and he felt certain that in time the final appeal in the House of Lords would reduce the award just to printing costs. He often went over the 1600 pages of the closely-printed records of the two trials.

The Germans have often been accused of being the only people who felt it necessary to devise a single word—*schaden-freude* to denote "malignant joy" in the misfortunes of others. What Sir William needed now was a word, an expression, for a much more complicated emotion. Ever since he left Waterlow's in 1928 the firm's annual net profits had dropped steadily:

$$
\begin{array}{lll}
1928 & \ldots & \pounds\,190{,}000 \\
1929 & \ldots & \pounds\,171{,}000 \\
1930 & \ldots & \pounds\,162{,}000 \\
\end{array}
$$

and from what he could learn, 1931 was going to be disastrous. (It was; profits fell to £87,000.) There was a fierce joy in the steady fall after his guiding hand had been forcibly removed from the helm. This was tempered, considerably, by the knowledge that one-third of his fortune was in Waterlow stock. Possibly, too, he may have admitted to himself that the fall in profits came *after* the enormously adverse publicity the case gave Waterlow's.

Early in July he felt severe abdominal pains and his physician advised immediate hospitalization and surgery. Peritonitis set in after surgery—as it all too often did in days prior to the antibiotics—and on July 6th Sir William was dead. He was 60.

The obituaries were lengthy, muted and most respectful. The Portuguese business was played down greatly. Not one obituary noted that Sir William's motto as a Baronet, *Per Mortem Vinco* ("I conquer through death") hardly seemed fulfilled in this case.

When his will was probated in August the papers announced that Sir William had left a comparatively modest estate of £58,000, reduced after death duties to £38,000 (about $190,-000). Most of it went to his wife and two sons. There were minor bequests to loyal aides: £200 to his secretary, Miss Shaw; and £100 to his chauffeur, Wensley, and £500 to his old public school, Marlborough.

Waterlow & Sons felt obliged to issue a statement to the press:

> Some surprise may be expressed at the small amount left by Sir William. . . . But the damages and costs of the law action brought by the Bank of Portugal did not in any way affect his personal estate. All the costs were borne by the company.

Strictly speaking, the statement was correct but in an indirect way the case had affected Sir William's estate. As his older son, James—who inherited the title—explained to friends later, the case had caused Waterlow shares to drop considerably. And since one-third of Sir William's estate consisted of shares in Waterlow the drop was directly felt. In addition, there had been the £10,000 Sir William had to spend on entertainment and charities during his year as Lord Mayor, plus the extra cost of ceremonial visits to Belgium, France and Denmark. His reign as Lord Mayor, said *The Times,* had been "one of the most brilliant of modern times."

The funeral was held in St. Paul's Cathedral with considerable pomp. There was a condolence message from the royal family, and hundreds of prominent Britons attended—*The Times* list ran more than a column. From Waterlow and Sons there was only one official representative, a minor executive named Smith.

Sir William was buried in the Harrow Weald churchyard, not far from the fine home he had once owned.

Another Waterlow went three months later. On September 20, 1931, Sir Philip H. Waterlow , Bart., who had been Sir William's predecessor as chairman of the family firm, died. "Fifty senior members of the staff of Waterlow and Sons attended his funeral" reported *The Times*. His title was inherited by his son, Edgar, now the chairman of Waterlow & Sons. Sir Philip left an estate of £255,000 after taxes.

Edgar had not spoken to Sir William from 1928 until his death. Every time Edgar looked at his 1931 year-end balance sheet with its reserve fund of £650,000 to meet a possible adverse decision in the House of Lords, he felt anew resentment at the incredible blundering of his cousin who had already cost the firm so much in reputation and might cost them the loss of more than three million dollars.

* * * * *

LONDON / April 28, 1932

THE LORD CHANCELLOR selects the Law Lords to sit on a case that is to be heard on final appeal in the House of Lords. Viscount Sankey, the then Lord Chancellor, was the highest legal officer in the realm, a member of the Prime Minister's Cabinet, and the Presiding Officer of the House of Lords.

Sankey, a draper's son like Birkett, had become Lord Chancellor in 1929 when the Labour Party came to power for a second time. Although he was a Conservative he was appreciated by Labour because he once headed a national commission which had first recommended nationalization of the nation's coal industry, a venerable Labour goal.

The Lord Chancellor selected four Law Lords—Lord Warrington of Clyffe; Lord Atkin; Lord Russell of Killowen and Lord

MacMillan—to sit with him on the case of the Bank of Portugal vs. Waterlow and Sons Limited.

All had been K.C.'s and had extensive civil litigation experience. Four of them had been civil court justices and the one who had not, Lord MacMillan, had been Lord Advocate in the first Labour government of 1924.

There were some changes in the line-up of Waterlow's counsel; Sir John Simon had to leave the team when he became Foreign Secretary. He was replaced by Gavin Simonds, K.C., with Norman Birkett again in a secondary position. The Bank held on to its original combination with Stuart Bevan.

Another change in the economic atmosphere might have had some influence on the outcome. In September, 1931, Great Britain in the middle of a severe depression, went off the gold standard. No longer could Britons exchange pound notes at the Bank of England for gold sovereigns or—with lots of pound notes—for a gold bar. Now in England, as in Portugal, banknotes were convertible only into other banknotes.

The consolidated appeals—the Bank and Waterlow were both appealing—were heard in the 45-foot high Chamber of the House of Lords. Here on the opening of Parliament, the Sovereign is seated on the throne at the end of the room, wearing the Imperial Crown. The assembled Lords and Commons seated on the tufted red leather benches listen to the Gracious Speech.

The speeches were presented by the opposing K.C.'s somewhat less graciously but very much to the point.

Stuart Bevan drew the obvious analogy early in his argument before the Lords, to Britain's new state of inconvertibility:

> It is a rather startling proposition that if the Bank of England were deprived by theft or otherwise of certain notes in circulation the Bank would be only entitled to the costs of paper and printing . . . If in the ordinary way the Bank of Portugal had handed out 200,000 notes they would have received assets of corresponding value, whereas here they had received nothing except worthless pieces of paper.

The trial before Justice Wright had taken 21 days; the one in the Court of Appeals, 11 days and, finally, in the House of Lords only 9 days were needed. There were no witnesses heard, of course. The Law Lords had the 1600 pages of testimony, the prior judgments and the cogent arguments of opposing counsel to go on.

On April 28, 1932, the split 3-2 decision was given. Speaking for the majority, the Lord Chancellor, Viscount Sankey, held that the Bank of Portugal was entitled to recover.

As he saw it, the simplest analogy was to

> imagine two persons coming into the Bank of Portugal at the same time, each of them wanting a good 500-escudos note. The first was an Englishman who wanted to get some Portuguese money. He handed over to the Bank five English pounds and got in return a 500-escudos note. The other person handed over one of the forged notes and he also got a 500-escudos note. What was the position of the Bank? In the first case they had got in exchange for the 500-escudos note five pounds in English money; in the second place they had gotten in exchange for the 500-escudos note a worthless forged note. It was not possible to say that in the second place the Bank had suffered no damage because they could print and issue a third 500-escudos note should they desire to do so. For that note they could also have obtained value. In truth they had lost the face value of the second note by reason of the fact that they had only got a worthless note in exchange.

Accordingly, he found that the Bank of Portugal should recover its entire claim against Waterlow, less the amount received from the conspirators, or a total recovery of £610,392 (about $3,000,000). And since it was the loser, Waterlow would also have to pay the costs of the two appeals.

He was joined by Lord Atkin and Lord MacMillan. The latter in his separate judgment observed a point that no one else had yet touched on in any of the trials—the accumulations by the conspirators and their Bank of Angola & Metropole. They, he said

> constituted themselves an illegal bank of issue for the spurious notes which cost them nothing but the cost of paper and printing, yet they seem to have made half a million sterling and probably much more by the issue of these notes. Why, it occurs to me to ask, should it be said that the Bank of Portugal would not equally have received value in return if it had issued a corre-

sponding number of genuine notes in ordinary course and that it had been deprived of nothing by having had to issue them gratuitously?

The minority dissenters, Lord Warrington of Clyffe and Lord Russell of Killowen, felt that the Bank had no right to recover anything except the cost of replacing the notes, some £8900.

Waterlow's paid the Bank the money plus the trial costs soon after. The 41 days of trial was estimated to have come to £95,000 (about $460,000) in costs which meant that the reserve fund of £650,000 that Waterlow had set aside for a possible adverse verdict wasn't quite enough.*

The verdict got understandably mixed reactions. In the City of London the general view was that the decision was most unfair, that the Bank of Portugal had been given an undeserved windfall of several million dollars. In a terribly roundabout way he'd never contemplated, Alves Reis' plan to bring fresh capital to Portugal and its colonies had succeeded.

The case was reviewed in *The Economic Journal* published by the Royal Economic Society. Ralph G. Hawtrey who was later to become president of the Society and *Sir* Ralph, thought the Lords' verdict in this "peculiarly audacious conspiracy" was an eminently just one:

> A manufacturer of explosives assumes a certain liability for accidents, and he cannot pass it on to his customers on the ground that they procured him to manufacture the dangerous product. The apparatus for the manufacture of bank notes has an explosive quality, and whoever undertakes the business does so at his peril.

But another expert, Sir Cecil Kisch, disagreed. As a British Foreign Office authority on central banks he had followed the three trials closely. In fact, after Waterlow lost the case in Justice Wright's court, Sir Cecil's advice had been sought by Francis Muir, the Waterlow director. But Sir Cecil felt it was too late to be of much help. He thought, though, that if Sir John Simon had been able to carry the case for Waterlow's to the House of Lords the banknote firm would have won.

---

* Waterlow's was well-insured against the normal risks of fire, theft and embezzlement. But who would sell you insurance against gullibility— or dare suggest you needed it?

Years later, in his London home on quiet Kensington Square, Sir Cecil talked to a visitor about what he called "the greatest swindle ever perpetrated." At the time his comments were not for quotation but with his death in 1961 that restriction is gone. He regarded "the stupidity of Sir William as being largely responsible for the complete success of this great confidence trick. He was a pompous man and like all pompous men, preferred to rely on his own judgment rather than trust that of others."

Sir Cecil felt the firm's defense had been mishandled. "They should have concentrated on the question of actual loss suffered by the Bank of Portugal instead of on the technical details. Sir John Simon intended to do this in the House of Lords appeal and just before he had to remove himself to become Foreign Secretary he told me he was confident Waterlow would win on this issue alone."

❄   ❄   ❄   ❄   ❄

EPILOGUE

BERLIN / September 20, 1932

NONE OF DÖRING'S ventures turned out well. The Chinese arms deal had been a costly waste of time. There had been a venture in Paris that soured and set him back $50,000. And now a grandiose scheme to settle Germans in Bolivia fell through dismally and cost another $25,000. With the severe fall in German securities he also had a great paper loss. He went to Kassel early in 1932 to get the securities which he held in a vault at the Landeskredit Bank. He had paid 1,000,000 marks (about $250,000) for them and now they had fallen to less than $50,000 in value. The Austrian Credit-Anstalt failure in Vienna marked the beginning of the financial collapse of all central Europe. By the beginning of 1932 there were more than six million unemployed. In the July, 1932, Reichstag elections the Nazis won 320 seats and some of Döring's old friends who were now influential in the rising National Socialist Party assured him that they would be in power before long.

From a friendly source Döring heard that the Portuguese were still anxious to try him in Lisbon. In anticipation of such a calamity Döring gave a power of attorney over his securities to an old friend, Heinrich K——— a Berliner.*

Early in September, 1932, Döring spotted his former mistress Annaliese Angold, on the Kurfürstendam in Berlin. It had been years since their liaison ended but he was curious. He followed her to her comfortable home in Zehlendorf and made some discreet inquiries. She had married a prosperous medical specialist and was now a well-dressed, middle-class housewife.

A few days later Döring phoned her and insisted they have a drink together for "old times' sake." A little apprehensively, she agreed and they met in the Cafe Kranzler on the Koo-Dam.

After going over the good old days in The Hague and Am-

---

* I avoid naming him because he is alive and the serious charges made against him later in this narrative are still unproven.

sterdam, he got down to his proposal: he had a foolproof system to beat the roulette wheel in Monte Carlo. But he needed a stake of $1,000 to get it started. *When* he won he and Frau Doktor ——— (he mentioned her married name with studied casualness) would share equally in the great winnings.

Annaliese kept calm. She would need a few days to think it over. Where could she get in touch with him? He was at the little Hotel Kiel, on Mittelstrasse. Things weren't going too well with him, he admitted. His pride wouldn't let him add that he had managed to get himself on the dole: he was drawing 20 marks a week (about $5) as one of the unemployed.

Annaliese knew it was the beginning of blackmail. There was only one way to handle such an affair. She left her former lover and went to the Portuguese Embassy in Berlin.

She spoke to the Vice-Consul: was there still a reward for information about Adolf Hennies, the missing criminal in the famous Bank of Angola & Metropole swindle? The consul asked her to wait while he checked with the Ambassador, Dr. Costa Cabral. The Ambassador wired Lisbon and the consul asked Annaliese to return in two days.

Lisbon replied that Adolf Hennies was very much wanted in Portugal to stand trial.

When Annaliese returned, she was told the Bank of Portugal was ready to offer a $500 reward. She informed the consul that Adolf Hennies who was really Johann Döring, was now living in the Hotel Kiel, room 57, on the third floor.

The Portuguese Ambassador phoned the Berlin police commissioner who, in turn, checked with legal officials in the Foreign Ministry. The situation was complicated. Although the Weimar Republic would not extradite its citizens to face jail in foreign countries, it had signed a League of Nations Convention of April 20, 1929. This established that each signatory country would punish equally the counterfeiting of national or foreign currency. In effect, if Germany would not send Döring to Portugal it would have to try him on a counterfeiting charge.

On the morning of September 20, 1932, Döring was arrested in his hotel room. He was quickly taken to the Berlin-Moabit Prison. The news made the Berlin, Paris and Lisbon papers.

In Paris, Mme. Karel Marang spotted the small item and

showed it to her husband. He shrugged and talked about some planned new factory additions, now that they were expanding their quite profitable manufacture of electric heaters. No sense worrying his wife. Early in September, Hennies had come to Paris to talk to Marang about "some business." Marang sensed only trouble and told his secretary that he would be "out" when Herr Hennies phoned again. He congratulated himself on his prescience.

*   *   *   *   *

SEAFORD, SUSSEX, ENGLAND /
December 22, 1933

WHEN HENRY ROMER submitted his resignation to Waterlow's after twenty years of service he received news from Lisbon. His old "bird dog" there, Walker, died on September 3rd. They had not gotten on too well but he liked Walker and everything considered, he wasn't a bad fellow, even if he was half-Portuguese. Romer sent Walker's widow a condolence note. The stationery was on that of the Sutton Nurseries, Seaford.

Romer was now growing carnations commercially. At least this was going better than the cacao plantation he had owned for a year in Trinidad. He sent his wife, two sons and daughter out to help run it but things hadn't worked out too well and he had to sell it.

His older son, John, had joined Waterlow's as an apprentice in 1922. Then after the traditional five-year indenture he was assigned to the legal publications end of the firm. He stayed only until 1929 when he left to help run his father's plantation in Trinidad.

Now in 1933 there was no longer a Romer with Waterlow's. But the old firm hadn't forgotten. There was a pension and early in December, 1933, Romer received an illuminated scroll signed by 112 of his former colleagues at Waterlow's. Included were Sir Edgar Waterlow and Philip Waterlow, the latter's son, now a director of the firm. It read:

TO
HENRY G. W. ROMER, ESQUIRE, F.R.G.S., F.R.H.S.*

On the occasion of your retirement after twenty years as Foreign Representative, the Chairman, Directors and Staff of Waterlow and Sons Limited, who have subscribed their names hereto, desire your acceptance of this address, together with the accompanying Piece of Plate, as a token of their esteem and goodwill.

They desire to place on record their appreciation of the services you have rendered the Company, of the distinction with which you have consistently upheld the dignity of your office . . .

Now on this December day Romer framed his reply carefully. He was quite moved.

My dear friends and colleagues,

I have to thank you from the bottom of my heart for the beautiful epergne which I have just received, together with the extremely handsome illuminated address, . . . it has always been a matter of great pride to me to have had the honour of carrying the flag of this great firm into many parts of the world.

Tremendous happenings in the history of your great Firm have unfortunately occurred within the last few years, and which, in my humble opinion, make it difficult, if not altogether impossible, for me to speak to you all as I should desire . . .

He ended his letter with a *momento mori:* "The day is far spent, the night is at hand when no man can work."

The night came a few months later, on April 5, 1934, when he collapsed and died in an Eastbourne hotel. A delegation from Waterlow's came down to his funeral service.

*   *   *   *   *

* He was a Fellow of the Royal Geographical and Royal Horticultural Societies.

LISBON / 1935

SINCE July, 1932, Portugal had been firmly and dictatorially ruled by Premier Salazar and his National Union Party. Salazar's powers were clearly established in 1928 when he took the appointment as an all-powerful Minister of Finance but he didn't become Premier until 1932. The following year, 1933, his government promulgated a new constitution which was approved by plebiscite. Among its provisions were a National Assembly elected by heads of families who had a certain degree of education and a corporative chamber representing occupations in the Italian fascist style.

In January, 1934, the General Confederation of Labor and the Communists led a revolutionary movement that was suppressed bloodily. At the end of the year voters were permitted to choose among the candidates put forward by the National Union Party only.

Salazar balanced the Portuguese budget and ended the inflation of the escudo. But in the process he engendered considerable unemployment. In 1935 a popular joke in Lisbon told about an old friend visiting Salazar. The Premier was upset about the sad state of the country's economy. His friend said: "It's no problem at all. I can solve it for ten escudos." How, asked Salazar. "We just spend it on cab fare," his friend went on. "We go to the penitentiary by cab, take out Alves Reis—and put you in his place."

Reis heard the joke several times from visitors. After the two years in solitary when he was permitted only one visit a week, his allowable visits increased considerably. His wife would come to see him two or three times a week. She was now living with her three sons in her mother's apartment in Lisbon. A few old friends remained loyal but for the most part she and her sons were shunned. Guilherme, the oldest, had frequent fights at school because he was always being taunted as the son of the "500-escudos man." To add to the boy's troubles, an arthritic spine condition set in.

"When men grow virtuous in their old age," Alexander Pope

wrote cynically, "they only make a sacrifice to God of the devil's leavings." But Alves Reis seemed able to endure these new onslaughts of misfortune because he had acquired a new and virtuous faith. He had become a far-out Protestant, a Fundamentalist. A fellow prisoner had given him some Evangelical tracts. "The Lord had sent them to me," he wrote, "just when I was in the greatest need of the 'communion of saints.'"

> Though now my horizon is limited by the narrow outlook of a convict, I am able, nonetheless, to see how the Spirit of God is at work in the world. . . . Whoever, like myself, has lived for years in sin and is miraculously converted to Christ through the Bible, grows in grace day by day by learning from His Word and seeks communion with Him in order the better to serve Him.

But it wasn't easy to be an Evangelical Protestant in Catholic Portugal or even in the cell.

> Alas, however, one's lower nature is not slain, and if I fail to nourish my spirit by reading God's Word, meditation and prayer, if I permit anything to hinder my communion with the One Who upholds me, my sinful nature immediately asserts itself urging me to throw off the easy yoke of my Lord: the Prince of this world strives to renew my slavery to sin by false promises in the wilderness of temptation.

The two years of solitary had been a particularly difficult period

> When I found myself shut up in my cell, my hair prison-cropped, dressed in convict uniform marked with the number by which alone I was thenceforth to be known, thank God I felt no resentment toward Him or toward man, yet my nature chafed at the confinement to which human justice had condemned me. As it were a leaden weight oppressed my heart, and I had the feeling that the twenty cubic meters or so which my cell measured comprised a moral vacuum. In the oppressive silence my spirit was asphyxiated, whilst dormant fleshly lusts and passions were aroused. . . . Such an environment is calculated to engender in an unregenerate man hatred of his fellows and blasphemy against God and the only solace for the Christain is to fall on his knees and seek solace.

He acquired ugly calluses on his knees from his frequent kneelings on the stone floor. In 1933 his wife and sons were also converted to the Evangelical Protestant faith. Reis' extraordinary zeal communicated itself to some other prisoners and he even effected a conversion of one of his fellow-conspirators, Adriano Silva. José Bandeira wasn't interested.

At night Reis wrote evangelical tracts and articles for an irregularly circulated newspaper financed by the Evangelical movement. Since he couldn't afford the $1.50 necessary to install an electric light in his cell—or the 25¢ a month to pay the electric bill—he worked with

> a small and very economical paraffin lamp, by the light of which I could not read or write without difficulty as my eyes had suffered from the effect of the poison I had taken in the attempt to end my life. . . . But once again the Lord came to my assistance. A fellow-convict, without infringing any regulations, made me a present of all that was necessary for installing electric light in my cell, and a relative at the same time made me a small monthly allowance as prison pocket-money.

He concluded a series of articles he wrote for *World Dominion,* a London-published monthly circulated among Evangelists, with:

> About a year ago [1933] I passed to an upper form in the school of grace, where I continue to learn what I need to be taught, in order that I may be "cleansed from all filthiness of the flesh and spirit, perfecting holiness in the fear of God," being confident of this very thing, that He which hath begun a good work in me will perform it until the day of Jesus Christ.
> Friends, pray for me and for my family!

They did and Alves Reis, possibly the best-known convert to the faith in the Thirties got correspondence and even visits from others in the faith. George Howes, an Englishman who had financed the work of conversion to the Evangelical faith in Portugal, interceded with Salazar for an earlier release for Alves Reis. But Salazar, an ardent Catholic and economic conservative, found the new Alves Reis even more heinous than he had been as an atheist, arch-criminal and economic innovator. Alves Reis would have to serve his full twenty year sentence.

But other compromises were possible. Towards the end of 1935 Sir Edgar Waterlow began making some direct approaches to the governor of the Bank of Portugal. He pointed out that the old contract between the Bank and Waterlow's had not been completed. Admittedly, certain best-forgotten incidents had intervened but now that the matter had been finally and honorably adjudicated surely it was time to complete the contract. For its part, Waterlow was ready to continue printing the 1000-escudo notes or any other the Bank would desire.

With the consent of Salazar, the Bank of Portugal entered into negotiations with Waterlow's for the printing of new banknote series. Understandably, many new precautions were employed: provisions for certain code words to be used on all correspondence and frequent telegraphic confirmations. No word of the *volte-face* was allowed to appear in the Portuguese press and Waterlow's was cautioned about making a public announcement. But somehow one London reporter did learn of the new contract between the old adversaries and on November 3, 1936, the *News Chronicle* carried a one-paragraph item about Waterlow's getting a "big order" for banknotes from the Bank of Portugal.

BERLIN / August 29, 1936

DÖRING REMAINED in the Moabit Prison for nearly a year. He was visited in January, 1933, by his daughter Anna and her husband, who had become an important police officer. Döring's relations with his daughters were never very warm but the visits served to cool them even more. But they did consult attorneys on how they could get their father out of prison.

The Portuguese continued to insist Döring either be sent under guard to Lisbon to stand trial again or that he be released only on high bail: 4,000,000 marks, say (about $1,000,000). But Döring still had some good connections with some old colleagues who had risen to power in the Nazi Party and in August, 1934, he was released from Moabit Prison with a letter stating there was "insufficient evidence" to try him in Lisbon.

Annaliese Angold never turned up for reward at the Portuguese Embassy. It was just as well. Portugal decided it would pay the reward only when Hennies-Döring was actually brought to Lisbon.

Döring rented a modest room in Berlin on the Kaiserallee. When he tried to get back possession of his funds he found great difficulties. He became bitter and desperate. In June, 1936, he sought out his old friend Karl Lampe who had a comfortable flat in Schaperstrasse in Berlin. Lampe had long since given up his import-export business in Nice because the boycott against Nazi merchandise, particularly textiles, had ruined profits. He had returned to Germany and bought a 60% interest in a textile firm.

Lampe visited Döring occasionally for old times' sake and to hear some of Döring's tales of his adventures before misfortune hit. Once Döring tried to interest Lampe in a proposition to export German silver spoons as sterling silver—to Switzerland. The idea that the canny Swiss wouldn't know the difference made Lampe think Döring was joking. But he wasn't and the men saw each other less frequently.

On one June day in 1936 a desperate Döring decided that Lampe was his only hope. As Lampe recalls, Döring

offered me a participation in a big garage in Berlin. He said the garage was about ready and all they needed was 5000 marks [about $1250]. So I said: 'Tell me more.' His answer was rambling and obscure and I finally realized that he really wanted me to *give* him the money; there wasn't any garage deal.

So I said to him, 'Well, Herr Döring, this is no business at all.'

'All right,' he said, 'I can get you a bank opinion and a bank letter on this enterprise. Let me make a phone call.' He called someone and asked me to talk to the person. I said, I am not interested in getting information on a proposition this way. What are you trying to do, cheat me, or something? I was pretty disgusted with him and I just refused to give him any money.

He stood up and said: 'All right, I will now go to the police and turn you in because of violating foreign currency regulations. You remember that we went to France a few years ago and you had illegal money with you.'

Well, I wasn't going to let him blackmail me with that kind of nonsense. After I ordered him out of my apartment I went to the Police Station to swear out a complaint against him, charging extortion. Two hours later Police detectives came to visit me. They were a little embarrassed.

'Herr Lampe,' they said, 'we're afraid there can be no proceedings against Herr Döring. We got in touch with central Police headquarters and the orders are not to arrest Herr Döring. It appears that he did great things for Germany in the War by getting foodstuffs illegally from Holland and Denmark.'

That was the last time Lampe saw Döring.

On August 25, 1936, Döring was admitted to the Westend Krankenhaus (hospital) for some undiagnosed ailment. His daughter Elizabeth who then lived in Berlin, visited him and she thought he didn't look very ill, but more as if he just needed a rest. Another visitor was Döring's old friend, Heinrich K_____. According to information pieced together from interviews with others, K. promised he would repay the great debt to Döring with monthly installments of 600 marks (about $150). He also gave Döring a few thousand marks. K_____ is believed to have been the last person to have seen Döring alive.

On the afternoon of August 29th Döring died suddenly. The hospital's death certificate diagnosis was "cardiac arrest."

Döring listed his brother, Wilhelm, as next of kin, rather than his two daughters. When the hospital notified Wilhelm he didn't go to Berlin from Kassel. Instead he told his niece, Anna Schluter, who also lived in Kassel. She and her husband went to Berlin and saw the corpse of her father. They thought it was a dark blue, which caused her husband—the police official—to suspect that death was not natural. He talked to the hospital personnel and they said that the dead man's last visitor had been Heinrich K_____. When K_____ was interviewed he said Döring was already unconscious when he came. But a doctor and nurse said they had been in Döring's room then and he was conscious and in good spirits.

To this day Döring's two daughters are convinced that their father was poisoned by Heinrich K_____. They also believe that K_____ retrieved the money he had given their father in the hospital and a small black diary in which Döring had listed all of his debtors and the securities he still owned.

They went through their father's furnished room and found nothing of value. Only a slip with Karl Lampe's phone number.

The millions of escudos, pounds, francs and marks had vanished despite the family's best efforts to uncover Döring's assets. The day before the funeral Karl Lampe got a call from Döring's daughter, Elizabeth. She begged him to visit her on a matter of importance. Lampe recalls that when

> I drove there I saw it was some kind of boarding house and she seemed to be the manager. She had a few girls working under her. She said her father had left nothing behind and she needed money. Would I lend her some? She had spent her money and wasn't making too much on the job. I gave her 300 marks—all I had with me. I felt very sorry for her and her whole family. Her father had not been a good father; nor a good friend. And now it turned out that he wasn't even a good businessman when it came to handling his money. But he did tell good stories about his adventures.

On September 1, 1936, Johann Georg Adolf Döring, alias Adolf Gustav Hennies, was buried in Berlin's Kissel'sches Feld cemetery in Row 9, Grave 16. It was the loneliest burial of the day. None of Döring's family, friends or former business associates accompanied the coffin. The funeral had been paid for by his main debtor and suspected murderer, Heinrich K_____.

❋　　❋　　❋　　❋　　❋

LISBON / May 7, 1945

WHEN ALVES REIS was released from the penitentiary at 4 P.M. on May 7th the city was joyously celebrating—the end of the Second

World War in Europe. Admiral Doenitz had accepted the Allied ultimatum for Germany and the Rossio was filled with thousands of Lisboetas waving flags and cheering wildly. Although Portugal had been officially neutral during the War the people were mainly anti-Axis. Still, the flags were at half-mast on Lisbon's public buildings when Hitler committed suicide. After all he had been the head of a friendly state.

During his last five years in prison, Alves Reis had been a trusty allowed the run of the prison. He had personally converted several prisoners to the Evangelical faith. He was rather popular and even respected. As a trusty he was in charge of the inventory of the prisoners' canteen and kept their accounts. He had long since given up cigarettes and coffee.

His liver kept giving him trouble. He also had a bad case of hemorrhoids and occasionally was allowed out to see a medical specialist. He put on about 30 pounds in prison and when he came out—after 19½ years—he was quite portly and nearly bald.

The adjustment was difficult. At first he kept to the ingrained habits of confinement. He stayed in his bedroom and had meals —as in prison—at 11 A.M. and 6 P.M.—and went to bed at 6:30 P.M. Many of his prison friends came to see him for advice on how to get started and Reis told his sons it had been a serious mistake when they introduced a certain prison reform in 1850. Until then all prisoners in Portugal had to wear white face masks. "With such a mask," he sighed, "no one would know me and hundreds of ex-inmates wouldn't be able to identify me as one of them."

He was also pursued by some shady characters with illegal schemes that only needed Alves Reis' "brilliant touch" to make them succeed. They didn't really believe in his conversion.

He spent much time as a lay preacher for the Evangelical faith. His sermons were well attended, particularly in Oporto. He was only paid expenses. There were then a dozen small Evangelical churches in Lisbon alone and he spoke at all of them. Mostly he repeated the details of his conversion.

In November, 1945, the head of a local bank sent Reis a message: if he would give up his Evangelical preaching he could get a job with the bank. Reis refused.

His three sons—now 27, 26, and 21—invited him to join their

business—Guilherme Reis and Company, a small import-export firm run from their apartment at 71 Rua Latino Coelho, in a middle-class neighborhood. During the war they exported wolf-ram, a source of much-needed tungsten. They had a contract with four marginal mines in Portugal and the business was quite profitable. After the war he helped them expand to rice and sugar imports.

Portugal was going through another of its periodic economic crises. There had been a ruinously poor sardine catch, a disastrous wheat crop and an adverse balance of payments. The lustre of Premier Salazar's financial genius had been smudged long ago.

In May, 1947, Reis and his sons worked out a deal with a Lisbon firm to import rice from Brazil. A million dollar credit was arranged and Alves Reis and his wife flew to Rio de Janeiro. For the first time since he got out of prison he felt himself caught up pleasurably in the exciting whirl of a big deal. But even now he couldn't resist shortcuts.

Brazil required Portuguese visitors to post a deposit covering their return trip so that there would be no danger of their becoming public charges. To save this deposit Alves Reis simply applied for a transit visa to Peru which meant that he could stay in Brazil 30 days.

With his bifocals and bow-tie he looked very much like the American businessman in Rio. He even inquired at the American consulate about possible migration to the United States. J. Edwin Orr, a prominent California Evangelical who had visited Alves Reis in prison several times, had encouraged him to emigrate. He felt that Reis could do great things for the faith in America. But Reis discovered that his jail sentence would be an adverse factor in coming as an immigrant to the U.S.

In Rio he learned the firm they were dealing with was nearly bankrupt and had no export license for the rice they had contracted to sell Reis and his group. He cabled his son and the latter managed to get a 45-day extension of the letter of credit. Now the old Alves Reis emerged gradually: an export license could be obtained only by a bribe. He paid for one and received the valuable permit. A day later he signed the contract for 83,000 bags of rice —only to learn that evening his letter of credit had been canceled. He was now obligated for 29 million escudos or about

$1,000,000. Returning to his hotel he picked up a local paper and read that a Cuban government commission was in town to buy rice and was staying at a nearby hotel. They were interested but could only pay exactly the price that Reis had bought his rice at. He had to accept though it meant he was out his considerable expenses and the cost of the export permit—about $25,000 in all.

To add to his troubles the police were after him for overstaying his one-month visitor's stay. He and his wife were expelled from Brazil in June. Shortly after the Reis' left a well-informed Rio columnist gave his readers the "real reasons" for the expulsion:

> I found the whole rice affair rather strange. This fellow Reis had served his term. What else could there be against him? Nothing—but Pedro Pereira [the Portuguese Ambassador to Brazil] got busy and had poor Reis expelled. Why? Because Reis managed to get a great rice export deal for Portugal. As is well known these deals in Salazar's domains can only be undertaken by Salazar sympathizers. Pero [a nickname for Pedro] flew to Lisbon and told his boss about the low trick Alves Reis was playing on him and preventing him from earning millions of escudos in the deal . . . Salazar took pity on his Ambassador . . . so Pereira returned to Rio with permission to have Reis kicked out. He also told the bigwigs of the Portuguese colony here that all big deals with Portugal could only be carried out through him . . . , Why doesn't Salazar make Pereira the Portuguese Ambassador to Chicago?

Someone sent Alves Reis a clipping but it wasn't any consolation. "No," he told his sons firmly. "It was all my fault. I had forgotten my good Christian principles and the Lord punished me. Only in prison could I be a good Christian. Outside, I failed."

Late in 1947 the Reis family firm failed with some $140,000 of outstanding debts. Reis had his first angina attack. Somehow the family kept going on petty deals. They sold things on commission and the sons got jobs. In August, 1951, when Senhora Reis died—in a mental hospital—her husband finally gave up. As he told friends, "I am just living from day to day." A second and more severe attack of angina hit him a month after his wife died.

In 1953 another attack left him paralyzed in his right arm

and leg for several weeks. He could no longer shave himself and grew a beard.

On the evening of July 8, 1955, Artur Virgilio Alves Reis had his final heart attack and died soon after. He had asked to be buried in a sheet so that his suit could be saved for his eldest son. The funeral services and simple pine coffin cost 800 escudos ($32) but the family was hard put to raise even that.

On the hot morning of July 10, 1955, the man who had dreamed the most dangerous, the most logical dream in counterfeiting history was put to rest in an unmarked grave in the cemetery of Alto de São João. The Evangelicals don't believe in lavish funerals: after death the soul is brought into the presence of God. The earthly remains are unimportant. They are among the few—there are some 20,000 of the faith in Portugal—who don't hire *Crepideiras,* paid mourners, to cry aloud all the good points of the dead on All Souls Day, November 2nd.

The obituaries pointed to the lessons to be learned from the dead man's life. Warned *Diario Popular:*

> The author of the most fantastic fraud of all time who had flooded the country with 500-escudos notes did not even have a few miserly pennies in the end.

And the *Diaria de Lisbon* added the final dirge-like coda:

> Death has eliminated a man who lived and died under an evil star.

Only abroad was there some appreciation of his goals. The London *Economist* said that "The perpetrators, however reprehensible their motives, did Portugal a very good turn according to the best Keynesian principles."

CANNES / February 13, 1960

THE LATER YEARS had been bountiful, kind, almost carefree. When his sons and daughter and their families came to Cannes for the annual Christmas reunion there were 12 grandchildren. Grand-père Marang, the founder of the family fortune, was dearly loved by his grandchildren. He always had surprise presents.

Oh, there had been some difficulties during the war years, but who didn't have troubles *then?* Enemies and business competitors spread the word Marang had collaborated with the Germans during 1942–3 but that canard was laid to rest when he became a naturalized French citizen in 1946. Surely they wouldn't have granted him that privilege if there had been a blot on his record.

There was a distant past, of course. But even that had been obliterated. His attorney in The Hague, Rolandus Hagedoorn, sent him a cheerful note in 1946. He checked the police files and made a happy discovery. The Dutch police automatically destroy the fingerprint record of unincarcerated criminals who are past 60. Karel Marang had turned 60 in 1944.

Marang prided himself on how French he had become. Not just in nationality but in outlook, manners and thinking. But one custom he would not observe. Every Frenchman knows he has a solemn duty to put chrysanthemums on his mother's grave on November 1st. But Karel Marang wouldn't go back to Dordrecht, Holland for this. There was no longer any danger of his being arrested, he knew, but there were just too many scarifying memories associated with Holland.

The business he had created in 1929 had grown steadily but not too quickly. It had taken small, safe, sure steps and now as Compagnie d'Appareils de Chauffage Electrique (S.A.) or more familiarly in the trade, "Chaufelec" it had a firm, respected place in the manufacture of electric heaters and irons.

At the modern plant they had in Château Thierry more than 150 hands were employed. Under the wise guidance of his sons, "Chaufelec" was now selling at least 9,000,000 francs (about

$1,800,000) worth of electrical appliances a year—and increasing every year.

His oldest son, Carel Marang, Jr., was president and general manager, a role he took over when his father retired in the mid-1950s. Like many a self-made businessman Marang loved to see the reports the leading credit agencies issued on his firm—just to make sure they had things right. The reports were even more favorable than the ones Sir William had drawn so many years ago on Marang & Collignon. The credit reports on Chaufelec always read:

> Management is well regarded. . . . Payments prompt. . . . Considered reliable for good credit facilities. . . . Financial condition is satisfactory and sufficient funds are available to meet obligations.

His sons, of course, knew about the old scandal but it was never discussed. Even their wives didn't know about it.

M. and Mme. Marang had first rented an apartment in Cannes for the winter in the modern Palais des Dunes, the first big apartment erected in Cannes. It's right on the Croisette, the city's fine sea-front boulevard. Then in 1954 the Marangs rented a large apartment in the Palais l'Augusta, a handsome three-story building with a large ornamental facade and a garden filled with flowers. It is on Rue du Canada near the Carlton, Cannes' leading hotel.

The Marangs loved the apartment so much they bought it. Then in 1956 they paid an additional large sum for the right to install an elevator in the building so that M. Marang wouldn't have to walk the two flights of stairs to the apartment. He had his first heart attack, a mild one, in 1956.

The Marangs played bridge with friends and Marang had a reputation for having a great knack with finesses. His other hobby was collecting fine antique furniture. There were several Chippendale pieces in the luxuriously furnished apartment.

Mainly, the Marangs loved walking together along the Croisette. His tall, solidly-built figure, his ruddy complexion, his impeccable manners often suggested to people who first met M. Marang that surely he had been a diplomat before retirement. "Yes," he would murmur, "but that was very long ago."

The final heart attack came at 5 P.M. on February 13, 1960. The death certificate described him as a manufacturer. As a solid, respectable French bourgeois *industriel* his death naturally called for a notice in *Le Figaro*. It appeared on February 18th:

> Mme. Charles Marang, Mr. and Mrs. Carel Marang, Mr. and Mrs. Florent Marang, Mr. and Mrs. R. H. MacDonald, Mr. and Mrs. Ido Marang and his 12 grand-children announce with great sorrow the death of Mr. Charles Marang, who died at his home, 8 rue du Canada in Cannes on Feb. 13, after a long illness. He was 76.
>
> The funeral was held in Cannes with only family and close friends attending.

❂   ❂   ❂   ❂   ❂

LONDON / March 17, 1960

THE RUMORS HAD BEEN floating around the City for months: someone was out to get control of Waterlow & Sons. The Lord alone knew why: Waterlow's had been sliding downhill for years and had a net loss of £252,000 (about $720,000) in 1959. The firm still had profitable and continuing contracts to print the widely-circulated *Radio Times* and *The Listener* for the BBC but the railroad ticket-printing side of the business had fallen off and the stamp and banknote end had become disastrous. In fact, most of the losses were incurred on the security printing side.

On this day the mysterious purchaser of Waterlow shares in the market disclosed himself as Wilfred Harvey, chairman of the much larger printing and publishing combine of Purnell & Sons. Purnell was offering Waterlow shareholders a small premium—about 65¢—over the market price for their shares. In effect, Purnell had offered £2,147,000 for all of Waterlow.

Sir Philip Alexander Waterlow who became chairman and managing director of the firm in 1954 when his father, Sir Edgar, died, urged his stockholders not to accept the "inadequate" offer.

Philip Waterlow "does not use title" his recent *Who's Who* listing points out. He had been born in 1897 and attended Harrow and Sandhurst, the British West Point. The difficulties of his business were matched only by those of his private life. Both his marriages had been unsuccessful. His first wife obtained a divorce and his second a judicial separation.

The Waterlow take-over bid had been carefully planned in advance and Purnell & Sons found little trouble in convincing the unhapppy Waterlow stockholders. As *The Economist* told it on June 11, 1960:

THE END OF THE AFFAIR

A long drawn out battle among master printers is over. It was clear last month that Purnell had won the day when its control of votes . . . was sufficient to defeat proposals of the Waterlow directors. . . .

Agreement has now been reached on the reconstruction of the Board of Waterlow. Mr. Wilfred Harvey, the chairman of Purnell will become the new chairman and he will bring with him on to the Board three other directors of Purnell as well as one other . . . Mr. Philip A. Waterlow, the present chairman will retire. . . .

A few months later a careful audit revealed that the Waterlow losses had continued into 1960. In the year ending September 30th, Waterlow had a loss of £220,000, mostly on the security printing side.

Inevitably Purnell got rid of the incubus that was causing Waterlow's losses. On January 11, 1961, Thomas de la Rue announced that it was buying that part of the Waterlow business dealing with the printing of banknotes, postage stamps, traveler's checks and bonds. No price was given. Among the continuing banknote contracts taken over by de la Rue were those of Eire, the West African Currency Board and Switzerland.

In 1964, Purnell & Sons, which had absorbed Waterlow's, became part of the giant British Printing Corporation. The merger of Purnell and Hazell Sun was rough and on December 1, 1965,

Wilfred Harvey, the chairman of Purnell who drew a salary of $770,000 plus 8% of the firm's net profits in 1964, was ousted by majority shareholders. They also filed a suit against him to recover $800,000 and they suspended his $140,000 a year pension.

De la Rue also seems to be having its own difficulties. According to a July, 1965, comment in *The Economist*, de la Rue profits between 1960 and 1964 have been advancing with "glacial speed." All the profits came mainly from a subsidiary manufacturing Formica. "De la Rue is a company with a wide range of apparently promising products, good research facilities and a go-ahead attitude that somehow never seems to get going," said *The Economist*.

De la Rue now claims it is the world's foremost banknote printer, turning out some 30 million notes a week. Very profitably, too, they say. Apparently it is still possible to make money by making money.

LISBON / March 30, 1960

JOSÉ BANDEIRA had emerged from the penitentiary about the same time that Alves Reis did. They saw each other in prison but had little to say. José had come to despise his former partner for what he thought was his hypocritical conversion.

There had been occasional correspondence with his old love, Fie Carelsen. He had aged greatly and put on considerable weight in prison. He was 64 and from a picture he had taken shortly after his release he appeared white-haired but his face was comparatively unlined.

His family helped support him for a few years. His older brother, Antonio, had died in Madeira in 1936 where he had gone to start a weekly newspaper after being sentenced to exile there. His wife was with him at his death.

In 1955 Fie began sending José a "petit cadeau" every month of 100 guilders, about $28, which went a good distance in the very low-cost Lisbon of the period.

He had also managed to buy a partnership in the Olympia Club in Lisbon, a cheap nightclub whose prime purpose was to facilitate pickups by prostitutes. They paid the management a percentage of their fees. José was the maître d'.

The Club didn't do well and José sold his interest, taking a loss. He took cheap lodgings in downtown Lisbon but still managed to keep two or three women friends. A woman cousin, a postal clerk, helped support him.

In March, 1960, he had a bad fall and broke a thigh bone. He was taken to the ward of the São José Hospital, one of Lisbon's oldest and dreariest. He wrote Fie of his accident and she sent him some money to buy a little radio to while away the time during recuperation. On March 21, 1960, he wrote:

> Ma Chère Amour,
> Thank you for the money for the radio . . . I couldn't walk . . . I should love to hear your voice. That would make me very happy. . . . For your birthday I send a big kiss. . . . How sad I am that I can't send you a little present. It is so against my nature and feeling . . . I finish and send you a big kiss and a hug. . . .

On March 29th, Fie got another letter from Lisbon. This one was from José's cousin, Maria:

> I have the sad news to give you: my cousin, José, died today. . . . You have been really the best and most sincere friend, faithful to the end. . . . He loved you deeply. . . .

Under his hospital pillow they found a worn cherished, memento. It was a picture of Fie Carelsen at the Longchamps track in Paris in that great time of May, 1925. In her cloche hat, low-waisted white silk afternoon dress she is smiling beyond the photographer at her lover, that dashing sudden millionaire, José dos Santos Bandeira.

CARACAS, VENEZUELA / May, 1964

THE LARGE TWO-STORY yellow stucco house with imposing white pillars was built by Simon Planas-Suarez when he returned permanently to Caracas in 1936. After he was abruptly requested to leave Lisbon late in 1925 he moved to Paris and he lived there quietly. In 1936 Venezuela's oil boom was well under way and Don Simon found that several Caracas properties his father bequeathed to him had risen enormously in value and now required his personal attention. He had become a millionaire.

The house in the staid, prosperous suburb of El Paraiso is surrounded by a large lawn and hidden behind a sturdy, high fence. Senora Planas died in 1957 and since then he has been living alone with two servants, a maid and a housekeeper.

Although he was separated from the Venezuelan Foreign Service immediately after the Portuguese banknote case broke, no other penalties were imposed on Don Simon. An investigation into his role in the affair was conducted by the Venezuelan Ambassador to London but the Jesuit librarians of the Venezuelan Foreign Office regretfully refuse to let outsiders look at the report: "Not until Don Simon's death."

In 1963 Don Simon had a bad fall in his house and his right thigh still has a metal plate so that he now walks with a cane and is rather stooped. His remaining hair is gray but he is still remarkably vigorous for an octogenarian. His mornings are given over to writing and in the afternoon he reads and is visited by old friends. The old scandal is, of course, never mentioned.

His latest book, published in 1964, is about Venezuela's various conflicts with Italy, England and Germany. He lists all 20 books in his latest entry in *Who's Who in Latin America* where Don Simon also proudly notes that he "commands English, French, Portuguese and Castilian Spanish."

Don Simon dressed in a gray suit and black bow tie, received a North American visitor cordially. He talked animatedly about his books and various honors he had received but the one he was looking forward to most was being made an honorary member of

294

the Institute of International Law which has only six honorary members. (At the September, 1965, meeting of the Institute in Warsaw he was elected.)

The honor was made known to several Caracas dailies and they praised his work. Don Simon showed the visitor some recent clippings: *El Universal* called him a "distinguished Venezuela intellectual and internationalist . . . his work is a highly appreciated scientific contribution to the formation of a new conscience in international juridical organizations." *El Nacional* added "The high and merited honor given to Dr. Suarez by the Institute of International Law satisfies and gives great pride to Venezuela's intellectual life."

When the visitor incautiously raised the subject of the Portuguese affair Don Simon lost his urbanity and cordiality. He flew into a rage: "Is that what you came here for?" and tried to tear the visitor's notebook away. He pushed forcibly for a man of 82 and soon had the visitor outside the door: "Out . . . out . . ." out!"

A few minutes later the Plana maid came out to apologize for her master's conduct. "He is very sensitive and gets terribly angry at anything that doesn't please him. Better do not try to see him again. I have not seen him so angry in a long time."

In another part of Caracas an old friend of Don Simon's was readier to discuss the past. He, too, had been in the Venezuelan diplomatic service and knew of the scandal.

"I believe Don Simon to be an honest man," he began. "I can only think that he was taken in by the gang. After all, when a fellow diplomat asks you to do him a great favor you are only too glad to oblige. It was a common thing then to bring in liquors, wines and coffee in diplomatic luggage. I'm sure Don Simon thought it was nothing more serious than that." He had the impression that the Venezuelan courts, although pressured by Portugal, had finally absolved Don Simon of any culpability in the affair.

"These things happen, you know. I'm sure Don Simon's obituaries here will be very long, very respectful and very discreet about the Portuguese matter. After all, we don't have any other Venezuelans who have writen twenty weighty books—and are also millionaires."

LONDON / July 30, 1964

T———, A FORMER Waterlow banknote special representative who is now retired, came up to London to lunch with me at my hotel and fill me in on the troubles the banknote business had been having since the end of World War II. T——— has a comfortable retirement cottage but occasionally likes to do special work for banknote companies as a "consultant." He is tall, lean, tanned and doesn't look the 70-odd I know he is.

Since it is a small and highly specialized field the banknote printing business has never had a trade publication of its own to record victories, defeats and promotions. To a certain extent the peripatetic special representatives fill the gap as world carriers of news and gossip in the trade.

I asked T——— the question that had been puzzling me most: how could he sell Waterlow banknotes to *any* country after the Bank of Portugal debacle?

"It was even harder than you think, thanks to some jiggery-pokery," he smiled. "Some of the opposition got up a neat booklet made up of clips on the case and the judgment and sent them to every central bank that didn't print its own banknotes—just in case they hadn't heard yet. One firm sent out 50 copies of Sir Cecil Kisch's 1932 analysis of the case. He felt Waterlow's really shouldn't have had to pay a shilling but he had enough bare details in the book to show how Waterlow was taken in.

"I handled the problem two ways. First, I stressed Waterlow's *did* pay up. Handsomely, too. Doesn't that show they're reliable? Then I knocked the Bank of Portugal a little. Imagine a central bank that didn't keep a register of large denomination banknotes so that duplicate numbers turning up would have to be detected right away!

"Still, the stink was there and Waterlow's often could get the business only by sharp price-cutting and that, eventually, led to their getting out of the security printing in 1961."

We talked about the bitter divisions in the Waterlow family and T——— commented that Sir William's two sons didn't suffer from not being able to go into the family business. The oldest son, James, who inherited the title did quite well on his own. He became deputy director of Amalgamated Press, a huge publishing combine, and then went on to become chairman of Corson's, a large printing firm. The younger son, Thomas Gordon, did even better. After serving heroically as an RAF pilot in the Battle of Britain and rising to Group Captain, he went to Edinburgh where his mother's family was well-connected and rose rapidly in the city's important financial world. He became chairman of the important Standard Life Assurance Company and was now managing director of William Thyne Holdings, Ltd., a powerful financial house. And a director of the Royal Bank of Scotland. Since Sir James is a bachelor the title will be inherited by his younger brother, Thomas Gordon. One of the latter's sons has entered the printing trade, making it seven generations of Waterlows in the field.

T_____ went on to talk of the secret work banknote companies are asked to do during wartime. "Sir William was proud of his role in helping the British Secret Service counterfeit German stamps and currency in the First World War but in the Second de la Rue found that it could be a great embarrassment."

When the Allies were advancing in Thailand, de la Rue was asked to supply currency, using official plates in the banknote company's possession. De la Rue which had been printing Siam's notes since 1902 refused until instructed by the Central Bank but since the latter was still Japanese-dominated such approval wasn't forthcoming. The British forced de la Rue to turn out some 500,000 notes anyway. They were air-dropped over Thailand to underground forces.

The affair engendered considerable criticism among some Siamese officials and from some other banknote companies but T_____ thought the company had no choice. "All banknote companies depend upon the good-will and surreptitious help of their home governments too much to be able to say no to special requests."

T_____ thought Waterlow's should have had closer liaison with the Foreign Office. That might have made them less anxious to get the banknote printing order for Tschombe's new Republic of Katanga, created when he seceded from the Congo Republic in 1960. The order was only half-filled and when de la Rue took over the Waterlow banknote business it was dropped completely mainly because the Republic of the Congo employed de la Rue to print its notes and one of the charges against Tschombe was "counterfeiting." The Katanga banknote order was never paid for.

"Terribly unlucky all around," T—— sighed. "Near the end every order went sour or was turned out at a great loss like the big one for Malaya Federation. Absorbing Waterlow's doesn't seem to have done de la Rue or Purnell or British Printing much good. A superstitious soul might even say Waterlow had a curse on it ever since Sir William received Marang on that December morning in 1924."

LISBON / August, 1964

AT 46, Guilherme Joaquim Alves Reis, the oldest son of the banknote fraud planner, is a leading figure in the small Protestant Fundamentalist world of Portugal. He writes regularly for *Espada do Senhor* (Sword of the Lord) a Portuguese counterpart of a U.S. Fundamentalist publication edited by John D. Rice. *Espada do Senhor*'s masthead makes clear it is an

> independent Christian weekly, standing for the Verbal Inspiration of the Bible, the Deity of God, His Blood Atonement, Salvation by Faith, New Testament Soul Winning and Premillenial Return of Christ. Opposes Modernism, Worldliness and Formalism.

Guilherme has to write standing up. After extensive surgery in 1956 for his rheumatic-arthritic condition he was able to walk only with the help of two canes. There are other great misfortunes among the sons of Alves Reis. The middle son, Manuel Filipe, also has rheumatoid arthritis and is confined to a hospital wheelchair. The two older brothers have spent many of their adult years in and out of hospitals.

The youngest, José Luis—named after his father's partner, José Bandeira—works for his father's brother, Alvara, who manages a hotel in Setubal, southeast of Lisbon. Alvara who had been provided with a business and languages education in Amsterdam —until he was arrested for possible complicity—is still convinced that his older brother, Artur, had accomplices within the Bank of Portugal.

But his nephew, Guilherme, can't accept this:

> I must believe my father. My father had no one else in on the secret. Each of his accomplices knew only a little of the plot.

Guilherme married in 1961 when he was 43. He met his wife, an attractive widow, at the Brothers Assembly, a Fundamentalist group. She has a teenage daughter who lives with them. When his wife, Pelina, became pregnant the doctors feared for her life because she suffers from a heart condition, called mitral valve strangulation. But Guilherme knew the pregnancy would work out fine for mother and child: "You are pregnant because God allowed it," he told her. She not only had that child safely but another, too.

With the $140,000 indebtedness incurred by the failure of G. Reis Limitado still hanging over him, Guilherme is in the strange position of a man who must watch carefully how and what he earns. The large apartment's low rental is met by the $20 a month he gets from a hospital charity in lieu of his staying in the hospital. He has translated a few American Fundamentalist books into Portuguese and occasionally does bookkeeping for friends and translations for businessmen. But he is handicapped without a phone. He could probably afford it—about $2 a month—but as he tells friends: "I owe too much to even display possession of a phone."

He often talks about how hard it is to live in a materialistic world. "It's easier to make a sermon out of the Bible than to live by full Christian standards." When he got out of the hospital after his operation he thought of opening a liquor store which some friends were ready to set up for him. "But as a good Christian I knew I couldn't sell liquor . . ."

Guilherme's apartment which he inherited from his mother's family is filled with relics of his father: his malacca cane, the old style six-row keyboard typewriter, the stand-up cut-out picture taken in Carlsbad in 1925.

Although he dearly loved his father, Guilherme can speak of him and his deeds with reasonable detachment. Only when he is asked for an assessment of his father does he become the special pleader:

"My father went to jail only because he worked too hard."

The statement is never accompanied by a smile.

* * * * *

Relics of the great Alves Reis scheme are still to be found all over Lisbon. The Menino d'Ouro, Reis's Golden Boy Palace, is now the home of the British Institute in Lisbon where Lisboetas attend classes in English and listen to visiting British lecturers discuss the Lake poets and Shaw. The Ajube Prison where Senhora Alves Reis spent nearly a year is now one of the two prisons in Lisbon given over solely to political prisoners. One unfriendly estimate is that more than 1000 prisoners are held in them. A recent report on them by a London investigator, barrister Neville Vincent, said the

> "statue" torture is widely employed. A prisoner is stood against a wall for up to seven days and nights. If he falls (legs begin to swell after two or three days) he is kicked until he gets up.
>
> Another torture is to be put into a dark and filthy cell and after a few days moved to a cell where the lower part is painted yellow, the upper blue. Many prisoners believe the blue is sky and take crazed running-jumps at it.

The Royal British Club of Lisbon where Romer spent many casual hours still has some 350 members who are mainly Lisbon-based Britons. But since 1963 the Club is no longer surrounded by a great collection of tolerated brothels. These were closed by the government on New Year's Day, 1963, and since then the city's 40,000 formerly licensed prostitutes have become outside free-lancers. Some police officials and newspaper editors believe closing resulted in a considerable increase in sex crimes. Others even blame it for the apparent rise in homosexuality. "The Portuguese man was always proud of being virile, an older official explained. "But the new generation of boys and men, it doesn't matter to them."

The shirtmaker José Bandeira bought into is still in business and in its windows, just as in the other better men's shops in Lisbon, the price tags are artfully hidden—in defiance of a law which stipulates that all prices must be shown clearly in the window display. José's barber shop which he bought because he once had an affair with the manicurist is still cutting hair at the same place. And Lisbon manicurists still make much more from their outside love-making than from holding hands in the shop.

There are still whispers of certain families who benefitted greatly from Alves Reis' crime. Family A's fortune, they say, began when an ancestor was one of the raiding detectives who unearthed the banknote hoard in the Golden Boy Palace, secretly cached several hundred notes—and converted them for good notes at the Bank of Portugal. Family B, about to go bankrupt because its Angola investments were failing, was able to recoup after making a suspiciously favorable deal with the Liquidating Commission on some of the Alves Reis investments in the colony.

As in most dictatorships rumors and whispers are an important medium of communication. They help negate the Law of the Corks which cynical Portuguese tell you means that "difficult subjects are bottled up."

In Lisbon all public buildings put up after the great earthquake of 1755 are considered national monuments and cannot have their facades altered. But the Bank of Portugal did get a much needed paint job in 1956 when the Queen of England visited Lisbon. The press censorship saw to it that there were no untoward references to the old banknote case when she came. During my visit the Bank of Portugal building was being painted and patched again. Pimply air conditioners jut out of certain office windows—status symbols for the top officials and the directors. You can no longer find Vasco da Gama on any Portuguese banknotes: the latest 500-escudos note features Dom Francisco de Almeida who was once viceroy of Portuguese India.

Alves Reis's office building which housed his firm is now the headquarters of the auto repairmen's union. The old Angola & Metropole Bank building now holds another bank, engaged in more orthodox financing. When I took some photos of the building an elderly shoe-shine man guessed quickly why I was staring at the building. "Alves Reis?" he said.

Just around the corner from the Angola & Metropole building is the new Bank of Angola, now the official bank of issue for the colony.* Thanks to the discovery of oil and considerable successful mineral exploitation in the colony, including diamonds, Angola is now prosperous with a $40,000,000 trade balance in its favor. In 1964 it produced 1½ million tons of iron ore and its diamond exports exceeded $25,000,000. If he could have held on to them, Alves Reis' Angola properties and claims would now be worth well over $50,000,000.

✲　✲　✲　✲　✲

HAARLEM / August 24, 1964

THE GREAT PRINTING FIRM of Joh. Enschedé en Zonen N.V. has grown since Karel Marang visited it 40 years ago but in physical appearance the plant has changed surprisingly little. It still forms a solid block-square fine-printing enclave in the heart of Haarlem.

My host, Wim van Andringa de Kempenaer, a nephew of the Enschedé family, is managing director and since 1947 has been in charge of sales development and public relations.

Since Enschedé has been printing banknotes for the Netherlands for more than 150 years it was inevitable that on one of his frequent business visits to New York, Wim Kempenaer, a hearty,

---

* It was created in 1926 to help the colony somewhat along the path outlined by Alves Reis. To make sure there is never another Reis-like plot, Angola's local unit of currency is the Angolar rather than the Portuguese escudo.

ardent salesman, found himself a guest on the *What's My Line* show. None of the probing panelists could guess that Kempenaer was "a man who made his own money." I had lunch with the present head of Enschedé, Boudawijn Franciscus Enschedé, Kempenaer's uncle. The 70-year-old president who looks like an older Ed Sullivan, recalled the long phone call he had received from Marang in 1924.

> I had been a director only one or two years then and I suppose normally I might have dealt with Marang if I wasn't so busy. You know, he even begged me to go to Waterlow's with him. But fortunately we never met and I am properly grateful for *that*.

He read and re-read the letter of introduction Marang had been given with its troublesome line, "the delivery of the notes is to take place by the intermedium of our firm." He still found it quite incredible that his firm had written such a note for a stranger. But he had to admit it had.

Later I put it to Wim Kempenaer and he concluded, reluctantly, that

> the Partners at the time, not prepared and probably not in a position to undertake the job themselves, were hinting at the possibility of being granted a commission in case the pending order would finally turn out to have been a profitable deal for Waterlow . . .

There was no commission, of course.

Enschedé now prints fine banknotes for Israel as well as the Netherlands. In the recent past they've done the notes for Syria and Luxembourg. The firm had competed with de la Rue for a large Iranian banknote order. "We brought in an Iranian artist, did many elaborate designs and spent some $10,000 in the speculative preparation of our bid but we lost to de la Rue. We lost on price. That's part of our trouble, I suppose. We're the Rolls Royce of the banknote business. Perhaps our quality is *too* high," Kempenaer explained.

When I was about to leave the plant I remembered something I had forgotten. I asked Wim Kempenaer who now printed the banknotes for the Bank of Portugal.

"Well, Bradbury, Wilkinson in London does part of it but the high denomination notes are done by us here."

It didn't seem possible Fate had closed the circle with total perfection. "Including the 500-escudos note?" I asked.

His smile covered a small blush.

"Including the 500-escudos."

❖   ❖   ❖   ❖   ❖

THE HAGUE / August 25, 1964

TO THE DUTCH Fie Carelsen is what an improbable mixture of Ethel Barrymore *and* Ruth Draper would have been in the United States from the Twenties through the Forties. For most of her professional life she was one of the leading actresses *and* the great monologist of the Dutch-speaking world. When she retired a few years ago—after 40 years in the theater—she received unusual honors for an actress in the Netherlands. She was made an Officer of the high-ranking Order of Orange and Nassau and the cities of Arnhem and The Hague gave her gold medals.

As she aged she sometimes had to move from a major role to a lesser one in the same repertory vehicle. For years she did the ingenue in *Outward Bound* and when the time came she gracefully retreated to the lesser role of the snobbish, middle-aged Mrs. Cliveden-Banks. But in the great banknote drama she played out the romantic lead extemporaneously. There never was a synopsis and she had no idea how Act III would develop. For that matter, most of the male leads didn't know much more. And because each saw the "play" quite differently there was a terrible conflict of styles. Even a Pirandello might have drawn the line at a drama in which the male lead directed even as he created new scenes and lines—on opening night.

Her involvement in the great banknote case didn't do her much professional damage. The staid Dutch *expect* their dramatic stars to lead more exciting and racier lives. At 75, Fie is still very much a national figure. A recent series she did for a leading Dutch magazine on people she had known—but nothing about José Bandeira—received a wide readership. A popular biography of her a few years ago sold well. (It gave a brief but frank account of her involvement in the banknote affair.) Her recorded monologues have a steady sale and the local radio networks seek her out occasionally for talks about the Dutch theater.

She now lives in a modern three-story apartment house in one of The Hague's newer suburbs. She no longer has the Javanese maid she had for years and the apartment is more modest than the fine band-box house she once owned. Her figure is filled-out, of course, but the wide mouth, the enormous black eyes, the restless face still mark Fie. She is proud her hair still has its original color and that her teeth are still her own.

When the Nazis ordered the closing of all Dutch theaters in 1942 she wrote and toured in her popular monologue, *A Woman Telephones.** She gave the one-hour show hundreds of times during the war and afterwards all over Europe and Latin America before Dutch-speaking audiences. The record's royalties plus her pension from the Royal Theater of The Hague are the mainstays of her current modest income.

She falls into monologue easily:

"The men in the banknote ring were a good-looking bunch with the exception of Hennies. Marang was tall, almost handsome but inclined to be pudgy. And now it turns out he was also the wisest. He became the richest and the one who suffered the least.

"In 1949 when I was touring with *A Woman Telephones* I was in Paris and some Dutch friends told me the Marangs were now major contributors to the Dutch Church in Paris. He was *very* wealthy, they said. So I decided why shouldn't he help poor

* Fie's synopsis of *A Woman Telephones:* "A woman answers the phone in her home. It's her former husband whom she's been divorced from 20 years ago. He asks her about their daughter who now wants a divorce. Then she phones her lover and it turns out that he now has a new little friend. Then she phones her dressmaker on whom she takes out all her aggressions against men. Then her daughter calls and she gives her this advice: perhaps a bad marriage is better than a good divorce . . . then she phones her granddaughter who is 14 and she tells grandma she's in love with a man of 41 . . ."

José who was having such a miserable time in Lisbon. I phoned Marang but could only get Madame Marang. Could they do something for José? Oh yes: she offered me 100 francs. I said something impolite and slammed the receiver.

"If José had listened to me he could have emerged from the whole affair very rich. Poor José could never believe the whole thing was crooked. He loved to call me stupid as a door when I questioned the wisdom of working with men like Hennies and Reis. But José was the only one who turned over his gains to Portugal voluntarily. Not very smart, was it? If he had known the whole thing was crooked he would have given me the money to hold.

"I think their *amour propre* couldn't allow them to think Alves Reis, the provincial businessman who spoke French so badly, could have tricked them just as he did the Bank of Portugal and Waterlow. Of course, towards the end they must have known the whole thing was crooked but by then it didn't matter: there was so much money coming in, no one wanted to ask too many questions. And it was such a *lot* of money.

"With a little luck they could all have become wealthy, respected businessmen and financiers just as Marang did. Imagine, whole financial dynasties begun because a magnificent Portuguese liar dreamed up such an impossible scheme . . ."